DATE DUE

OC 15 '99			
JY 26 '01			
JE 17 '03			
OC 28 '04			
JE 4 '08			

More than any of his predecessors in the White House, Franklin D. Roosevelt drew heavily on the thinking of economists as he sought to combat the Great Depression, to mobilize the American economy for war, and to chart a new order for the postwar world. *Designs within Disorder* is an inquiry into how divergent analytic perspectives competed for official favor and how the President chose among them when formulating economic policies.

During the Roosevelt years, two "revolutions" were underway simultaneously. One of them involved a fundamental restructuring of the American economy and of the role government was to play in it. A second was an intellectual "revolution," which engaged economists in reconceptualizing the nature of their discipline. Most of the programmatic initiatives Roosevelt put in place displayed a remarkable staying power for over a half century.

Designs within Disorder

Historical Perspectives on Modern Economics
General Editor: Craufurd D. Goodwin, Duke University

This series contains original works that challenge and enlighten historians of economics. For the profession as a whole, it promotes better understanding of the origin and content of modern economics.

Other books in the series:

William J. Barber, *From New Era to New Deal: Herbert Hoover, the Economists, and American Economic Policy, 1921–1933*

M. June Flanders, *International Monetary Economics, 1870–1950*

J. Daniel Hammond, *Theory and Measurement: Causality Issues in Milton Friedman's Monetary Economics*

Lars Jonung (ed.), *The Stockholm School of Economics Revisited*

Kyun Kim, *Equilibrium Business Cycle Theory in Historical Perspective*

Gerald M. Koot, *English Historical Economics, 1870–1926: The Rise of Economic History and Mercantilism*

Philip Mirowski, *More Heat Than Light: Economics as Social Physics, Physics as Nature's Economics*

Philip Mirowski (ed.), *Natural Images in Economic Thought: "Markets Read in Tooth and Claw"*

Mary S. Morgan, *The History of Econometric Ideas*

Takashi Negishi, *Economic Theories in a Non-Walrasian Tradition*

Malcolm Rutherford, *Institutions in Economics: The Old and the New Institutionalism*

E. Roy Weintraub, *Stabilizing Dynamics: Constructing Economic Knowledge*

Juan Gabriel Valdés, *Pinochet's Economists: The Chicago School of Economics in Chile*

Karen Vaughn, *Austrian Economics in America: The Migration of a Tradition*

Designs within Disorder

Franklin D. Roosevelt, the Economists, and the
Shaping of American Economic Policy, 1933–1945

WILLIAM J. BARBER

CAMBRIDGE
UNIVERSITY PRESS

e of the University of Cambridge
Street, Cambridge CB2 1RP
NY 10011-4211, USA
lelbourne 3166, Australia

© Cambridge University Press 1996

First Published 1996

Printed in the United States of America

Library of Congress Cataloging-in-Publication Data
Barber, William J.
   Designs within disorder : Franklin D. Roosevelt, the economists,
and the shaping of American economic policy, 1933–1945 / William J.
Barber.
      p. cm. – (Historical perspectives on modern economics)
   Includes bibliographical references.
   ISBN 0-521-56078-0 (hardcover)
   1. United States – Economic policy – To 1933. 2. United States –
Economic policy – 1933–1945. 3. United States – Politics and
government – 1933–1945. 4. Roosevelt, Franklin D. (Franklin Delano),
1882–1945. I. Title. II. Series.
HC106.3.B269   1996
338.9—dc20   95-45049
                                                             CIP

A catalog record for this book is available from the British Library

ISBN   0-521-56078-0   Hardback

Contents

Preface

Some years ago, I set out to write a study of the role of economists in shaping and reshaping American economic policies during the New Deal years. As that project proceeded, it became apparent that an introductory chapter setting out what Franklin D. Roosevelt inherited from the Hoover administration was needed. That consideration led me to the Herbert Hoover Presidential Library in West Branch, Iowa. What I found there resulted in a book entitled *From New Era to New Deal: Herbert Hoover, the Economists, and American Economic Policy, 1921–1933* (Cambridge University Press, 1985). In the preface to the work, I wrote that the sequel would "have to wait a bit." Claims on time imposed by other professional obligations have meant that the sequel has been delayed longer than I would have wished it to be.

In the preparation of this book, I have accumulated an extraordinary array of debts. I am especially grateful to friends and colleagues who have viewed the manuscript with a sympathetically critical eye: Robert W. Dimand, Burton C. Hallowell, Richard A. Miller, James Tobin, and Robert Wood. They, of course, bear no responsibility for any errors of fact or interpretation that may remain. I have also been greatly blessed to have had the benefit of the exceptional secretarial skills of Frances Warren.

I wish also to record my gratitude for the wonderful services to scholarship provided by the staffs of the Franklin D. Roosevelt Presidential Library (Hyde Park, New York), the National Archives (Washington, D.C.), and the Manuscripts and Archives Division of the Yale University Library (New Haven, Connecticut). I am indebted as well for the support provided by the faculty research grants funded by the Trustees of Wesleyan University and by a grant from the National Endowment for Humanities under its Travel to Collections program.

The kind permission of the following publishers to reprint materials originally prepared for their use is acknowledged with thanks: the Duke University Press (for extracts from articles that appeared in *History of Political Economy* under the titles "The Career of Alvin H. Hansen in the 1920s and 1930s: a Study in Intellectual Transformation" and "The Divergent Fates of Two Strands of 'Institutionalist' Doctrine during the New Deal Years"); the Woodrow Wilson Center Press (for extracts from an essay that appeared in *The State and Economic Knowledge,* edited by Barry Supple and Mary O. Furner); and the Truman Library Institute (for extracts from a chapter entitled "Presuppositions, Realities, and Creative Ad-Hoc-ery: the Road to the Unplanned Plan" to appear in *The United States and Integration of Europe).*

W. J. B.

Guide to abbreviations in citations of sources

FDRPL   Franklin D. Roosevelt Presidential Library, Hyde Park, New York

NA   National Archives, Washington, D.C.

PPA   Public Papers and Addresses of Franklin D. Roosevelt

YUA   Yale University Archives

Prologue

This study is concerned with the interplay of economic ideas and events during a dozen years of extraordinary turbulence in the American economy. The administrations of Franklin D. Roosevelt confronted formidable challenges, including persisting depression, a major downturn in economic activity (in 1937–38) which the received learning could not readily explain, mobilizing resources for war while leaning against runaway inflation, and preparing for a postwar order from which the nightmares of the 1930s would be banished.

When he entered the White House in 1933, Roosevelt inherited a disorderly economy whose behavior was at odds with textbook teaching. At his death, he bequeathed a restructured economy – in which the role of government had been redefined – that would inspire a rewriting of the textbooks. Along the way, he was to execute more than one "U-turn" in his economic strategies. It is small wonder that this apparent disorder induced his critics to question whether Roosevelt's economic thinking was rooted in any coherent analytic perspective. His behavior also gave ammunition to those who would argue that his policies were driven solely by political opportunism.

Roosevelt never committed himself irrevocably to any single economic doctrine. He was certainly not immune, however, from intellectual influences. On the contrary, he was remarkably receptive to a broad spectrum of economic ideas. More than any of his predecessors in the American presidency, he was prepared to listen to the designs put before him by members of the economics profession. Indeed he was receptive to advice based on a remarkably broad spectrum of analytic perspectives – some of which were mutually incompatible. He never claimed standing as a producer of economic ideas. Instead he saw himself as their consumer and, on these matters, he was an uncompromising champion of consumer sovereignty.

1

These were years of disarray – not just for the economy, but also for practitioners of the discipline of economics. For economists, the impact of the Great Depression has been perceptively likened to that of the Big Bang for theoretical physicists. The cataclysmic events of the 1930s called into question most of the established verities of the orthodoxies of the day. There could be no escaping the disjunction between the realities of the observable world and the mainstream theoretical construct in which conditions of full employment were taken to be the "norm." The awkwardness of brute facts, however, was not sufficient to shake the faith of true believers in the fundamental validity of the basic "model." Stubbornly persisting unemployment, it could be argued, was the result of "rigidities" in price and wage making. As these phenomena were incompatible with the competitive conditions presupposed in the theory, one could conclude that the world – but not the model – was out of joint. This intellectual maneuver had the virtue of logical tidiness. But it could offer little comfort to a distressed populace or to economic policy makers pressured to find solutions to real problems.

The economic environment of the early 1930s proved to be auspicious for economic thinkers with heterodox leanings who then found some attentive listeners. Though their arguments were not identical in their substantive properties, they were projected from a shared point of view: namely, that it was futile to pretend that the nation's economic health could be restored without unconventional interventions by government. Given the conditions of the times, it was not surprising that Roosevelt should have provided house room for heterodoxies. The apparent bankruptcy of the old-fashioned remedies suggested that it was time to try something different. Roosevelt's willingness to experiment was one of the most engaging aspects of his presidential style. When doing so, he was prepared to break the inherited rules delineating the appropriate spheres for the private and public sectors in economic activity, as well as those defining the respective jurisdictions of various echelons of government within a federal system.

Roosevelt's activism always sparked intense controversy. But, much of the time, it had a positive effect in bracing badly bruised public morale. The experiments in economic policy in the early going were failures – or, at the minimum, produced results quite different from those that had been anticipated. Even the disappointments had compensating features. New learning emerged when economists tried to understand what had gone wrong. This could be a slow and uneven process. It was accelerated, however, in the president's second term.

Roosevelt's Washington was a laboratory affording economists an opportunity to make hands-on contact with the world of events. Their activities yielded a noteworthy payoff in 1937–38. Economists were then challenged by a fresh set of perplexities and the response that a number of the "insiders" came up with was to inspire the formulation of a "model" to guide economic policy.

This left a significant mark on the flow of events. It also proved to be a catalyst to a revolutionary transformation in the discipline itself. The perspective then proclaimed insisted that a promised land was in sight if government intelligently deployed the tools of aggregate demand management.

At the time of Roosevelt's death, an Americanized version of Keynesian macroeconomics framed the agenda at the highest levels of economic policy making. Its conceptual categories had not been available when the course of the first New Deal had been charted in 1933. Even had they been at hand, the temper at that moment would have precluded their use. Post-1938, fundamental change in the atmosphere and in the inventory of analytic tools was in evidence. But there was still a sniff of heresy about this version of a "new economics" and it did not lack for critics. Within the bureaucracy, doctrinal innovation made considerable headway – indeed its insights were sharpened and refined in the management of wartime mobilization and in the preparations for a postwar economic order. Domesticated Keynesianism did not enjoy such repute in the academy. When Roosevelt left the scene, it was regarded as suspect by the bulk of the academic establishment.

The Roosevelt years marked a watershed in the development of policies to reshape the American economy and in the development of economic analysis as well. The chapters to follow aim to tell the story of how these outcomes were influenced by the competition between rival economic ideas – and by the creation of new ones – during a period of exceptional ferment.

1

Stage setting in the presidential campaign of 1932

In the presidential campaigns of 1932 and 1992, Democratic challengers opposed Republican incumbents. In 1932, the slogan that was intended to keep the 1992 challenger's campaign staff focused – i.e., "It's the economy, stupid!" – would have been redundant. No alert observer could entertain any doubt that the economy was the central issue in Franklin D. Roosevelt's first campaign for the presidency. The wreckage wrought by three years of depression had a distressing immediacy in the form of mass unemployment, idled industrial capacity, collapsed farm prices, real estate foreclosures, and bank failures.

It is now a part of the conventional wisdom that a president running for re-election is in trouble if the "economic discomfort index" – defined as the sum of the unemployment rate and the inflation rate – is in double digits. (In the environment of 1932, it would have been fitting to rewrite this formula by substituting the deflation rate, which was then responsible for major economic distress, for the inflation rate.) By these standards, contemporaries might easily have concluded that the Hoover administration's economic performance meant that it was automatically doomed. Before the fact, however, the electoral result was less than self-evident. The electorate clearly had ample reasons to reject the party in power. But observers at the time also had valid grounds for wondering what a Democratic administration would bring. Only four times in the preceding eighteen presidential contests had the Democrats won control of the White House. By 1932, the party's core constituencies amounted to a coalition of contradictions: among them, boss-dominated big city machines that offended the champions of "clean government"; Southern landholders committed to perpetuation of racial segregation; Northern workers for whom advancing the rights of labor took high priority; groupings of intellectuals who were eager to promote economic and social reforms. The philosopher-comedian

Will Rogers captured the flavor of this when he remarked, "I belong to no organized party: I am a Democrat."

In the second half of the twentieth century, it has become standard practice for presidential candidates to invite academic social scientists – and particularly economists – to assist them in preparing position papers and speech drafts. Candidate Roosevelt broke new ground when he took that step in 1932. In his choice of academic advisers, he signaled that he was hospitable to heterodoxy. The three charter members of his Brains Trust were drawn from the Columbia University professoriate. Their selection had an obvious logistical recommendation – i.e., geographical proximity to the candidate. Nevertheless, if a professional organization (such as the American Economic Association) had been asked to nominate persons competent to advise a potential president, the names of those to whom Roosevelt turned would not have been on the list.

1   Designs for the industrial order

The original Brains Trusters shared a common perspective. As each saw matters, the deranged condition of the American economy reflected fundamental structural imbalances that could be corrected only through actions by government. They brought differing professional specialties to their assignment. Raymond Moley, who had served Governor Roosevelt as an advisor on reform of the criminal justice system in the state of New York, identified himself as a political scientist. Though he served as the coordinator of this experiment in idea brokerage, his substantive contribution to an economic model to inform campaign strategy was slight. Nonetheless, the moral of the one that was developed – i.e., the imperative need for public intervention to promote economic balance – was one that he could readily embrace. Adolf A. Berle, Jr., professor in Columbia's School of Law, and Rexford Guy Tugwell, professor in the university's economics department, were on hand to supply the economic arguments.

Berle and Tugwell converged in their readings of the dimensions of disorder in the industrial sector, though they did not begin from the same starting point. Berle's point of view reflected his background as a lawyer, a career he had embarked on following his graduation from Harvard Law School in 1916 at the age of 21. As the youngest graduate in its history, he had quickly acquired a reputation as an infant prodigy. (Some of his critics were later to assert that he remained an infant long after he ceased to be a prodigy.) By the late 1920s – and informed by his work in corporate law – he was persuaded that a "major shift in civilization" was underway as a by-product of the power acquired by large corporations.[1] In his search for a richer understanding of the implications of this phenomenon, he enlisted the aid of a graduate student in economics at Harvard, Gardiner C. Means, to conduct empirical studies of cor-

1. A. A. Berle, Jr., assisted by Gardiner C. Means, "Corporations and the Public Investor," *American Economic Review,* March 1930, pp. 54–71.

porate concentration. The fruits of this collaboration appeared in 1932 in a book entitled *The Modern Corporation and Private Property* and were to cause a mild sensation.

Through Berle, the essential arguments of this work were put before Roosevelt in memoranda and oral briefings early in the 1932 campaign. In a 39-page document of May 1932, for example, Roosevelt was informed that:

> Concentration has proceeded to a point at which 65% of American industry is owned and operated by about six hundred corporations. ... Nearly 50% of American industry is owned and operated by two hundred large corporations. ... This means that some six thousand men, as directors of these corporations virtually control American industry ...[2]

In light of this, Berle anticipated that "at the present rate of trend, the American and Russian systems will look very much alike within a comparatively short period – say twenty years." And he added that "there is no great difference between having all industry run by a committee of Commissars and by a small group of Directors."[3]

The trends notwithstanding, there was nothing predetermined about this outcome. Governmental policies should be deployed to ensure that the public interest was better protected. Berle rejected totally the traditional trustbusters' solution to the problem of concentration. Bigness should be accepted as a fact of life in modern industry. He proposed instead that the antitrust laws be amended to permit consolidations and "even monopolies at will" – subject to the condition that federal regulation would be applied when the two-firm concentration ratio exceeded 50 percent. And he specified that such regulation "should include power to require uniform prices; to control security issues; and to control further consolidation."[4]

Rexford Guy Tugwell could embellish these themes as a prolific critic of mainstream economics. Throughout his academic career, he had championed his version of a "new economics," which rejected the doctrines of laissez-faire as unrealistic, wasteful, and socially immoral. He had cast himself as a promoter of a *Methodenstreit* in which the objective was no less than the banishment of standard neoclassical teaching, which, in his view, blinded those under its influence to correct perceptions of crucial economic problems.

Tugwell's thinking had its roots in a well-established body of home-grown American heterodoxy. Thorstein Veblen had pioneered this tradition with such trenchant works as *The Theory of Business Enterprise* and *Engineers and the Price System.* Within his analytic framework, the interests of those in business (as profit maximizers) and of "engineers" (as output and efficiency maximiz-

2. Berle (assisted by Louis Faulkner), "The Nature of the Difficulty," May 1932, Berle Papers, FDRPL.
3. Ibid., p. 30.
4. Ibid., pp. 34, 35.

are) were fundamentally opposed. Indeed, business – in the pursuit of maximum profits – could be expected to practice "industrial sabotage." This was systematic waste that took the form of restricting outputs (with the sacrifice of cost-minimizing utilization of capacity) and of suppressing technical innovations to protect the value of the existing capital stock. For Veblen, these socially undesirable outcomes were inherent in the capitalistic industrial system and could be corrected only if decisions on resource allocation were transferred to technical experts. In the early 1920s, Veblen had called for a "Soviet of Engineers" to perform this planning function. Tugwell distanced himself from this emotionally charged terminology, though his style of thinking owed much to his study of Veblen.

Tugwell had articulated his vision of a new economic order in some detail before the December 1931 meeting of the American Economic Association. He then endorsed a system of comprehensive national planning, which he characterized as follows:

> Planning is by definition the opposite of conflict; its meaning is aligned to co-ordination, to rationality, to publicly defined and expertly approached aims; but not to private money-making ventures; and not to the guidance of a hidden hand. ... Planning implies the guidance of capital uses; this would limit entrance into or expansion of operations. Planning also implies adjustment of production to consumption; and there is no way of accomplishing this except through a control of prices and of profit margins. It would never be sufficient to plan production for an estimated demand if that demand were likely to fail for lack of purchasing power. The insurance of adequate buying capacity would be a first and most essential task of any plan which was expected to work.[5]

Lest anyone mistake the meaning of this message, Tugwell emphatically asserted that:

> business will be logically required to disappear. ... To take away from business the freedom of venture and of expansion, and to limit the profits it may acquire, is to destroy it as business and to make of it something else. ... The traditional incentives, hope of money-making, and fear of money loss, will be weakened; and a kind of civil-service loyalty and fervor will need to grow gradually into acceptance. New industries will not just happen as the automobile industry did; they will have to be foreseen, to be argued for, to seem probably desirable features of the whole economy before they can be entered upon.[6]

5. R. G. Tugwell, "The Principle of Planning and the Institution of Laissez-faire," *American Economic Review Supplement,* March 1932, pp. 89–90.
6. Ibid., pp. 89–90.

This was strong stuff. Predictably, it drew fire from the mainstream professionals.[7] Tugwell, however, was undeterred by harsh criticism. He remained supremely self-confident about the "rightness" of his views, which, he maintained, had been validated by the course of events. In mid-1928, he had been one of the few to forecast an imminent downturn in economic activity. The hey-day of "new era" prosperity, he had then argued, had been associated with haphazard investment and mistaken business expectations about the demand for outputs that could be produced from newly created facilities. This had led to excess capacity and increases in overhead costs. To achieve profitability, industries had then cut back on their operations and set prices at levels that were needlessly high. This line of adjustment both choked off production and cost jobs. Tugwell predicted that presidential candidates in the election of 1928 "were going to have to talk to unemployed people, people, perhaps, who are hungry and who next winter will be cold."[8] But this outcome could have been avoided if proper public direction of the flow of private investment, combined with controls to compel producers to reduce prices as average costs fell, had been in place.

In a book completed in 1932 (though not published until May 1933), Tugwell added some refinements to the general positions he had set out earlier. Reiterating one of his standard themes, he argued that the problems of excess capacity and unemployment in industry could be traced to "inexpert allocation of capital." The remedy should be sought in a planning system that "allocated to specific industries capital sufficient to produce an amount of goods which would be taken by consumers at the price possible with capacity production, and no more ..."[9]

How, then, could the right balance be struck? In Tugwell's judgment, properly administered capital allocation "would depend on knowledge, from some planning agency, of how much for a measured future period ought to be put to one use rather than to another." He recognized that the issue was not solely the determination of the optimal future output of an industry as a whole. Decisions would also have to be made about the distribution of the industry's target production between its participating firms. This matter would be difficult unless

7. The University of Chicago's Frank Knight, for example, spoofed Tugwell's presentation to the American Economic Association: "... I think it is a most excellent oration of its kind, and a most excellent kind; also that in the time, place, and circumstances it was altogether appropriate. A little high-grade utopian-reformist soap-boxing should provide excellent – let us say – messianic relief from the nerve-strain of the solemn stodginess of a meeting of a learned society. But – perhaps it is out of place to remark as to how out of place it would be to think of such a performance in the light of a contribution to the solution of any social problem." (Frank H. Knight, "The Newer Economics and the Control of Economic Activity," *Journal of Political Economy,* August 1932, p. 475n.)

8. Tugwell, "Hunger, Cold and Candidates," *The New Republic,* 54 (May 2, 1928), pp. 323–4.

9. Tugwell, *The Industrial System and the Governmental Arts* (New York: Columbia University Press, 1933), p. 204.

firms within the industry were "either combined or sufficiently closely associated for practical action."[10]

When the industry was effectively integrated for planning purposes, the guiding principle should be to "drive corporate surpluses into the open investment market." This could be done through a tax on undistributed corporate profits. Such an innovation, he insisted, would automatically correct what he took to be a major flaw in the existing system: "self-allocation" of retained corporate earnings. But another step would be required to reach the overall objective. Government and its planning authorities would need to be empowered to control new capital issues.[11]

This was only the beginning of the comprehensive scheme of controls Tugwell had in mind. While industrial integration should be encouraged, it was imperative that producers should be denied the power to be price makers: "otherwise the advantage of efficiency will result in corporate profits, but not in lower prices."[12] Hence governmentally determined price controls were essential.

Tugwell was under no illusions that the totality of his grand design could be put in place quickly. But he hoped that some interim steps could be taken with little delay. As an initial one, he proposed that a governmental agency be empowered "to issue certificates of convenience and necessity" to industrial associations permitting them to "set up their own planning boards and central management devices for maintaining standards of competition and for controlling maximum prices and minimum wages." All of the individual industrial groupings would be subject to oversight and control by a central body – he suggested that it be named the Industrial Integration Board – which would be directed by representatives of affiliated industries and representatives of the government. The board would be charged to review policies on prices and security issues and be empowered to assess fines on firms failing to comply with the common policy. Administrative costs of this exercise could be met by an excise tax on industrial products, the proceeds of which would be paid into an Industrial Reserve Fund.[13]

10. Ibid., p. 205. Action before the desired degree of industrial integration had been accomplished would require, he argued, the adoption of some principle of apportionment between firms, such as relative size, relative contribution to the industry's total output, and perhaps "some recognition of the superior efficiency of one over the others." (Ibid., p. 205.)
11. Ibid., p. 206–7.
12. Ibid., p. 210.
13. Resources thus accumulated were to serve other purposes as well. Tugwell envisaged a tripartite division of the residuals (after administrative expenses had been met). One-third would be distributed to industries that had complied with the overall plan, scaled in proportion to the tax collected on their products. One-third would be retained as a reserve for dividend payments to corporate shareholders. One-third would be allocated to a wage reserve fund to be distributed to states that had organized programs of unemployment insurance. (Ibid., p. 215.)

All this amounted to an appeal for a radical reconstruction of the industrial order. There was some overlap between Tugwell's thinking and proposals then being floated by various business groups. The scheme most prominent in contemporary discussion was known as the Swope Plan, which had been proposed by Gerard Swope, President of the General Electric Company. When it was unveiled in September 1931, President Hoover had denounced it as "the most gigantic proposal of monopoly ever made in American history." Under its terms, trade associations would be invited to coordinate supply and demand with immunity from prosecution under the antitrust laws for the purpose of "stabilizing prices and sustaining wages." Swope and Tugwell parted company on a crucial point. Tugwell's version of planning provided no room for business autonomy. The ultimate decisions on resource allocation would be made by public authorities. There was no need for the state to own the means of production. But it was imperative that it should control their use.

When projecting their visions of industrial reconstruction, the Brains Trusters of 1932 left many questions unanswered. But they were unambiguous when distancing themselves from doctrines to which they were fundamentally opposed. They were united in insisting that their candidate for the presidency should purge his party's historic affiliation with economic thinking associated with Louis D. Brandeis (then an Associate Justice of the Supreme Court). In that view of the world, industrial bigness was a "curse" that should be banished through rigorous enforcement of the antitrust laws and the promotion of other procompetitive policies. Much to the consternation of Tugwell and Berle, Professor Felix Frankfurter of the Harvard Law School (who also aspired to gain access to the candidate's inner circle) kept reminding Roosevelt of the Brandeisian message. The Brains Trusters were also at one when denouncing mainstream neoclassical teaching on the virtues of vigorously competitive markets kept vital through surveillance by the Justice Department's Anti-Trust Division. There was no place in their world for the call for reinvigorated antitrust enforcement issued in 1932 under the leadership of Princeton's Frank A. Fetter, which was endorsed by 127 signators (including seven former presidents of the American Economic Association). Sound industrial policy, in the view of the Brains Trusters, called instead for "concentration and control" to replace "competition and conflict."

2   Competing designs for a new deal for farmers

For more than a decade, agriculture had been the economy's "sick sector." American farmers enjoyed boom conditions during and immediately after World War I. The upsurge in demand for farm products had then boosted prices and induced enlarged production. In the process, farmers had borrowed heavily to expand land holdings (purchased at abnormally high prices) and to add to their stock of equipment. This episode of euphoria had been short-lived. When European producers recovered from the devastation of war, export markets for American agricultural commodities collapsed. From the early 1920s onwards, farmers had suffered from reduced prices for their products and from the increased real burdens of debts incurred in happier times.

A fundamental imbalance between the agricultural sector's capacity to produce and the ability of the domestic market to absorb its output was abundantly apparent. In addition, a structural fault line could be identified that separated the agricultural and industrial sectors. Farming, with a large number of small producers, effectively replicated the conditions of the textbook model of perfect competition. Whereas farmers were price takers, manufacturers were not: The latter typically were able to exercise some measure of market power by reducing outputs in face of softening demand. Farmers could not do so: When agricultural prices fell, they typically expanded production in an attempt to service their debts. This response – given the relatively inelastic demand for staple food products – shrank their income still further. A case could thus be made that laissez-faire worked perversely in agriculture and that intervention was therefore imperative. With the fortunes of roughly a quarter of the population linked to the livelihood of farmers, no candidate for national office could be indifferent to these considerations.

Consensus, however, was difficult to reach on an appropriate strategy. Tugwell had already given the matter some attention and his approach to this issue was of a piece with his thinking about industrial reform: The visible hand of government should again coordinate supply and demand. The objectives of intervention were not identical in the two cases. In the industrial sector, the planner's target was to press sticky prices downward and to stimulate increased outputs at reduced unit costs. With respect to the staple farm commodities then in surplus, on the other hand, the planner should restrict outputs in the interest of raising prices. In 1928, Tugwell had sketched a technique for doing this. He had then offered a blueprint for a system of production controls with the following features:

> (1) A survey of the amounts necessary to meet normal needs and which will command a profitable price. (2) Notice of limitation of planting, on a basis of ten-year averages, by local (probably county) agents of a Farm Board. (3) Enforcement through denial of the use of railways and warehouses to produce grown on unauthorized acreages.[14]

In July 1932, Tugwell made common cause with two agricultural economists: M. L. Wilson, then at Montana State College, who had formerly served with the Bureau of Agricultural Economics, and Mordecai Ezekiel, another veteran of the Bureau of Agricultural Economics who was then an official at the Federal Farm Board. An important programmatic ingredient was added: di-

14. Tugwell, "Reflections on Farm Relief," *Political Science Quarterly,* December 1928, p. 490.

rect payments to farmers who complied with recommended restrictions on production. To finance this initiative, a tax would be levied on processors of farm products (e.g., on wheat millers, on cotton ginners, and the like). Packaged in this form, this scheme was labeled the Domestic Allotment Plan. No longer would farmers make production decisions on their own; the planners would do that. Farmers would be rewarded twice over: first, through benefit payments received from retiring acreages, and again through the higher prices for marketed outputs that would follow from supply restriction. There was, of course, more than a slight overtone of regimentation in this procedure. But it was hoped that the troubling aspect of this intervention could be neutralized with an understanding that it would not be implemented unless a majority of the producers of specified crops agreed to its implementation.

In 1932, the vision of planning the agricultural sector through the Domestic Allotment Plan was novel. But other forms of governmental action to relieve the plight of farmers were also on offer. Depressed conditions in the farm sector were already more than a decade old. Over that span of time, two schemes of special significance were spawned. Each, in its own way, was also a challenge to laissez-faire orthodoxy.

The plan for farm relief with the greatest appeal to farm lobbyists dated from a pamphlet issued in 1922, entitled *Equality for Agriculture,* produced by George N. Peek and General Hugh S. Johnson. The authors, both of whom were alumni of the War Industries Board, subsequently migrated to Illinois to enter the farm implement manufacturing business. The postwar break in farm prices had had a direct and forceful impact on their personal fortunes. Their response took the form of advocacy of a plan to raise farm prices: Translated into legislative form, it became known as the McNary-Haugen Bill. Though the scheme went through a number of iterations – the bill twice passed both houses of Congress and was twice vetoed by President Coolidge – there was continuity in its basic structure. The core idea held that the economy was fundamentally imbalanced as a by-product of the nation's tariff policies. The manufacturing sector had enjoyed systematic protection, whereas the agricultural sector had not. Elementary fairness, it could thus be argued, meant that government should even the scales. Moreover, were farmers to enjoy "tariff equivalence," their circumstances would be bound to improve. In the home market, prices of staple commodities would be raised above the world market price by the average amount of the tariff on manufactured goods. Surpluses that did not clear at home would then be sold abroad for what they would fetch – and the ultimate payout to farmers would be struck as a weighted average of the returns from domestic and foreign sales. Under Republican presidents – doctrinally hostile to such manipulative price fixing – this scheme had been stymied. The McNary-Haugen approach nonetheless remained alive and well in political discourse in 1932. It called for intervention, but in a form totally at odds with that of the Domestic Allotment Plan. To the McNary-Haugenites, supply restrictions mandated by government were abhorrent.

Yet another approach to the farm problem competed for attention. The central source of this doctrine was the University of Wisconsin and the tradition of "institutionalist" economics established there by Richard T. Ely. He certainly did not disguise his sympathies for governmental intervention to uplift the farm economy. The type of planning he advocated, however, was distinct from the programs championed by both the advocates of McNary-Haugenism and of Domestic Allotment. Price raising through "tariff equivalence for agriculture" was misguided: It would simply encourage more production. The farm problem should instead be attacked from a recognition that acreage under the plough was far in excess of that needed to satisfy normal demand for farm products. But that was not the sole difficulty. Agrarian distress was compounded because much of the acreage in use was ill-suited to cultivation and incapable of generating decent living standards for those who tilled it.

The Wisconsin vision for the uplift of the agricultural economy placed the emphasis on land use planning. From this perspective, the attention of government should focus, in the first instance, on discouraging extensions in the cultivated acreage. Immediate repeal of the Homestead Acts should properly be an initial step in that direction. In addition, government should sponsor surveys to classify the nation's land resources and to identify their best uses. Then aggressive measures should be taken to retire submarginal lands from cultivation and to convert them to pasture or forest. Land reclaimed for tax delinquencies should not be resold, but withdrawn from tillage. Governments should also invoke powers of eminent domain to buy misused lands and to withdraw them from tillage. Ultimately, the downdraft on farm prices could thus be checked and reversed. This kind of planning offered a solution for the longer term – and one that was compatible with conserving the nation's land resources. And, by contrast with the Domestic Allotment Plan, it shied away from direct manipulation of prices.

The land use management approach had infiltrated one of the lower echelons of the federal bureaucracy in the 1920s. When the Bureau of Agricultural Economics was established within the Department of Agriculture in 1921, an Ely-trained Wisconsin Ph.D., Henry C. Taylor, became its first chief. He was soon joined by L. C. Gray, another Ely protégé, who headed the Division of Land Economics. The Wisconsin perspective also left its mark on two other economists in the agricultural bureaucracy: M. L. Wilson (who had studied with Ely) and Howard Tolley (who had not, but who had absorbed its message from those who had). Their collaborative efforts had shaped the language of a bill, sponsored by Representative Victor Christgau of Minnesota in 1930, calling upon the federal government to launch a research program to provide a base for rational land utilization. The immediate objective was to educate farmers about the crops they could best produce in their respective land "zones," pointing toward the ultimate goal of retiring the submarginal lands altogether. This modest proposal went nowhere. By 1932, a number of its original champions – most notably M. L. Wilson – made a tactical adjustment by supporting the Domestic Allotment Plan. In his judgment at the time, the Domestic Allotment approach was far from ideal: The quota method of reducing planting by a specified percentage from a prior base period was at odds with promoting the most efficient land usage. Nevertheless, he went along with Domestic Allotment as a second-best emergency measure, hoping that its adoption would rekindle interest in a more enlightened land policy for the longer term.

These designs were obviously different. Even so, they shared one attribute: All of them had been opposed by Herbert Hoover. He was to describe Henry C. Wallace, Secretary of Agriculture from 1921 to 1924 (and whose son was to serve Roosevelt in that capacity), as "a Fascist, but did not know it" for expressing sympathy for the McNary-Haugen plan.[15] As Secretary of Commerce, he had also played a leading role in the preparation of Coolidge's messages vetoing the McNary-Haugen Bills of 1927 and 1928. As president, he had opposed the modest program for land use planning proposed in the Christgau Bill. To his mind, direct controls over production, such as those called for in the Domestic Allotment Plan, were absolutely unthinkable.

3   Visions of salvation through monetary manipulation

The Columbia group of Brains Trusters were "sound money men." Their sights were set on the alleged structural distortions of the economy. They had no patience with nostrums pressed by another strand of heterodoxy, i.e., by those calling for monetary measures to manipulate the general price level.

Advocates of monetary solutions to depression were kept off-stage in Roosevelt's campaign entourage. Nonetheless, they made their presence felt from the wings. Indeed some of the agitators for farm relief actively preferred monetary remedies to structural interventions. This attitude had deep roots in American history. In times of economic distress, farm lobbies had often sought solutions through monetary manipulation. They had done so in the 1870s when supporting the Greenback movement to expand the currency issue. They had done so again in the 1890s when rallying behind William Jennings Bryan's campaigns for "free silver."

In 1932, this tradition had a renewed vitality. The argument for inflationary policies to pump up farm prices was now articulated in more sophisticated form. Through the work of the Cornell agricultural economist, George F. Warren, and his Cornell collaborator, F. A. Pearson, doctrines that could formerly have been dismissed as the work of "cranks" and "amateurs" could be given at least a pseudoscientific veneer. Operating from their base at the state of New York's land

15. Herbert Hoover, *The Memoirs of Herbert Hoover: the Cabinet and the Presidency, 1920–1933* (New York: Macmillan, 1952), p. 174.

grant college, Warren and Pearson enjoyed proximity and visibility to the state's political establishment. And they had won converts to their views among some who were later to fill high positions in Roosevelt's administrations – most notably, Henry Morgenthau, Jr., a future Secretary of the Treasury.

Warren and Pearson rested their arguments on elaborate statistical investigations of the behavior of commodity prices on the one hand and of the price of gold on the other. These findings suggested that there was a high positive correlation between the two. It thus seemed to follow that the answer to depressed farm prices could be found in raising the price of gold.[16] This argument implied that there was an easy road to farm relief, which would make special programs of supply restriction superfluous. The policy remedy, however, would be incompatible with a U.S. commitment to gold convertibility at a fixed parity.

A variation on this theme – and one with potentially greater persuasive power – was offered by Yale's Irving Fisher. Unlike Warren and Pearson, Fisher's professional stature – thanks to his pioneering contributions to general equilibrium theory, to monetary economics, and to the construction of index numbers – placed him in the front rank of the international community of economists. He was also an inveterate champion of "causes," including prohibition, world peace, life extension through scientific diet and exercise. In the same reformist spirit, he had throughout his career pressed his views on economic policy to any who would listen – and certainly with insistence on those who held or aspired to high public office. The advice he offered in conversations and correspondence with candidate Roosevelt during the campaign of 1932 was self-initiated. Whether his thinking was welcomed or not, Fisher was still an intellectual force to be reckoned with.[17] Moreover, he had standing among leaders in farm organizations. In October 1931, he had been engaged by the American Farm Bureau Federation to draft legislation that it could support before Congress to elevate the general price level.[18]

By 1932, Fisher was convinced that he could provide both an explanation for the persistence of depression and a solution that would promise a quick recovery. The root of the problem, as he saw matters, could be traced to two diseases: the "debt disease" and the "dollar disease." The American economy of 1929 was vulnerable because of overindebtedness: Too much spending had

16. See, for example, George F. Warren and F. A. Pearson, "The Future of the General Price Level," *Journal of Farm Economics,* June 1932 and "Relationship of Gold to Prices," *Journal of the American Statistical Association* (Supplement), March 1933.

17. Fisher came away from interviews with Hoover and Roosevelt in 1932 persuaded that the latter would be the more receptive to the monetary policies he was then sponsoring. Even so, largely on the grounds that Roosevelt was a "wet" and Hoover a "dry," he voted for Hoover.

18. Fisher, "Three Bills to Stabilize Prices," October 26, 1931, Fisher Papers, YUA.

been financed with borrowed money. Once this phenomenon had been recognized, alarm had been triggered among some debtors and creditors, which had sparked an initial round of liquidation. This, in turn, had set off a chain reaction involving distress selling, contraction in bank deposits as loans were paid off or called in, and a consequent fall in the price level. At this point, difficulties were aggravated by the "dollar disease"; i.e., as prices fell, the real burden of debts increased. Deflation then became cumulative. Fisher had worked out the central logic of these deflationary mechanisms in a book entitled *Booms and Depressions,* published in mid-1932, copies of which he made available to Roosevelt and to members of his campaign staff. As he summarized its central message in an article appearing in 1933:

> *the very effort of individuals to lessen their burden of debts increases it, because of the mass effect of the stampede to liquidate in swelling each dollar owed.* Then we have the great paradox which, I submit, is the chief secret of most, if not all, great depressions: *The more debtors pay, the more they owe.*[19]

Fisher had arrived at this insight the hard way. As late as the early autumn of 1929, he had been an enthusiast for the permanence of "new era" prosperity. That conviction had inspired him to plunge heavily in the stock market on margin, a decision with disastrous consequences for his personal finances.

In Fisher's judgment, the most arresting finding of the analytic position he had reached in 1932 was that deflation simply generated more deflation, with no end in sight, short of universal bankruptcy. Bankruptcies and shrinking profits led to reductions in output and employment. These conditions bred pessimism, hoarding, and a further slowdown in the velocity of monetary circulation. But these circumstances need not be tolerated. The remedy was implicit in the diagnosis: "reflating the price level up to the average level at which outstanding debts were contracted by existing debtors and assumed by existing creditors, and then maintaining that level unchanged."[20] Debt burdens would thereby be relieved and liquidations brought to a halt. Debtors would then have more discretionary income available for spending on goods and services, and the resulting resurgence in purchasing power would reinvigorate production and employment.

The ideas that Fisher presented in 1932 and 1933 were of a piece with doctrines he had worked out in the preceding decade when he had argued that the business cycle could be tamed if the proper monetary policy were adopted. Based on statistical investigations in the 1920s, he had then concluded that fluctuations in the volume of trade were linked with the rate of change in the general price level. Periods of rising prices were associated – with an average lag of seven months or so – with expansion in production. Reductions in the

19. Irving Fisher, "The Debt-Deflation Theory of Great Depressions," *Econometrica,* October, 1933, p. 344. Italics in the original.
20. Ibid., p. 346.

general price level were followed by contractions in total output. This suggested that the task of stabilizing the economy could be reduced to one of stabilizing the price level. He was confident that this could be accomplished if the Federal Reserve System were compelled to manage the money supply through its open market operations to ensure overall price stability.[21]

During the 1920s, Fisher had lobbied persistently, albeit unsuccessfully, for legislation that would oblige the central bankers to behave in this manner. This proposal was vigorously resisted: Central bankers typically have little enthusiasm for formulas that would override their judgment calls. It also was summarily rejected by the Hoover administration. Hoover took it to be a categorical imperative that the United States should defend the gold standard, even after most of the rest of the world had lapsed from it. Its "rules of the game" prescribed that price level variations – downward for deficit countries, upward for surplus countries – were important responses to imbalances in international trade and payments. Central bank intervention to maintain a stable domestic price level (as called for by Fisher) would be at odds with this component of the gold standard mechanism of adjustment.

Fisher's position in 1932 and 1933 differed in details from analyses he had worked out in the preceding decade, but maintained a continuity in theme. The call for stabilization in the 1920s had now become a call for "reflation." The latter term, he insisted, should not be confused with "inflation." The objective was simply to restore an earlier price level – say, that of 1926. Once that had been accomplished, price stabilization would again be the order of the day. He recognized, however, that the weapons of monetary control on which he had depended in his recommendations in the 1920s (open market interventions by the Federal Reserve System) might require reinforcement in a deflationary environment. In particular, measures to stimulate the velocity of circulation might also be needed. He was soon to be attracted to a scheme for "stamped money." Under this arrangement, the government would issue a special series of dollar bills that would depreciate in value by 2 cents each week unless a 2 cent stamp were affixed to them. This was calculated to be a direct attack on the hoarding of currency: obviously the holder of "stamp-scrip" had an incentive to move it before its value depreciated.[22]

21. Fisher, "Our Unstable Dollar and the So-Called Business Cycle," *Journal of the American Statistical Association,* June 1925. By contrast with a doctrine of monetarism of later vintage, no prespecified rate of growth in the money supply would be mandated. Fisher saw no reason to believe that the velocity of monetary circulation would be stable; on the contrary, he expected that it would be likely to vary. The task of the Federal Reserve System was thus to adjust the money supply to compensate for fluctuations in velocity to ensure overall price stability.

22. The stamped money idea was not, however, original to Fisher. Silvio Gesell, a German businessman operating in Argentina, had advanced this proposal in 1890. Fisher hit on it in mid-1932 and quickly assimilated it into his program.

Thanks to Warren's access to the world of New York politics, his version of the reflation message had more privileged status in the Roosevelt entourage than did Fisher's. Fisher's argument, on the other hand, had greater analytic depth to reinforce it. Differences in their emphases were apparent: Warren was preoccupied with the alleged link between the gold price and commodity prices (particularly those of agricultural products), while Fisher called for a broad array of monetary weapons to elevate the general price level. In the atmosphere of 1932, however, these differences were suppressed. Fisher then spoke approvingly of Warren's position, characterizing it "as *exactly* my doctrine."[23] Fisher could be faulted for some interpretive elasticity when offering that assessment. There was a kinship between Warren's position and the one Fisher had first presented in *The Purchasing Power of Money* (1911) and subsequently embellished in *Stabilizing the Dollar* (1920). In those works, he had set out the case for varying the gold content of the dollar to offset changes in its real purchasing power. From the mid-1920s onwards, however, his policies for stabilization had stressed control of the money supply (through the open market operations of the central bank) and, later, stimulants to velocity (through the use of stamped scrip). While Fisher had moved away from the "compensated dollar" as a policy instrument, Warren insisted that reduction in the gold content of the dollar was the only device through which commodity prices could effectively be elevated.

How much of a hearing the monetarists' message would receive at Roosevelt's headquarters remained an open question. Berle, for example, was at pains to caution Roosevelt against embracing it. In his view, inflation would "not necessarily stimulate business in any way" and would "be cruelly unjust to those individuals who had already been wiped out" through foreclosures and receiverships. In addition, it would reduce the real wages of workers. Though farmers, as sellers, might benefit, they too would lose to the extent that they held savings. In his judgment in August 1932, the existing federal deficit was already fueling an inflationary momentum that should be resisted.[24] For his part, Fisher had put on record his dissatisfaction with the thinking of the Columbia Brains Trusters. From his perspective, the depression could not be explained by "overproduction" or by "maladjustment between agricultural and industrial prices." Those who advanced those arguments were guilty of "mistaking too little money for too much goods."[25]

23. Fisher used this description in a letter to his wife when commenting on Warren's testimony to the Senate Committee on Banking. (Irving Fisher to Margaret Hazard Fisher, May 12, 1932, Fisher Papers, YUA.)
24. Berle to Roosevelt, "The Policy Regarding Inflation of Currency," August 10, 1932, Berle Papers, FDRPL. Berle, however, did concede that "conceivably the situation may be so bad by March fourth next that inflation is the only way out. But that bridge can be crossed when we get to it."
25. Fisher, "The Debt-Deflation Theory of Great Depressions," loc. cit., p. 340.

4   **Economic arguments and campaign rhetoric**

Roosevelt left the electorate in no doubt that his election would bring a shift in style. He pledged to practice "bold, persistent experimentation" and to offer a "New Deal" which he defined as "plain English for a changed concept of the duty and responsibility of government toward economic life."[26] But it was far from clear what the substance of that change would be.

There were, to be sure, a fair number of targeted campaign promises, including support for reforestation in the interests of both reemployment and conservation, legislation to bring "daylight" to security issues, tighter regulation of the interstate operations of public utilities, provision of federal resources to bolster the nation's financial fabric and to ease the burdens of farm and home mortgages. These pledges did indeed point toward an extended jurisdiction for the federal government. Whatever their merits as measures of relief and reform, they did not speak directly to the management of policy for economic recovery.

Roosevelt chose to speak with extraordinary specificity on one aspect of his recovery strategy. There could be no ambiguity about the words he uttered in Pittsburgh, Pennsylvania on October 19, 1932 when he asserted that "a complete and honest balancing of the Federal budget" was "the one sound foundation of permanent economic recovery." Moreover, he pledged to reduce the cost of the "current Federal government operations by 25 percent." He allowed himself an escape hatch: Appropriations needed to address "starvation and dire need" should be treated as emergency outlays and not chargeable against his commitment to match ordinary spending with receipts. These statements still had the ring of old-fashioned fiscal orthodoxy.[27] They also seemed to be saying that fiscal activism would have no part to play in a Roosevelt recovery program. The Democratic candidate thus appeared to have turned a deaf ear to the many calls for an aggressive acceleration of expenditure on public works. By 1932, this type of spending as a depression remedy had won support among a fair number of professional economists, including many who subscribed to budget balancing in principle but who had concluded that the usual rules should be suspended in conditions of emergency.

Roosevelt and his Columbia Brains Trusters were later to regret that the 1932 Pittsburgh speech was ever delivered. Yet, at the time, its content was not out of tune with their thinking. After all, Hoover had tolerated unbalanced budgets, and there were partisan debating points to be won by denouncing him as a reckless deficit spender. Nor did a commitment to fiscal responsibility seem then to be particularly bothersome. The "structuralists" in Roosevelt's

---

26. Roosevelt, Radio Address to the Business and Professional Men's League, October 6, 1932, PPA, Vol. I, p. 782.
27. Roosevelt, Campaign Address on the Federal Budget, Pittsburgh, Pennsylvania, October 19, 1932, PPA, Vol. I, pp. 807–10.

entourage could live with it. As Moley was to observe, "none of us, then, was a member of the 'borrow and spend' school."[28] Tugwell could also accept a posture of fiscal orthodoxy as appropriate.[29] Even the monetary "reflationists" could accommodate "budget-balancing." From their perspective, it was possible to take the "balanced budget" goal on board and to turn it to advantage by arguing that it was achievable only when the economy had been revitalized through monetary stimulation.

In his campaign comments on farm problems, Roosevelt paid more than lip service to structuralist arguments on supply management. His address on this subject at Topeka, Kansas on September 14, 1932 clearly bore the fingerprints of Tugwell and Wilson. The language was artfully crafted to make contact with the more popular schemes for farm relief then in circulation. Thus, the principle of long-term planning for rational land usage was endorsed. In phrasing with overtones of McNary-Haugenism, farmers were promised a "tariff benefit over world prices ... equivalent to the benefit given by the tariff to industrial products." But something new had been added. Roosevelt's specifications for a fresh approach explicitly rejected resort to "dumping" farm surpluses abroad – a key feature of the McNary-Haugen approach. Though "domestic allotment" was not mentioned, direct supply management was implicit in Roosevelt's comments on the importance of designing a program to raise the prices of "staple surplus commodities" – those enumerated were wheat, cotton, corn in the form of hogs, tobacco – in a manner that would be self-financing and operated "in so far as possible" on the basis of voluntary cooperation among producers.[30]

With respect to the course a new administration might chart for the industrial sector, Roosevelt spoke even more guardedly. On various occasions, he lamented the growth in industrial concentration and its dangers, drawing on materials supplied by Berle.[31] In addition, he made frequent reference to the

28. Raymond Moley, *After Seven Years* (New York: Harper and Brothers, 1939), p. 62.
29. On this point, Tugwell later wrote: "At the moment, even to those of us who were more realistic about the future need for relief and public works, fiscal conservatism did not seem an impossible policy. To me for instance, it seemed in order to pay for these expanded programs from increased taxation. I was against inflation. My concert-of-interests theory required that, in the interests of parity, some prices come down as others went up." Tugwell, *The Democratic Roosevelt* (Garden City, N.Y.: Doubleday and Co., 1957), p. 240.
30. Roosevelt, Campaign Address on the Farm Problem, Topeka, Kansas, September 14, 1932, PPA, Vol. I, p. 704.
31. For example, he spoke as follows in Columbus, Ohio on August 20, 1932: "We find two-thirds of American industry concentrated in a few hundred corporations, and actually managed by not more than five hundred individuals. ... In other words, we find concentrated economic power in a few hands, the precise opposite of the individualism of which the President speaks." (Roosevelt, PPA, Vol. I, p. 679.)

importance of "balance" to the stabilization of business. The handiwork of Berle and Tugwell showed through in his call for government to lead in creating a new "economic constitutional order" and in his insistence that "private economic power is ... a public trust as well." In that spirit, he observed that "some enlightened industries" – those interested in seeing wages restored and unemployment ended – were already endeavoring "to limit the freedom of action of each man and business group within the industry in the common interest of all ..." This was "why business men everywhere are asking a form of organization which will bring the scheme of things into balance, even though it may in some measure qualify the freedom of action of individual units within the business."[32]

Despite the obvious genuflections toward doctrines put before him by the structural interventionists, some who worked closely with Roosevelt in shaping these messages were uncertain about their impact on his thinking. Tugwell and Wilson, for example, had their doubts about what their candidate would ultimately prescribe as a farm program. They drew some satisfaction from the position Roosevelt had adopted in his Topeka speech. Both were still fearful that Roosevelt might succumb to the "reflationist" remedy for farm problems and allow supply management to go by the board. In Wilson's judgment at the time, "the farm fellows are going to keep pressing for inflation and a cheaper dollar" to circumvent controls over production.[33] Tugwell shared this concern, observing that farmers would "try to get what they want" while "giving very little in return in the way of restricted production. If Governor Roosevelt does not show the utmost firmness in that situation everything will be lost and I have difficulty in believing that he will find the requisite firmness."[34]

Roosevelt had largely steered clear of the reflation question in his public utterances. He did give a *pro forma* endorsement to the language in the Democratic platform pledging "a sound currency to be preserved at all hazards, and an international monetary conference called, on the invitation of our Government, to consider the rehabilitation of silver and other questions."[35] This begged the question of the criterion of soundness. When campaign strategies were being mapped in August 1932, staff members tentatively scheduled a set speech on the currency question. It was subsequently scratched.[36] By mid-October, Roosevelt, in private conversations with his aides, made it clear that

32. Roosevelt, Campaign Address on Progressive Government at the Commonwealth Club, San Francisco, California, September 23, 1932, PPA, Vol. I, pp. 752–3.
33. Wilson to Tugwell, October 8, 1932, FDRPL.
34. Tugwell to Wilson, November 3, 1932, FDRPL.
35. Roosevelt, Discussion of the National Democratic Platform, Radio Address, Albany, New York, July 30, 1932, PPA, Vol. I, pp. 661–2.
36. Berle, Memorandum of August 5, 1932, Berle Papers, FDRPL. Berle then anticipated that this speech would probably be drafted by General Hugh S. Johnson, aided by Tugwell and James Angell of Columbia University.

references to the gold standard should be purged from speech drafts. "I do not want to be committed to the gold standard," he reportedly said, adding that he had not "the faintest idea whether we will be on the gold standard on March 4th or not; nobody can foresee where we shall be."[37]

From the vantage point of Fisher and Warren, Roosevelt's performance had been an acute disappointment. Monetary issues – crucial, in their view, to economic recovery – seemed to have been ignored. Shortly after the election, Warren soothed Fisher's bruised feelings by assuring him that there was no Roosevelt "black list." In Warren's appraisal, "he is a man who appreciates people who do not agree with him. I think he is somewhat interested in money but the stumbling block is economists." (Warren was here obviously referring to economists of orthodox persuasion whom he characterized as believing "that our money troubles are merely a matter of credit and that prosperity is just around the corner.")[38]

Fisher treated the electoral outcome in November as the moment to launch a campaign for "reflation" in earnest. Roosevelt's neglect of monetary issues, he wrote, had meant that "campaign arguments" had been "economically superficial" – indeed "the whole drama … was acted like Hamlet with Hamlet left out." The president-elect could be forgiven on the grounds that he needed to avoid any taint of "Bryanism."[39] It was now time to move forward. Though he had made no secret of the fact that he had voted for Hoover, Fisher hastened to seek entry into the president-elect's inner circle. On November 14, 1932, he dispatched a copy of *Booms and Depressions* to Moley and requested an opportunity to talk with him "while the plans of the new administration are still in flux."[40]

In the American polity, presidential campaign rhetoric has seldom been a reliable predictor of subsequent economic policy performance. It was certainly not to be the case in 1932.

37. As quoted by Berle, Memorandum of October 17, 1932, Berle Papers, FDRPL. Berle observed that he "gathered that the Governor would rather stay on the gold standard than not. But he is not undertaking to say now what the policy will be. In this connection note that Felix Frankfurter and his friends have been arguing for a managed currency along the line of Maynard Keynes."
38. Warren to Fisher, November 18, 1932, Fisher Papers, YUA. Warren differentiated his position from that of the "economists": "Our prices are definitely tied to gold and cannot be disassociated from it except temporarily. I see no hope whatever thru credit management of any kind."
39. Fisher, "Our Rubber Dollar Did It," Weekly Article of the Index Number Institute, November 14, 1932.
40. Fisher to Moley, November 14, 1932, Berle Papers, FDRPL.

2

Curtain raising in the first hundred days

In the annals of the United States government, the first hundred days of Roosevelt's New Deal hold an unbroken record for governmental activism in peacetime. No contemporary observer could be left in any doubt that the new administration meant business, but not business as usual. Bold experimentation was the order of the day. The president asked for a lot and Congress gave it to him with extraordinary dispatch.

In his opening moves, Roosevelt kept faith with his campaign pledge to redefine the role of government in economic life. Many of his early actions were driven by the imperative to provide relief for distress, both to individuals and to institutions. Directly or indirectly, few citizens were left untouched. The unemployed were made eligible for direct federal assistance, and the strains on state governments – beleaguered by this burden – were eased. Indebted householders and farmers were aided by governmental financial backstopping to arrest foreclosures. Guarantees to railroads both helped to keep the transport system alive and defended those who would have been seriously damaged by default on railway obligations, particularly the insurance companies and their policyholders. Bank depositors were shortly to become the beneficiaries of a governmental program to insure their deposits. The very structure of the nation's financial institutions was also transformed through legislation requiring the divorce of investment banking from commercial banking.

Though many of the early initiatives were hastily improvised, a number of them had been foreshadowed during the campaign. With passage of legislation creating the Civilian Conservation Corps, Roosevelt redeemed his pledge to create jobs in reforestation and to promote conservation. He also delivered on his promise to press for "economy in government" when reducing the pay scales of Federal employees and pensioners by 15 percent, thus signaling that

23

he took fiscal prudence seriously. To be sure, his emergency programs added massively to governmental expenditures. But these outlays were treated as "extraordinary." In the official bookkeeping, Roosevelt's commitment on budget balancing referred to the "ordinary" activities of government.

The New Deal was also quick off the mark in extending the role of government as a regulator. Speedy passage of the Securities and Exchange Act promised to protect the investing public from fraudulent manipulators by bringing the stock markets under governmental surveillance. In addition, the regulatory authority of the Federal Power Commission was strengthened. This was a fast beginning.

Even so, the most arresting features of the New Deal agenda during its curtain-raising phase were its initiatives to spark economic recovery. In its policies toward industry and agriculture and in its approaches to monetary problems, the Roosevelt administration adopted precedent-shattering measures.

1   Monetary issues at center stage

In Roosevelt's campaign headquarters, monetary issues had been treated *sotto voce*. They acquired a fresh lease on life during the post-election interregnum. Part of the attention they then received stemmed from the fact that the incoming administration would be obliged to develop an official American position for the forthcoming World Economic Conference. Hoover had proposed this gathering and he had hoped to use it primarily as a vehicle for regrouping the international community around the gold standard. Members of the Roosevelt team had not been present at the creation; the Democratic platform, however, had endorsed the principle of American participation. Just how the U.S. delegation should be instructed was a matter that remained to be worked out.

Events on the domestic scene during the interregnum gave still greater prominence to monetary issues. In mid-February 1933, another alarming epidemic of bank failures set in. In the preceding three years, the public had become accustomed to runs on banks. But the dimensions of this latest episode broke all previous records. The gravity of the situation was initially exposed in Michigan where its governor declared a bank moratorium, convinced that otherwise virtually all of the state's banks would be wiped out. This sparked a chain reaction throughout the country. Depositors' demands for cash and/or gold exceeded the banking system's capacity to honor them. Something had to give. During his last days in office Hoover considered issuing an executive proclamation declaring a national bank holiday. He refused to do so, however, without the prior endorsement of the president-elect, which was not forthcoming. Roosevelt insisted, as he had throughout the interregnum, that he would take no responsibilities for policies until the powers of the presidency were constitutionally his.

While this was a moment of crisis, it could also be perceived as one of opportunity (at least by those who had long believed that the fundamental redirection of monetary policy was imperative). Fisher certainly saw it as such. Writing to Roosevelt on February 25, 1933 (at the request of the president-elect), he maintained that the "right sort of announcement or proclamation" on inauguration day on March 4, 1933 "would reverse the present deflation overnight and would set us on the path toward new peaks of prosperity ..." He implored Roosevelt to seize "the opportunity of a generation to serve your fellow men and make a place in history beside Washington and Lincoln, having rescued your Country and the World from debt slavery and pauperism and safeguarded them against such disasters in the future."[1]

What then should a presidential proclamation contain? Fisher urged a complete break from gold in favor of "a managed currency (and 'pegged' foreign exchanges)" based on "a commodity standard without any remaining fiction of a gold standard." Though this was his preferred course, he recognized that it might be too drastic to be politically acceptable. Hence, he drew attention to a fall-back position that was compatible with views he had long since expressed. The place gold had come to occupy in economic life was irrational, the argument went, but there still might be negative psychological repercussions on public confidence were it to be completely demonetized. As a second-best option, a link to gold could be preserved, but on different terms; the president should proclaim that the content of the dollar was instantaneously cut in two. This, Fisher noted, would not double the price level – a point on which he and Warren appeared to differ – but it would have substantial positive effects, such as "an immediate rise in the prices of wheat, cotton, and other products dependent on world markets;" "an immediate sympathetic rise in many other prices;" "an immediate rise in the stock market;" "within a week other price rises;" "within a few weeks increases in velocity of circulation of money and credit and stopping of hoarding;" "within a month much reabsorption of idle labor and idle plants."[2]

Fisher was not alone in his perception that a fundamental break from the established monetary order was both desirable and within reach. Though their positions differed on points of detail, he and kindred spirits – Warren of Cornell and John R. Commons of the University of Wisconsin, in particular – agreed wholeheartedly that all gold payments should be suspended as a minimal first step in salvaging the financial system. Other measures could follow to repair "our broken-down price level."[3]

On March 6, 1933, in his first substantive action, Roosevelt issued an executive order suspending internal gold payments when declaring a bank holiday.

1. Fisher to Roosevelt, February 25, 1933, FDRPL.
2. Ibid. Fisher also drew attention to other measures – ones that could be taken quite independently from policy toward gold – that he deemed important. These included steps to unfreeze deposits in failed banks, to ensure deposits in existing banks, and to issue stamp scrip.
3. See Telegrams exchanged among Fisher, Commons, and Warren, March 4 and 5, 1933, Fisher Papers, YUA.

Normal banking operations were then out of the question, and would remain so until public confidence could be restored. Roosevelt aimed at rebuilding it when he proclaimed in his inaugural address that "we have nothing to fear but fear itself." Action followed with passage of the Emergency Banking Act of March 9, 1933, enacted into the law on the very day it was submitted to the Congress. Its provisions created the machinery to reopen banks, once federal inspectors had declared them to be sound. Heartening results followed. By the end of March, roughly two-thirds of the nation's banks, accounting for 90 percent of aggregate deposits, were functioning.[4]

When Roosevelt suspended internal gold payments, it was not initially clear whether this was to be a permanent departure or merely a temporary one. This uncertainty was soon to be removed. As banks began to resume business, there were solid grounds for believing that their fragility precluded a full return to the *status quo ante*. Under the preproclamation arrangements, the public had the right to demand conversion of currency into gold – and in the panic days had exercised it. Roosevelt, recognizing the damage that another round of gold hoarding would bring, outlawed private holdings of monetary gold by executive order on April 5, 1933.[5] External gold payments were a different matter. The Bank Moratorium Order had placed them under governmental jurisdiction, but they had not been banned altogether. It was thus still possible for informed observers to conclude that this feature of the gold standard regime had not been scrapped, but only held in abeyance. On April 18, 1933, however, Roosevelt confounded his more conservative advisers by announcing that licenses to export gold would no longer be issued (apart from authorizations earmarked for transfer to foreign governments before the moratorium had been declared) and that the United States was "off the gold standard." When asked about the further implications of this move at his press conference the following day, he explained that he was determined to raise commodity price levels, but added that "one of the things we hope to do is to get the world back on some form of gold standard."[6]

2   Action on the structuralist agenda: The agricultural component

During the electoral contest, Roosevelt put himself on record as committed to supporting a program of farm relief, though its precise form remained to be determined. Even after the passage of the Agricultural Adjustment Act of 1933, signed into law on May 12, 1933, there were lingering uncertainties about which model would guide intervention in the farm sector. The goal to be sought was not in doubt: to raise farmers' purchasing power and ultimately to restore the price ratio of farm products to nonfarm products that had prevailed

4. James P. Warburg, *The Money Muddle* (New York: Alfred A. Knopf, 1934), p. 94.
5. This action was supplemented by legislation in June 1933 to invalidate clauses in contracts that had stipulated payment in gold.
6. Roosevelt, Thirteenth Press Conference, April 19, 1933, PPA, Vol. II, p. 140.

in the years immediately before World War I. But which policy instruments would be deployed for this purpose? The legislation authorized use of any or all of the competing techniques then at the forefront of discussion: direct control over production (favored by advocates of Domestic Allotment), export promotion and negotiation of marketing agreements on terms favorable to farmers (championed by the residual McNary-Haugenites), and retirement of submarginal acreages (supported by enthusiasts for land use planning). The Secretary of Agriculture and/or his delegate were empowered with sweeping discretionary authority to implement the program as they deemed fit.

To Secretary of Agriculture Henry A. Wallace, this open-ended jurisdiction was an unmixed blessing. Policy makers were sailing in uncharted waters: the greater their freedom of maneuver to make adjustments, the better. Rexford Guy Tugwell, newly appointed as Assistant Secretary of Agriculture (then the number two post in the department), seconded this opinion. When testifying before a Senate committee, he emphasized the experimental character of all this when pressed on whether or not the provisions of the bill should be regarded as permanent or temporary. As Tugwell saw matters:

> ... it was thought best to leave it indefinite in this way, with discretion to withdraw the entire act, the provisions of the entire act or the provisions of any part of it at any time, in the discretion of the Executive. I might also say that it was felt that some provisions of the act it might be desired to leave permanently, unless Congress desired to repeal them ...[7]

Tugwell's support for the Domestic Allotment approach was in evidence in his testimony on behalf of the farm bill. He was, however, to touch some sensitive Senatorial nerves when defending the proposed tax on processors of those agricultural products selected for production controls. This revenue-raising device was essential to the funding of benefits paid to farmers who cooperated by restricting supply. It was thus imperative that it not be compromised by farmers who might short-circuit the usual processor – the butcher in the case of hogs, for example – by doing their own butchering on the farm. To forestall this potential leak, farmers were to be taxed on marketings of products that they had processed on their own. Some Senators expressed disquiet about this constraint on the income-maximizing opportunities of farmers. In rejoinder, Tugwell insisted that the farmer "cannot have his cake and eat it, too," pointing out that, if self-processed products were marketed "through tax-free channels, you would not get enough money to return in benefits to the farmer to induce him to reduce production."[8]

While the Agricultural Adjustment Bill was still under review in Congressional committees, a quite different attitude toward the processing tax –

7. Tugwell, Testimony before the Committee on Agriculture and Forestry, U.S. Senate, 73:1, March 17, 1933, p. 50.
8. Ibid., pp. 55, 60.

and more generally toward Domestic Allotment – was articulated by George N. Peek who testified at the request of Secretary of Agriculture Wallace. Peek did not then occupy any official position, though he was to be named the Agricultural Adjustment Administrator after the bill was passed. As a prime mover for McNary-Haugenism, he had earned a right to be heard when farm legislation was being deliberated. Peek made clear his distaste for a general program of output restriction (though he allowed that it might be necessary in certain exceptional instances). He also indicated his discomfort with the proposal to impose an immediate tax on processors to subsidize curtailment in production. "I think it would be better," he testified, "to make a gradual approach to it and give these processors to understand that they must pay the farmer a fair price, and if they don't pay the fair price, they will have to pay it through taxes. Then I think you would see the prices come up." Peek further challenged the view that "higher prices up to a reasonable level" would expand production. This point of view was obviously incompatible with the Domestic Allotment policy. Peek nonetheless urged Congress to equip the Agricultural Adjustment Administrator with the full arsenal of policy weapons.[9]

Yet another scheme for agricultural uplift was to be incorporated in the Agricultural Adjustment Act of 1933. Senator Elmer Thomas (Democrat of Oklahoma) put the matter squarely before Secretary Wallace who had been arguing for supply restriction to raise prices. Thomas inquired, "Is it or not your opinion that this could be reached immediately, directly, and easily through the placing of more money in circulation?"[10] Wallace accepted that a rising price level, generated through increased currency and credit, would benefit farmers by lightening their debt burdens, but this in itself would not dispose of the overhang of farm commodities. He added: "There are such things as monetary control and production control. They are both important. This bill, of course, addresses itself merely to the production control end."[11]

Thanks to the efforts of Senator Thomas, the final version of the Agricultural Adjustment Act of 1933 embraced more than just the "production control end" of the farm problem. The Thomas Amendment (appropriately named for its author) contained three provisions of special note: (1) that the President be empowered to issue greenbacks in amounts not to exceed $3 billion; (2) that he be authorized to establish the gold content of the dollar, with the restriction that it could not be reduced by more than 50 percent; and (3) that he be given broad powers to acquire silver and to establish bimetallism. There was plenty here to conjure up ghosts of Bryanism. Though some in Roosevelt's inner cir-

9. George N. Peek, Testimony before the Committee on Agriculture and Forestry, U.S. Senate, 73:1, March 24, 1933, pp. 80, 81.
10. Senator Elmer Thomas, Hearings of the Committee on Agriculture and Forestry, U.S. Senate, 73:1, March 25, 1933, p. 144.
11. Wallace, ibid., p. 144.

cle found this disturbing, the president felt comfortable with these powers as long as they were not binding. Battles over how they were to be used, if at all, could be postponed to another day.

Characteristically, Fisher believed that the president should take immediate advantage of the enlarged discretionary authority. "Congratulations with all my heart on the passage of the so-called inflation bill," he wrote to Roosevelt on the day after the Thomas Amendment was enacted. And he sought an early opportunity to discuss with Roosevelt the "personnel for administering reflation and stabilization." He disclaimed any "personal ambitions" in this regard, though he did claim competence to evaluate the qualifications of candidates.[12]

3 Action on the structuralist agenda: The National Industrial Recovery Act

When Roosevelt signed the National Industrial Recovery Act into law on June 16, 1933, he declared it to be "the most important and far-reaching legislation ever enacted by the American Congress."[13] Its stated purpose was "to promote cooperative action, eliminate unfair practices, increase purchasing power, expand production, reduce unemployment, and conserve natural resources." Title I of this legislation authorized the president, for a period of two years, to create an administrative apparatus to approve "codes of fair competition" submitted by trade and industrial associations. As long as the president or his delegate was satisfied that such codes were not contrived to promote monopolies or monopolistic practices, members of such associations could engage in agreed trade practices with immunity from antitrust prosecution. The act intended that each code set acceptable provisions for maximum hours, minimum wages, and socially desirable workplace conditions. The interests of workers were to be further protected through an understanding that employers who became parties to code authority would be obliged to bargain collectively with representatives of the workers' choosing. Members of the business community who had insisted that their ability to pay decent wages hinged on coordinated action in meshing supply with demand could take heart from this language. Representatives of organized labor anticipated that the act would prove to be a catalyst to the extension of unionism. The traditional trust busters were less than satisfied, notwithstanding the antimonopoly language that had been inserted to assuage their concerns. But their protests had been drowned out by the applause generated by leaders in the labor movement and in the business community. William Green, President of the American Federation of Labor, viewed the bill as "the most outstanding, advanced, and for-

12. Fisher to Roosevelt, May 13, 1933, YUA. Fisher's nominees included Warren, James Harvey Rogers of Yale, W. I. King of New York University, Jacob Viner of the University of Chicago, and John R. Commons (if in "vigorous health").
13. Roosevelt, PPA, Vol. II (1933), p. 246.

ward-looking legislation designed to promote economic recovery that has thus far been proposed."[14] The President of the United States Chamber of Commerce, Henry I. Harriman, lauded it as making an essential contribution to economic "balance" within the industrial sector and beyond: It was also needed to ensure the success of the AAA by making it "possible for the city man to pay the higher prices for the farm products."[15] Harriman hailed passage of the National Industrial Recovery Act as "a new business dispensation" to usher in an era of "constructive cooperation" from which the "industrial buccaneer," the "exploiter of labor," and the "unscrupulous price-cutter" would be banished.[16]

It did not follow, however, that the act's major architects shared a common understanding of the significance of this fundamental departure from traditional practice in the relation of government to business. One of the principal draftsmen – General Hugh S. Johnson (formerly of the War Industries Board and coauthor of *Equality for Agriculture,* who was to be appointed as NRA administrator) – saw it as a "charter of a new industrial self-government."[17] Tugwell, on the other hand, had something else in mind: not self-government by industry, but a rational procedure for collaborative planning in which champions of the public interest would enjoy supremacy. As of late May 1933, he was enthusiastic about the prospects. "The most interesting, in a way," he then wrote, "of all the legislation of this period to later observers, will probably be the National Recovery Act. It did not fix the design – the AAA Bill did that – but it carried it out even more perfectly."[18]

There was indeed a noteworthy common feature in the design of these two landmark pieces of legislation. Both provided maximum scope for administrative discretion in the development of policies and procedures. Donald R. Richberg, a labor lawyer from Chicago who was to become Johnson's deputy as NRA administrator, extolled the virtues of this flexibility when the bill was under Congressional consideration. Administrative machinery could be created to meet the needs of specific situations and the risk of "hopeless red tape" that might arise from "some rigid method of control" could be avoided. It also meant that the administrative challenge would be more manageable: "we do not have to go into the proposition of trying day after tomorrow to regulate all of the industries of the United States." Those that could readily agree on a "fair code" could quickly receive governmental

14. William Green, Testimony before the Ways and Means Committee, House of Representatives, 73:1, May 19, 1933, p. 118.
15. Ibid., p. 134.
16. As quoted in Ellis W. Hawley, *The New Deal and the Problem of Monopoly* (Princeton, N.J.: Princeton University Press, 1966), p. 19.
17. As quoted in ibid., p. 19.
18. Tugwell Diaries, May 30, 1933, FDRPL.

sanction for self-control. Official attention could thus be concentrated on industries in more troubled condition.[19]

Title II of the National Industrial Recovery Act spoke to another set of enthusiasms, and its provisions were welcomed by the advocates of an aggressive program of public works as an economic stimulant. An appropriation of $3.3 billion – a record for a single peacetime appropriation – was included therein. (This figure appears to have been struck as a compromise between the numbers of New York's Senator Robert Wagner, who had appealed for an emergency spending program of $5.5 billion, and the views of members of Roosevelt's inner circle who believed that only about $1 billion worth of socially justifiable projects could then be found.) The legislation gave the president wide latitude to allocate this appropriation through a Public Works Administrator of his choice. Several spending categories, however, were specifically enumerated, such as an enlarged program of naval construction or the retirement of submarginal lands from cultivation.

The haste with which Titles I and II had been patched together was to leave behind some confusion. A number of Roosevelt's advisers saw the two titles as integrally linked. In their view, the spending provided in Title II was essential to the fulfillment of the reemployment objectives of Title I. But it was not unreasonable to arrive at a different conclusion: namely, that policies entering the "mix" on separate tracks deserved to stay on separate tracks. If there was no necessary connection between the sectoral interventions and monetary policy authorizations (via the Thomas Amendment) in the Agricultural Adjustment Act, one could hold that there need be none between the sectoral interventions and fiscal policy authorizations in the National Industrial Recovery Act.

Title III of the act was intended to provide comfort to those fearing that the $3.3 billion in spending contained in Title II was not fiscally responsible. Roosevelt's commitment to budget balancing would not be compromised, as his Budget Director, Lewis W. Douglas, argued, because these expenditures were of an extraordinary and emergency character. Nevertheless, he insisted that soundness required new revenues to cover the service charges (estimated to be about $220 million per year) on the debt issued to finance the public works program.[20] Irving Fisher seized this opportunity to attempt to sell Congress on a technique for dealing with this problem. The debt service charges, he explained to the House Ways and Means Committee, could be paid for in stamp scrip, which would be self-liquidating. Thus, when government "issues $220,000,000 of this money [it] is not going to have to levy any tax to retire it." By requiring a 2-cent stamp each week to validate each dollar of scrip, the

19. Donald R. Richberg, Testimony before the Ways and Means Committee, House of Representatives, 73:1, May 18, 1933, p. 69.
20. Lewis W. Douglas, Testimony to the Ways and Means Committee, House of Representatives, 73:1, May 18, 1933, p. 34.

government would raise $1.04 in the course of a year which would permit re-
demption of the scrip and generate 4 cents per dollar's worth of scrip in net
revenue.[21] Fisher was no fan of public works spending as a reemployment device: He consistently maintained that jobs should be created in the private sector and that could best be accomplished through monetary stimuli. But if public works expenditures were to be the order of the day, he could tolerate them
if they had a monetary ingredient. Despite his advocacy, the stamp scrip formula did not make its way into Title III of the National Industrial Recovery
Act. Revenues to service the enlarged public debt were to be found in a new
scheme of capital stock and excess profit taxes.

4   Competing perspectives on the World Economic Conference

The domestic scene – particularly the fallout from the Bank Holiday and the preliminary designs for AAA and NRA – dominated the headlines in March and April 1933. Meanwhile preparation for the World Economic Conference, scheduled to convene in London in June, proceeded
behind the scenes.

Three figures played primary roles in preparing the administration's initial
brief: Oliver M. W. Sprague, a highly regarded professor of banking and finance at Harvard, who had been appointed as an economic adviser to the
Treasury;[22] James P. Warburg, a New York banker with broad experience in
international finance and son of Paul Warburg, a charter member of the Federal Reserve Board; and Herbert Feis, who had held the title of economic adviser to the Department of State for more than a decade. All three distanced
themselves from the views of Fisher and Warren. In the first instance, they
challenged the premise that monetary manipulation could control the behavior of the general price level. (Sprague, for example, had forcefully spelled
out his doubts on this point in testimony before Congressional Committees in
the 1920s when attacking legislation championed by Fisher and Commons
that would instruct the Federal Reserve to target price stability as its overriding objective.) They were even more skeptical – to the point of being derisive

---

21. Fisher, Testimony before the Committee on Ways and Means, House of Represen-
    tatives, 73:1, May 19, 1933, p. 172. When the House of Representatives did not
    warm to this proposal, Fisher put another version before the Senate Committee on
    Finance. In this instance, he suggested that the federal government should autho-
    rize state governments to issue stamp scrip to fund the latters' contribution to pub-
    lic works projects (in which the sharing was expected to be 70 percent federal, 30
    percent state). (Fisher, Testimony before the Committee on Finance, U.S. Senate,
    73:1, May 31, 1933, pp. 337–40.)
22. Sprague's other qualifications included sometime service as a consultant to the
    Bank of England and as one of Roosevelt's instructors during his undergraduate
    days at Harvard.

– of the Warren line of argument about an alleged link between the price of gold and the general price level. Reduction in the gold content of the dollar, it was recognized, could elevate the domestic price of commodities sold in volume abroad. Such action, however, could scarcely have significant impact on the broad range of products that lacked significant export markets.

Nor did the Sprague-Warburg-Feis strategy group have any tolerance for the Fisher ideal: the ultimate demonetization of gold. In their view, gold continued to have a vital role to play in international reconstruction. Nevertheless, they held it to be folly to attempt to roll the clock back to 1929. Some realignments in the gold content of currencies were in order. As far as the United States was concerned, much of the needed readjustment had already been accomplished with the depreciation of the dollar's exchange value following the suspension of gold exports. Fixed exchange rates – pegged to gold – remained as a goal, though the gold standard needed to be "modernized." Three departures from earlier practice were to be sought through international agreement. In the first instance, gold should henceforth be held exclusively by central banks and governments and withdrawn from private circulation. (The United States had already taken this step in April 1933.) Second, provision should be made for flexibility in the gold reserve ratios that governments chose to specify as backing for domestic currency. Thus, no country should be handicapped for reducing gold backing at home when growth in the world's demand for gold fell short of growth in its supply. Third, the international community should develop common rules to permit a currency's metallic base to be augmented through the use of silver as a reserve in a pre-specified proportion.

Not surprisingly, Fisher took vigorous exception to the Sprague-Warburg-Feis approach to an official American position at the London Conference. In a letter to Sprague (with a copy sent to Roosevelt) on June 1, 1933, Fisher called for an American "declaration of independence." The United States "should not wait for action by other countries, nor make our action dependent on theirs, nor tie up our standard to theirs irrevocably. Otherwise we shall again suffer deflation or inflation if they do." He reiterated the importance of declaring reflation to the 1926 price level to be the objective. And he further insisted that the United States should retain freedom to raise the price of gold until that objective had been reached. Preserving the ability to act unilaterally was important to the United States for another reason:

> in order to avoid the falling price level consequent on reducing our tariff. If, for instance, we adopt a new but fixed gold price in agreement with other countries, and then reduce our tariff, gold may flow out and our price level will fall.[23]

Such deflationary forces could not – and need not – be countenanced.

23. Fisher to O. M. W. Sprague (with a copy to Roosevelt), June 1, 1933, FDRPL.

There were many occasions during the Roosevelt years when the executive branch seemed to be operating at cross purposes. The London Economic Conference was conspicuous among them. As Sprague, Warburg, and Feis understood their task, they should press adoption of the "modernized" gold standard regime in which individual countries could be afforded considerable latitude in determining when their exchange rates would be stabilized. The reflationists at home, on the other hand, feared that the American delegation would commit the United States to stabilization prematurely and were not bashful in voicing their concerns. The Committee for the Nation, a lobbying group in which Fisher and Warren were influential members, cautioned Roosevelt against yielding to pressures from Britain and France to limit a reduction of the gold content of the dollar to 25 or 30 percent. The American government should not allow its hands to be tied, this group argued, when a much deeper cut was needed to stimulate reemployment and to restore the domestic price level to its 1926 altitude.[24]

Roosevelt's own cable to the London Economic Conference of July 3, 1933 effectively repudiated the groundwork laid by the American delegation and by his personal representative, Raymond Moley, who had been dispatched with fresh instructions at a point when the conference had appeared to be stalled. "I would regard it as a catastrophe amounting to a world tragedy," Roosevelt asserted, "if the Great Conference of Nations ... should ... allow itself to be diverted by the proposal of a purely artificial and temporary experiment affecting the monetary exchange of a few Nations only." Stabilization of the exchange value of the dollar, as he then saw matters, was incompatible with the objective of American policy to seek "the kind of dollar which a generation hence will have the same purchasing and debt-paying power as the dollar value we hope to attain in the near future."[25]

Moley, as well as the regular members of the American delegation, were nonplussed by this bombshell of a message. Only later were they able to comprehend what must have possessed the president. Roosevelt was at sea on a Navy cruiser when the cable was sent. Henry Morgenthau, Jr. was among his traveling companions, and he had come well armed with Professor Warren's charts tracking the prices of gold and of commodities.

The demise of the London Economic Conference left hurt feelings and bruised egos in its wake. But there were those who rejoiced at this outcome. John Maynard Keynes hailed the president as being "magnificently right." (Moley later countered with the observation that what Keynes really meant was

24. Cable from the Directing Committee of the "Committee for the Nation" to Roosevelt, June 30, 1933, FDRPL.
25. Roosevelt, "A Wireless to the London Conference," July 3, 1933, PPA, Vol. II, pp. 264–5.

"magnificently left."[26]) Fisher joined the rejoicing, informing Roosevelt that his message to the Economic Conference "makes me the happiest of men."[27]

Roosevelt had indeed kept his hands untied. Amidst all the confusion of the first hundred days, there was at least one common thread. All the initiatives embarked upon enlarged the president's freedom for economic policy maneuver. How that freedom would be exercised remained to be determined.

26. See Moley, *After Seven Years,* p. 262n.
27. Fisher to Roosevelt, July 5, 1933, FDRPL.

3

Deployments in the second half of 1933

Roosevelt's bombshell message to the London Economic Conference made clear that he was not willing to make commitments abroad that might put at risk his policies at home. The precise form that his domestic initiatives were to take had yet to be determined. The president did not suffer from a shortage of counsel about how the affairs of the National Recovery Administration and the Agricultural Adjustment Administration should be conducted or about what to do next with respect to the international exchange value of the dollar. These issues were to be at the top of the agenda for the remainder of 1933.

1   Activating the National Recovery Administration

Roosevelt told the nation in July 1933 that the National Industrial Recovery Program reflected careful planning for a "logical whole" of measures.[1] This put a strain on reality: The scissors and paste character of the act hardly justified such a description. This legislation, it will be recalled, had two central features. The first was concerned with the apparatus for code making, to be conducted under the supervision of a National Recovery Administrator. The second provided $3.3 billion to be spent under the direction of a Public Works Administrator. Some involved in shaping the language of the National Industrial Recovery Act – among them Alexander Sachs, who served as NRA's first Director of Research – did indeed regard these provisions as constituting a "logical whole." In this view, a spur to the economy from public works outlays was vital to the reemployment objectives of the act and to worthwhile results from code making.

---

1. Roosevelt, Third Fireside Chat, July 24, 1933, PPA, Vol. II, p. 296.

Roosevelt did not share that view. Had he done so, he would not have handed the portfolio of Public Works Administrator to Harold D. Ickes, Secretary of the Interior. Ickes had unimpeachable integrity, an admirable trait in a public official. He insisted that no government contract should be awarded without careful scrutiny to ensure that taxpayers were protected from corruption and waste. He also stood firm against authorizing projects before their long-run social utility had been clearly demonstrated. These qualities were not well calculated to produce timely action. Ickes's posture, however, was congenial to a president who was not then persuaded that public works spending could be a pump primer and who stood for budget balancing in the normal operations of government.

When filling the post of National Recovery Administrator, Roosevelt turned to General Hugh S. Johnson, a man whose style could not have contrasted more sharply with that of Ickes. Whereas Ickes was cautious and methodical, Johnson was impetuous, abrupt, and determined to produce quick results. This appointment was not universally applauded. Tugwell, for one, was particularly uncomfortable about Johnson's association with Bernard Baruch, the financier who had headed the War Industries Board in 1917–18. Yet, although he had reservations about the appointment, he ended up endorsing it. As he recorded his appraisal of Johnson at the time:

> I had gotten used to thinking of him as Baruch's man rather than as an independent personality, not doubting, of course, the strength of character and the real brilliance, which are obvious. I think his tendency to be gruff in personal relations will be a handicap and his occasional drunken sprees will not help any; but on the whole I am quite happy about it. ... It would doubtless have been better if he had been further removed from the Baruch speculative influence and if he believed more in social planning, but the one gives him an inside knowledge which will be useful in his dealings with business and the other is something that comes out as it is done. I doubt if one is a much better planner for believing in it as a principle.[2]

Roosevelt's decisions on the division of labor that would breathe life into the first two titles of the National Industrial Recovery Act meant that no significant stimulus to reemployment could be expected from the spending authorized in Title II. Where then was a boost to the economy to come from? The implicit model offered at the time called initially for a form of work spreading. The first step was to invite all employers to reduce the length of the workweek while maintaining the same weekly pay packet. Two results were anticipated: (1) Jobs would be created to absorb the unemployed, and (2) the increment in the aggregate wage bill would enlarge total purchasing power and augment demand for labor still further. Though this clearly meant that hourly wage rates would rise, it was argued that costs per unit of output would not necessarily go up.

2. Tugwell Diaries, May 30, 1933, FDRPL.

After all, excess capacity in the industrial sector was abundantly in evidence. Increased demand for a manufacturer's product – fed by an enlarged total wage bill – might well lead to lower average costs as production expanded into the range of more efficient operations. Success in executing this maneuver could lift the economy by its bootstraps. Roosevelt, presumably, had this in mind when he appealed for a speedy and united effort. In his words, "if all employers in each trade now bond themselves faithfully in these modern guilds – without exception – and agree to act together and at once, none will be hurt and millions of workers, so long deprived of their right to earn their bread in the sweat of their labor, can raise their heads again." But he cautioned that "the whole project will be set at naught" if prices were to rise at the same rate as wages.[3]

The atmosphere of the summer of 1933 had all the psychological trappings of a nation at war, but the enemy was at home, not overseas. All citizens were invited to mobilize in a common cause, and those who did not were to be stigmatized as unpatriotic shirkers. Employers were under pressure to sign the President's Reemployment Agreement, copies of which were available at every post office. Signers of this covenant committed themselves to abide by stipulated conditions on the maximum length of the workweek and to set pay scales no lower than specified minima.[4] The signators also committed themselves to "cooperate to the fullest extent" in preparing a "Code of Fair Competition" for their industry for submission no later than September 1, 1933. The Reemployment Agreement further called for universal compliance with the following standards for price behavior: Prices should not exceed those prevailing on July 1, 1933 except by the amount "made necessary by actual increases in production, replacement, or invoice costs of merchandise"; in the event that price increases could be so justified, the seller would agree "to give full weight to probable increases in sales volume and to refrain from taking profiteering advantage of the consuming public."

An employer's decision on participation in the president's program was technically voluntary. Not too subtly, there were both carrots and sticks. Com-

---

3. Roosevelt, Presidential Statement on the National Industrial Recovery Act, June 16, 1933, PPA, Vol. II, pp. 252, 255.
4. The formulas made allowance for special circumstances in particular trades: For example, the standard maximum workweek in factory employments was set at 35 hours, but registered pharmacists and those engaged in emergency repair and maintenance work were not subject to a ceiling. Similarly, minimum wage rates varied with community size: The weekly minimum was set at $15 in cities with a population of 500,000 or more; at the other extreme, employers in towns populated by fewer than 2,500 persons were expected "to increase all wages by not less than 20 percent, provided that this shall not require wages in excess of $12 per week." The agreement also included an "anti-child labor" provision: No minor under the age of 16 could be hired as a full-time worker. (President's Reemployment Agreement, July 27, 1933.)

pliers were entitled to display the Blue Eagle emblem, identifying them as "doing their part." Firms without this label risked boycott. Those interested in doing business with government agencies certainly knew where the action was. By executive order in August, Roosevelt directed that government's orders should go only to businesses that had joined the program. Altogether an impressive response was forthcoming. More than 2.3 million individual agreements were signed, covering about 16.3 million employees.[5]

Code drafting, on the other hand, got off to a slow start, Johnson's flair for drama notwithstanding. In the National Recovery Administration's first month, 103 codes were submitted (and of those only 65 dealt with industrial groupings of national scope). In the last half of July, 144 proposed national codes were received. The president's Reemployment Agreement, which obliged signers to submit a code by September 1, spurred activity. The number of submissions rose to 546 in August, and another 263 were received by September 23.[6]

Processing this traffic imposed a formidable administrative burden on NRA headquarters in Washington. In the typical case, the procedure for review went as follows: A Deputy Administrator, usually a person of business experience, would be assigned to review each proposed code. A representative of each of three Advisory Boards – one for labor (appointed by the Secretary of Labor), one for industry (appointed by the Secretary of Commerce), and one for consumers (appointed by Johnson) – would work with the Deputy Administrator in shepherding the code application. Although the Deputy Administrator was honor-bound to attempt to win the concurrence of these advisers before making a recommendation, he retained the authority to forward a code for Johnson's endorsement without their approval.

In principle, this apparatus ensured that all parties at interest had a voice in decision making. In practice, code approvals – in more cases than not – gave businesses what they wanted. It did not follow that the business community liked these procedures. There was considerable grumbling over the labor provisions, particularly over NRA's guarantee that workers had rights to bargain collectively. With respect to trade practice provisions in the codes, however, the industry's point of view tended to dominate. In the words of an expert committee conducting a postmortem on the NRA experience (which reported in 1937): "... in this code-making process during the early months, without express policy guides, industry had quite fully expressed what it wanted as to trade-practice provisions, and to a great extent it had received what it asked for."[7]

5. Roosevelt, PPA, Vol. II, p. 312.
6. *The National Recovery Administration: Report of the President's Committee of Industrial Analysis,* House Document 158, March 2, 1937, pp. 19, 21.
7. Ibid., p. 36. The members of this investigative team were John Maurice Clark, Professor of Economics at Columbia University; William H. Davis of Pennie, Davis, Marvin and Edmonds; George M. Harrison, President of the Brotherhood of Railway and Steamship Clerks; and George H. Mead, President of the Mead Corporation.

Trade practice provisions, which were to spark intense controversy, were far from uniform across industries. A few examples from the early rounds of code approvals will illustrate their character:

- *Cotton textile code:* Production was limited by prohibiting the operation of machinery for more than two 40-hour shifts per week.
- *Shipbuilding and shiprepairing code:* Sales of goods and services below their reasonable cost (which would be determined by accounting methods set by the industry) were proscribed as "unfair competition," and the use of rebates, refunds, unearned discounts, etc. was prohibited.
- *Wool textile code:* Production limitation as in the cotton textile code.
- *Electrical manufacturing industry code:* Sales below costs were prohibited, and firms were required to notify competitors – but not customers – of any intent to change prices. An obligatory waiting period of 10 days was specified before a price change became effective. Thereafter, sales below the filed price were prohibited.
- *Corset and brassiere code:* Sales below costs were prohibited, and myriad regulations – ranging from the standardization of packaging of merchandise, requirements on the registration of designs, and prohibitions against "enticing" away a competitor's sales employees – were promulgated.
- *Legitimate full-length dramatic and theatrical industry code:* Ticket "scalpers" were barred.
- *Lumber and timber products industry code:* Minimum prices were established and quotas allocated to individual producers.[8]

Before it was finished, NRA approved 557 basic codes, more than three-quarters of which were issued during the first year of operations.[9] Once a code had received blessing in Washington, day-to-day administration was thereafter assigned to code authorities set up by representatives of the industrial grouping in question. It was presupposed that the costs of this activity would be borne by trade association members. Virtually all codes provided that mandatory assessments could be made for this purpose. A few codes – only 26 of them – stipulated that funding for code authorities could be generated from payments for "damages" imposed for a code violation.[10] This was a very faint shadow of Tugwell's vision of an Industrial Integration Board in which non-compliers would be fined to reward cooperators.

The flurry of activity in the early months of NRA left behind confusion, but also some achievements. On the positive side, some 2,462,000 workers were reemployed between June and October 1933, generating an increase of 6.8 percent in total employment. Job growth in NRA industries – some 11.4 percent – was significantly higher than in industries not affiliated with NRA. All this occurred at a time when total industrial activity was declining, suggesting that increases in the number of persons at work could be largely attributed

8. Ibid., pp. 34–6.
9. Ibid., p. 27.
10. Ibid., p. 74.

to the work-spreading feature of the president's Reemployment Agreement.[11] On a less happy note, these findings indicated that productivity per worker had declined.

In the autumn of 1933, the NRA authorities elected to attack the problem of recovery via another route. They then mounted a Buy Now campaign which was intended to pressure consumers to increase their normal purchases by 10 percent. It was a resounding failure. Hoover had attempted a similar promotion in the spring of 1932, billed at the time as an antihoarding campaign, with no better results. The lessons of the earlier episode, if indeed they had ever been learned, seemed to have been forgotten. NRA's Buy Now campaign did not falter because it failed to think "big." One of its architects, Frank R. Wilson of its Bureau of Public Relations, had in mind a scheme in which 20 million or more consumer pledge cards would be distributed by NRA committees in all major cities. In a manner analogous to bond drives organized in wartime, quotas for supplementary spending pledges were to be assigned geographically. The public's tolerance for high-pressure boosterism had been pressed beyond its limit.[12]

Other difficulties were quick to surface. Complaints about the impact of codes on price making were legion. Representatives of farm organizations protested that gains in farm income flowing from New Deal agricultural programs were being eroded by unwarranted increases in the prices of goods farmers purchased. Labor organizations complained about a tendency of prices to rise faster than wages and about the underrepresentation of workers in code authorities. Government procurement officers drew attention to a tendency for competition to disappear in bidding on government contracts: Increasingly, it seemed, the bids turned out to be identical. Not only did this smack of collusive behavior, it also suggested that the purchasing power of funds appropriated for public works was being diminished by inflated price rigging. Meanwhile, the Federal Trade Commission began to register protests with the White House that NRA was sanctioning – most notably in the case of the steel code – price-fixing practices that the FTC had already outlawed.[13]

11. Ibid., p. 95.
12. Frank R. Wilson, Bureau of Public Relations of the National Recovery Administration, "Preliminary Report on Preparation for the 'Buy Now' Campaign," September 8, 1933, FDRPL.
13. Garland S. Ferguson, Jr., Acting Chairman of the Federal Trade Commission, to Roosevelt, December 30, 1933, FDRPL. Attorneys at the Federal Trade Commission elaborated as follows on the steel code: "Those members of the trade who adhere to price understandings are deemed fair competitors under the code. Adherents to similar understandings were formerly indictable and subjected to injunction and treble damage suits under the Sherman Act and were liable to proceedings and orders to cease and desist under the Federal Trade Commission Act. On the other hand those traders who now compete in price, in harmony with the spirit of the

Particularly vociferous was the indignation voiced by representatives of consumers. A confrontation between Johnson and a consumer spokesman, Leon Henderson, in December 1933 was to have lingering consequences. After what was described as a "shouting match" between the two men, Johnson posed a question to Henderson: "If you're so goddammed smart, why don't you come down here and be my assistant on consumer problems?"[14] Henderson joined the NRA payroll in Washington in January 1934 and was to play a formidable role in the ensuing chapter of its history.

2   Activating the Agricultural Adjustment Act

The language of the Agricultural Adjustment Act had made provision for a number of differing approaches to the elevation of farm prices, but had assigned to them no ordering of priorities. Roosevelt's initial choices of key players on the operating team also fell short of giving clear-cut focus to farm policy. The secretaryship in the Department of Agriculture went to Henry A. Wallace, an Iowan with high visibility among farmers who had recently been converted to the merits of domestic allotment while remaining sympathetic to monetary measures to raise farm prices. Tugwell was assigned the second-ranking post in the department (then styled as assistant secretary) Because of his interest in reshaping the industrial sector, he had originally believed that an appointment in the Department of Commerce might be better suited to his talents. An opportunity to engage in hands-on planning in the farm sector had its own magnetism in view of his fervent advocacy of supply restriction through domestic allotment. Roosevelt's decision to appoint George N. Peek as the Agricultural Adjustment Administrator ensured, however, that a distinctly different point of view would be represented in the high command. Peek's tireless campaigning for the McNary-Haugen Bill had won him a devoted following in the major farm organizations. He did not conceal his opposition to restrictions on farm output, and he was also on record in protesting that "farm leaders were being led off by economists."[15] Even so, one of the professors, M. L. Wilson, was appointed to a post in Peek's organization as administrator of the wheat program. Wilson had an abiding loyalty to land use planning as the long-term solution to the problem of crop surpluses, although he embraced supply restriction through domestic allotment as necessary in conditions of emergency.

anti-trust laws, and who reject understandings as to prices are deemed users of unfair practices and are subject to the code penalties therefor. And those who were formerly law breakers are now favored and given authority over their competitors' prices and practices." ("Memorandum for the Chairman in re: Steel Code, Approved under the National Recovery Act," December 29, 1933, FDRPL.)

14. As quoted by Hawley, op. cit., p. 77.
15. As quoted by Gilbert C. Fite, *George N. Peek and the Fight for Farm Parity* (Norman, Ok.: University of Oklahoma Press, 1954), p. 244.

This line-up had the political recommendation of ticket balancing, but it was decidedly not one to assure organizational harmony. Signs of strain were not long delayed. Wallace and Peek were at odds before the Agricultural Adjustment Act had been a fortnight old: Peek claimed the right to bypass the secretary's office and to approach the president directly, a procedure totally unacceptable to Wallace. Much of this friction reflected the jurisdictional jealousies of two strong personalities. At base, a point of principle was also at stake. Peek sought to expand markets and to avoid production controls. Wallace, with strong support from Tugwell, was convinced that export promotion, given the state of the international economy, would be wasted effort and that there was no feasible alternative to shrinking supply.[16]

Operationally, the central issue turned on the respective emphases to be assigned to different techniques for raising prices. One of them, championed by proponents of domestic allotment, authorized the government to make benefit payments (paid for by taxing processors) to farmers who reduced their outputs. A second, for which Peek's lobbying had been responsible, placed primary weight on marketing agreements, negotiated by government, under the terms of which processors and distributors would undertake to purchase farm products at prices approaching "parity" (as defined by the relationships between the prices of farm and nonfarm goods in 1909–14).

There was never any doubt about the course Peek preferred to pursue. Nevertheless he accepted that output restriction, in extraordinary circumstances, might be necessary as an option of last resort. And he practiced it in mid-1933 when subsidizing growers of cotton and tobacco to plough up a substantial fraction of the acreages already planted to these crops. To brace the price of hogs, he also ordered the purchase and destruction of some 6.2 million pigs and 222,000 sows. Even though much of the resulting inventory of edible pork was distributed as food relief, this manipulation to contrive scarcity aroused popular indignation.[17]

The marketing agreement approach, on the other hand, at least held out the possibility that farm prices could be raised without the unpleasantness asso-

16. It should be noted that Wallace and Tugwell were enthusiasts for seeking out novel ways to enlarge the demand for farm products at home. In April 1933, for example, they argued in favor of research funding to perfect the technology of gasohol. Success in such a venture, they observed, would not only create a new market for surplus corn, but would also serve the national interest by conserving exhaustible fossil fuels. With the repeal of prohibition, Tugwell also championed the consumption of wine produced from home-grown grapes. This bit of salesmanship – presented in an address to a Democratic Women's Club entitled "Wine, Women and Song" – prompted letters of protest to the White House from a group of Ohio clergymen.

17. For additional details on these points, see Murray R. Benedict, *Farm Policies of the United States, 1790–1950* (New York: The Twentieth Century Fund, 1953), especially pp. 306–8.

ciated with the deliberate destruction of farm products. The administration of marketing agreements, however, created other problems. In his enthusiasm to strike a better deal for farmers, Peek was not overly scrupulous in his oversight of processors. The NRA had transferred the authority to approve "codes of fair competition" for the agricultural processing industries to his office; Peek thus had the power to permit them to collude with immunity. In Tugwell's view, shared by the legal staff of the Department of Agriculture, Peek had used this power irresponsibly by allowing processors to expand their "spreads." This issue came to the boil in September 1933 over proposed marketing agreements for sugar and tobacco. The Legal Division advised Secretary Wallace, who had the final say in the matter, to deny his approval unless the processing companies opened their books for public inspection. Peek objected and prevailed in this round, after taking the dispute directly to Roosevelt. His undoing as Agricultural Adjustment Administrator was triggered soon thereafter when he sought to transfer $500,000 from processing tax revenues to subsidize the export of surplus butter to Europe. As Wallace and Tugwell saw things, receipts from processing taxes should subsidize American producers who curtailed outputs, not foreign consumers. Peek's scheme was objectionable for a further reason: It amounted to export "dumping," which should be rejected on principle. Roosevelt asked for Peek's resignation in mid-December 1933. In a face-saving gesture, Peek was appointed as a special adviser to the president on foreign trade.[18]

With Peek's departure from the agricultural bureaucracy, the dominance of supply restriction over the marketing agreement approach to elevating farm prices was established. Amid the confusion, one significant point emerged. For perhaps the first time in American history, the views of professional economists had made a formidable contribution to the shaping of fundamental policy strategy. Peek and the residual cohort of McNary-Haugenites had leverage in the farm constituencies, whereas the economists certainly did not. Though many thorny issues in farm policy remained on the agenda, at least part of the ambiguity built into the Agricultural Adjustment Act had been resolved. When forced to choose, Roosevelt backed the options presented to him by the economists, rather than those preferred by lobbyists of farm organizations.

While contention over rival strategies for short-term price manipulation commanded the headlines in 1933, supporters of the land use planning technique for supply management over the longer term still showed some positive vital signs. They scored a minor victory in the summer of 1933 when exposing a contradiction between the output reduction program of the Department of Agriculture on the one hand, and the operations of the Public Works Ad-

18. These episodes are recounted in Fite, op. cit., especially Chapter XV, and in Bernard Sternsher, *Rexford Tugwell and the New Deal* (New Brunswick, N.J.: Rutgers University Press, 1964), pp. 183–203.

ministration on the other. It made no sense for PWA to enlarge the cultivated area by funding irrigation and reclamation projects at a time when AAA was trying to shrink it. The upshot was an interdepartmental agreement that henceforth the productive capacity added by PWA's projects would be offset by eliminating an equivalent amount of production on submarginal lands.[19] Funds to purchase land for retirement would be provided by a transfer of appropriations from the Public Works Administrator to the Secretary of Agriculture. The sums involved were initially modest; $25 million was thus made available for land purchase in 1933. They still permitted a pilot program to go forward. In addition, the creation of a Program Planning Division within the Department of Agriculture, which was staffed principally by champions of land use planning, offered an institutional base for advocates of this point of view.

3   Reflationists and their critics: A return engagement

The London Economic Conference expired with the future of the dollar in international markets unresolved. Roosevelt had been unambiguous on one point: He was not prepared to fix an exchange value of the dollar in July 1933. His rhetoric still paid lip service to the desirability of international regrouping around a modified gold standard. But at what point in time and on what terms? In midsummer 1933, the reflationists and their opponents again mobilized to do battle on these issues. But there was a new twist to the disputation in this round. Members of both camps, in decidedly different ways, then argued that adoption of their respective recommendations was crucial to the success of the president's domestic program.

Warburg, who had left London in a huff, hoped to rally the "stabilizers." In a memorandum prepared for the president on the voyage home, Warburg warned that:

> the Administration has never faced a more serious situation than it does today. The entire recovery program, which is at the heart of its policy, is jeopardized by uncertainty and doubt in the monetary field. The National Recovery Act cannot possibly function to any useful end if there is fear of currency depreciation of an unknown amount and fear of monetary experimentation.

He called for a fresh analysis of the administration's monetary policy to design a definite program no later than October 1.[20]

A study group for this purpose was hastily assembled, under the chairmanship of Secretary of the Treasury Woodin. Its interim report, submitted on August 29, 1933, argued that it was unrealistic to expect "monetary action alone"

19. See M. L. Wilson to Harold Ickes, Public Works Administrator, August 31, 1933, Records of the Bureau of Agricultural Economics, NA.
20. Warburg to Roosevelt, "The Domestic Currency Problem," August 2, 1933, FDRPL.

to generate recovery; monetary policy could, however, either "create an environment favorable to the success of action along other lines" or an environment that would "frustrate such action." Conventional techniques of monetary stimulus via open market purchases by the Federal Reserve should be welcomed to support NRA's projected Buy Now campaign. But unconventional monetary experimentation, such as measures put at the president's disposal by the Thomas Amendment, should be avoided. A special issue of "greenbacks" would have particularly harmful effects on business confidence. For the longer term, this monetary advisory group recommended "establishment of an improved gold standard," after trade recovery had been achieved. Prospects for success in reaching both immediate and longer-run goals, its members concluded, would be enhanced "if there were some assurance that we were moving towards, rather than away from international cooperation."[21]

Treasury officials participating in this study resisted "inflationist" arguments for a further reason. Part of their charge was to manage the national debt. Refinancing a sizable volume of maturing obligations was shortly ahead, to say nothing of borrowing to cover the administration's current spending. An official signal of intent to raise the price level would jeopardize these operations. In principle, this problem could be addressed if the Treasury were authorized to issue "purchasing power" bonds, i.e., bonds with interest payments indexed to the general price level. Anticipating that the orthodox would claim that reflation would thwart public debt management, Fisher had put the indexing proposal on the table several months earlier.[22]

In a personal intervention, Warburg took his case to the president in late September with another note of alarm. Since the submission of the Interim Report of the Monetary Group, the dollar had depreciated further; altogether, its gold value had shrunk by about 35 percent since March. "Whatever benefits could be derived from depreciation of the currency," he argued, "would seem to have been realized." Already hopes aroused by NRA were being dashed as workers observed that the purchasing power of recently established wage minimums was being eroded. Now was the time to stabilize. This was "not a plea for capitalists [who] by and large will be able to protect themselves," he insisted. It was instead "a plea for the man who lives on wages or who has retired on the savings out of past wages."[23]

Meanwhile Roosevelt listened to other voices. In the week following his bombshell message, he conferred with Warren. Yale's James Harvey Rogers (who had gained notoriety in 1931 for predicting a month before the fact that Britain would be forced to leave the gold standard) was also drawn into the midsummer conversations. In addition, Fisher had an extended audience with

21. "Interim Money Report," transmitted to Roosevelt by Woodin, August 29, 1933, FDRPL.
22. Fisher to Sprague, June 1, 1933, FDRPL.
23. Warburg to Roosevelt, September 20, 1933, FDRPL.

the president at Hyde Park in August 1933. In his account of this meeting, Fisher reported that the president referred to his rejection of Warburg's request that he "fix a definite price of gold." The president asked Fisher if he "agreed with Warren and Rogers that if he [Roosevelt] got the Federal Reserve to buy newly mined gold at say $29 an ounce it would help raise commodity prices." Fisher replied that he did.[24]

By late September, Warren (then operating from an office at the Department of Commerce) argued with heightened urgency that a rise in prices was "essential" and could be accomplished in "only one way": i.e., "by reducing the gold content of the dollar." Restlessness among farmers, in particular, was growing. With the end of the harvest season at hand, farmers would not "receive the benefit on this year's crops" unless prices advanced before they had to sell them. Policy delay would simply increase the amount by which the gold content of the dollar would ultimately have to be cut. "A year ago," he maintained, "a cut of about one-third might have been sufficient. Now, a cut of nearly a half is likely to be necessary to get prompt results, to save banks, cities and other private and public credit, as well as public morale."[25]

Warren also had at hand a recommendation for a technique to produce quick results. The government should enter the gold market by purchasing gold at prices that would be moved upward week by week.[26] Fisher endorsed this approach, warning Roosevelt that America was losing ground on the "reflation job"; the remedy was an "open market for gold" and "announcement of the price sought – as $35 to $40, etc." He added that "a prompt resumption of rapid reflation will help enormously to make this N.R.A. a success."[27] There were, however, some lingering doubts about the legality of putting government in such a gold-buying business. Certainly Dean Acheson, then Acting Secretary of the Treasury, entertained them, and he questioned the effectiveness of a gold purchase program as well.[28]

In an address to the nation on October 22, 1933, Roosevelt announced his decision to instruct the Reconstruction Finance Corporation "to buy newly mined gold in the United States at prices to be determined from time to time. ... Whenever necessary to the end in view, we shall also buy and sell gold in the world market. ... This is a policy and not an expedient. It is not to be used merely to offset a temporary fall in prices. We are thus continuing to move toward a managed currency."[29] On each business day in the ensuing weeks,

24. Fisher to Margaret Hazard Fisher, August 9, 1933, YUA.
25. Warren to Roosevelt, September 20, 1933, FDRPL.
26. Warren to Roosevelt, September 20, 1933, FDRPL.
27. Fisher to Roosevelt, September 11, 1933, FDRPL.
28. Acheson to Roosevelt, October 21, 1933, FDRPL.
29. Roosevelt, the Fourth Fireside Chat, October 22, 1933, PPA, Vol. II, pp. 426–7.
    Warren and Rogers had been on hand when this speech was prepared. Though the

Morgenthau (who was to be named Acting Secretary of the Treasury in mid-November), Warren, and Jesse Jones (Director of the Reconstruction Finance Corporation) met with the president to fix the day's price of gold. Before the new policy was announced, the price on the London market stood at $29.01 an ounce. When this price-elevating bidding was terminated in January 1934, it had reached $35 per ounce.

The gold purchase program marked a policy-shaping triumph – at least momentarily – for advocates of reflation and, more particularly, for the Warren version of that doctrine. As might have been expected, this tilt toward heresy aroused the ire of the orthodox. For example, Princeton's Edwin W. Kemmerer – widely referred to as the "money doctor" by virtue of his advisory missions to position foreign governments on the gold standard in the 1920s – decried the futility of this experiment. In his view, the administration's actions had seriously damaged business confidence and thus had a negative impact on recovery.[30] But gold price manipulation also produced some blood letting within Roosevelt's official entourage. Acheson was so discomfited by this turn of events that he handed an undated letter of resignation to the president, which was accepted. Sprague resigned as a Treasury economic adviser and made no bones about his disgust with a policy that he held would not work, but that would imperil government credit and retard recovery.[31] Warburg also felt obliged to appeal to the public (which he hoped to arouse), having become persuaded that "the tide could not be turned by a tolerated opposition from within."[32]

two men collaborated on this project, they were not altogether of one mind. For Warren, the gold price was the variable controlling economic performance. Rogers, on the other hand, favored the ultimate demonetization of gold and assigned a major weight in recovery programs to public works spending financed by new money.

30. Edwin W. Kemmerer, "Controlled Inflation," *American Economic Review Supplement,* March 1934, pp. 90–100. His appraisal of the New Deal's monetary policy was initially presented at the meetings of the American Economic Association in December 1933.

31. Sprague maintained that the banking and business community was hesitant to make commitments "because it naturally fears that when the Warren program of depreciation of the dollar is seen to be ineffective, the Administration, instead of reverting to reasonably sane monetary policies, will either experiment with devaluation at the present or lower value of the dollar, as expressed in the price of gold, or resort to positive inflationary measures." [O. M. W. Sprague, *Recovery and Common Sense* (Boston: Houghton Mifflin Company, 1934), p. 60. The material in this volume was initially copyrighted in 1933 by the North American Newspaper Alliance.]

32. James P. Warburg, "Reply to Senator Elmer Thomas and Professor Irving Fisher," *The Annals,* January 1934, p. 145. This paper was originally presented at the meeting of the American Academy of Political and Social Science on November 22, 1933. On this occasion, Warburg challenged Fisher's credibility by reminding his audience of Fisher's statement of October 15, 1929 that stock prices had reached "what looks like a permanently high plateau." (Ibid., p. 148.)

Sprague and Warburg were on the warpath and, as former insiders, they attracted attention as informed authorities. Fisher appreciated the importance of blunting their arguments, lest they sour the public on the administration's monetary program. The appropriate response, as Fisher read the situation, was not to engage in open debate over the merits of rival theories. What mattered to the public was demonstrated results. It was thus all the more urgent, he informed Roosevelt, "to disprove Sprague's prediction that the gold policy cannot yield a rapid rise in prices" and to "silence the talk started by Sprague about the government needing to borrow and our bonds going down."

Again Fisher volunteered specific recommendations. If the government were to require the Federal Reserve Banks to surrender their gold holdings to the Treasury for payment at their original cost (i.e., $20.67), the Treasury would realize a "profit" on the appreciated price. New notes – designated as "yellowbacks" to be sharply distinguished from greenbacks – could be issued against this profit (which he estimated would exceed $2 billion). Holders of maturing debt could be offered a choice between new bond issues or redemption in yellowbacks. This, in Fisher's opinion, would both secure the government's credit and increase the number of dollars. Moreover, as the gold price continued to rise, the creation of dollars could be expanded "indefinitely." These measures, he believed, would "start prices upward with a bang."[33] Shortly thereafter, he modified this position in one respect. By December 1933, he was convinced that the time had come to remove uncertainty about the future price of gold by announcing an immediate devaluation of the dollar by 50 percent. Such action would mean that capital that had taken flight would "return as added buying power and the upsurge of prices, business and confidence will be the most rapid ever witnessed." As prices approached the 1926 level, the way would be paved for the introduction of a "stabilization bill," which would oblige government thereafter to fight inflation as well as deflation. Confidence in the soundness of the system would then be solidified. [34]

4   Aspects of the "policy mix," vintage late 1933

In his third fireside chat, delivered on July 24, 1933, Roosevelt observed:

> I have no sympathy for the professional economists who insist that
> things must run their course and that human agencies can have no
> influence on economic ills. One reason is that I happen to know that
> professional economists have changed their definition of economic
> laws every five or ten years for a very long time.[35]

33. Fisher to Roosevelt, November 24, 1933, FDRPL.
34. Fisher to Roosevelt, December 1, 1933, FDRPL.
35. Roosevelt, PPA, Vol. II, p. 302.

His decisions throughout 1933 had provided ample demonstration of his antipathy toward the economics then regarded as respectable in mainstream academia. In his support for structural interventions in industry and agriculture and in his monetary experimentation, he had embraced the recommendations of the heterodox.

But was substantive coherence to be found in this whirlwind of activity? His various policies, at one level, could be perceived as having a common thread: The designs of both the structuralists and the monetarists shared a price orientation in their diagnoses of and prescriptions for the economy's ills. The structuralists were preoccupied with price behavior in specific sectors: Thus, AAA's policies sought to raise the prices of farm outputs deemed to be "basic," and the NRA codes sought to stabilize the prices of manufactured goods and to banish "destructive" price wars. The gold purchase program, on the other hand, was intended to raise the general price level.

While the two schools of heterodoxy could coalesce in their focus on price behavior, one did not need to probe very far below the surface to detect signs of tension between the contributors to the policy mix of late 1933. Monetarists, for example, were unsympathetic to the suppressions of output encouraged by the New Deal's structural programs. Privately, Fisher read matters as follows:

> It's all a strange mixture. I am against the restriction of acreage but much in favor of inflation. Apparently FDR thinks of them as similar – merely two ways of raising prices! But one changes the monetary unit to restore it to normal while the other spells scarce food and clothing when many are starving or half-naked.[36]

Yet he was aware that Roosevelt had a heavy stake in AAA and NRA. Thus, it was tactful not to attack them head-on, but rather to emphasize that the objectives of these programs required "reflation" if they were to be met. Fisher had insisted that the reemployment goal of the NRA could best be reached when spending power was buttressed by monetary stimulants. Warren also had little use for structural interventions: He characterized AAA as "about 10 percent useful, 15 percent political expediency, 25 percent hot air, and 50 percent" a measure that would "result in violent action unless prices are raised ..."[37] It followed that the expectations AAA had aroused could be fulfilled only by radical monetary measures to elevate the commodity price level.

Similarly, leading advocates of the structural interventions within Roosevelt's official family were hostile to the reflationist nostrum. Tugwell, for example, had no use for the Warren-Fisher strategies. In his view, correcting price imbalances between sectors deserved top priority. Measures to pump up

36. Fisher to his son, Irving Norton Fisher, August 15, 1933, YUA.
37. Warren to Morgenthau, as quoted in John Morton Blum, *From the Morgenthau Diaries: Years of Crisis, 1928–1933* (Boston: Houghton Mifflin Company, 1959), pp. 66–7.

the general price level would not address this problem and indeed might divert attention from it. The Warren theory, Tugwell advised Roosevelt, was "non sense." When Roosevelt embarked on the gold purchase program, however, Tugwell presented himself as an administration loyalist by publicly supporting this policy and by describing it as a "logical step."[38]

The coalition that had provided the ingredients for the policy mix of 1933 was indeed a fragile one. Excitement about innovative boldness managed, however, to mute the public airing of internal dissent for a bit. By contrast, there was nothing muffled about the critiques of the early New Deal emanating from more orthodox economists in the academy. A number of Fisher's Yale colleagues, for example, derided the administration's enthusiasm for novelty, arguing that "what is needed is not a new body of principles, but the application of established principles to recent experiences and propaganda." In their view, the nation faced a choice between "competitive internationalism and relatively free markets" and "monopolistic nationalism with highly controlled markets." They left their readers in no doubt about which choice was correct. The Yale commentators were also harsh on the New Deal's tolerance toward deficits (its "double-budget" rhetoric distinguishing "ordinary" from "emergency" spending notwithstanding). This had tended to "brush aside traditional notions of economy" with the result that the American people faced heavy taxation in the years ahead.[39]

Nor could Roosevelt's economists find much to cheer about in appraisals offered by Harvard economists. Joseph A. Schumpeter, after a survey of historical characteristics of depressions, concluded that "our analysis leads us to believe that recovery is sound only if it does come by itself."[40] (By implication, the New Deal's approach was thus unsound.) Edward S. Mason expressed fear that NRA codes were encouraging restriction and threatening recovery.[41] In their treatments of the impact of public works spending, Harvard economists displayed an allegiance to a body of doctrine that would shortly be subjected to vigorous attack by John Maynard Keynes. From Edward Chamberlin's perspective, it was fitting to warn that incremental income produced by employing workers on public projects risked the "danger of creating for a period an artificial boom in the retail trades and in the industries close to the consumer, a boom which will mean reduced consumption on the

38. As described by Bernard Sternsher, *Rexford Guy Tugwell and the New Deal* (New Brunswick, N.J.: Rutgers University Press, 1964), pp. 314–16.
39. Fred Rogers Fairchild, Edgar Stevenson Furniss, Norman Sydney Buck, Chester Howard Wheldon, Jr., *A Description of the "New Deal"* (New York: The Macmillan Company, 1934), pp. 17, 96, 104.
40. Joseph A. Schumpeter in Douglas V. Brown, Edward Chamberlin, Seymour E. Harris, et al., *The Economics of the Recovery Program* (New York: McGraw-Hill, 1934), p. 20.
41. Edward S. Mason in ibid., p. 62.

part of everyone else (through higher prices) for the benefit of workers employed on public works."[42] Seymour E. Harris supported public works spending, but with a proviso:

> Expenditures on public works are to be heartily approved unless they stimulate production of capital goods relative to consumption goods for which a new demand is now induced to such an extent as to cause unhealthy increases in the price of consumption goods.[43]

Academic opinion tended to be no more receptive to New Deal initiatives when administration economists were afforded opportunities to explain the rationale for their programs at first hand. Events at Swarthmore College – which sponsored a series of nine public lectures by economists within the administration or close to it – are instructive. (The lecturers included two of the original Brains Trusters, Tugwell and Berle.) Members of Swarthmore's economics department assessed their handiwork in an editorial introduction to a volume in which the lectures were collected. They concluded "that a program of debt reduction, plus sound money, plus public works plus tariff reduction, without the National Industrial Recovery Act, would have offered us a shorter road to recovery than the one the Administration has chosen to take."[44]

One appraisal of the New Deal's first year was to attract more headlines than any of the others. John Maynard Keynes set out his thoughts in an "Open Letter to the President," published in the *New York Times* (and other U.S. newspapers) on December 31, 1933. Keynes made clear his view of what was at stake. "You have made yourself the trustee for those in every country who seek to mend the evils of our condition by reasoned experiment within the framework of the existing social system. … [I]f you succeed, new and bolder methods will be tried everywhere, and we may date the first chapter of a new economic era from your accession to office." He recognized that Roosevelt faced a double challenge – recovery and reform – but maintained that recovery should take precedence. He was critical of NRA's restrictive price raising and of the gold purchase scheme. Keynes characterized the latter as "more like the gold standard on the booze than the ideal managed currency of my dreams." The right way to promote recovery, he argued, was through the "increase of national purchasing power resulting from governmental expenditure, which is financed by loans and is not merely a transfer through taxation from existing incomes. Nothing else counts in comparison with this."[45]

42. Edward Chamberlin in ibid., pp. 27–8.
43. Seymour E. Harris in ibid., p. 116.
44. Clair Wilcox, Herbert F. Fraser, Patrick Murphy Malin, eds., *America's Recovery Program* (New York: Oxford University Press, 1934), p. 11.
45. Keynes, Open Letter to the President, *New York Times,* December 31, 1933.

4

Rethinking the structuralist agenda (I):
The fate of NRA, 1934–35

When the National Industrial Recovery Act was being designed in the spring of 1933, the enthusiasts for "concentration and control" – as opposed to "competition and conflict" – were riding the crest of the wave. A new industrial order appeared to be within reach. Tugwell and those like-minded saw this legislation as marking a sea change in the functioning of the American economy. At last it had been officially recognized that faith in the social benevolence of free markets was out of touch with the reality of mature industrialism. A brighter future could be anticipated when visible hands guided the allocation of resources.

By early 1934, much of this original enthusiasm had been spent. Results clearly did not measure up to expectations. Work had been spread, but output in the manufacturing sector had stagnated. NRA codes might have something to recommend them as instruments of reform, especially through their attacks on child labor and on sweat shop working conditions. But their impact on lifting the economy out of depression was increasingly perceived to be negative. Codes that encouraged firms to limit production and to postpone investment (out of fear that capital spending would simply add to excess capacity) offered no formula for a return to prosperity. In the press, NRA was being pilloried as standing for "No Recovery Allowed," "National Retardation Association," or "National Run Around."

These circumstances stimulated some fundamental rethinking of NRA's design, to which economists of a variety of persuasions were to contribute. In his capacity as National Recovery Administrator, Johnson was certainly aware that he needed either to deflect or to adapt himself to the arguments of his critics. In January 1934, he challenged them to come forward with constructive suggestions. He maintained that there was now "a welcome breathing spell";

"generally speaking, the dead cats are fewer in number and have lost some of their ripeness and velocity."[1] The breathing spell was short-lived. Two additional critiques of NRA's operations were gathering momentum: attacks from consumer advocacy organizations (with the charge that NRA's approach to price making was exploiting the public) and attacks from members of Congress (who maintained that NRA was "oppressing" small enterprises).

1   Economists as consumer advocates

The raucous exchanges between Johnson and consumer advocates in December 1933 had prompted him to offer Leon Henderson a position on the NRA staff. Henderson was well credentialed to speak for the interest of the consuming public. Since 1925, he had served as the Director of Consumer Credit Research at the Russell Sage Foundation in New York. From this base, he had been active in developing "model" laws, to be recommended to state governments, designed to protect the small loan borrower from sharp practices by money lenders. The underlying premise of this work was that installment buying, which had mushroomed since the early 1920s, performed a legitimate and important function in the modern economy, but that the borrowing public deserved protection from unscrupulous loan sharks.

Henderson thus brought to Washington a well-developed sensitivity to the welfare of consumers. His vision of a competitive order did not mean that the state should be removed from the marketplace. Government, he maintained, had a valid role to play as a regulator. He was not the first economist to be a consumer advocate within NRA. Corwin Edwards of New York University had been recruited by the Consumer Advisory Board in late 1933 to join its staff, and Paul Douglas of the University of Chicago had been engaged to organize consumer councils at the county level.[2] The circumstances of Henderson's appointment offered promise that his influence might be greater than that of those who had preceded him. Indeed his standing within the organization was enhanced soon after his arrival when, in February 1934, he was designated as Director of NRA's Research and Planning Division.

While Henderson's group in the Research and Planning Division was girding for action, two economists associated with NRA's Consumer Advisory Board were also exploring the impact of codes on price making. Edwards and Dexter Keezer (then on leave from his duties as President of Reed College) collaborated in a study that documented a high correlation between codes permitting open price provisions – i.e., those stipulating that firms planning to make price changes should give prior notice to trade association members – and the incidence of uniform bids. This result seemed to be explained by co-

---

1. General Hugh S. Johnson, Address to the National Retail Dry Goods Association, January 18, 1934 (as reported in the *New York Times,* January 19, 1934).
2. Hawley, *The New Deal and the Problem of Monopoly,* p. 76.

ercion experienced by firms signaling an intent to cut prices. Johnson initially brushed these findings aside. The economists pressing for reforms – and in the direction of policies to strengthen competition – still scored a breakthrough in the late spring. Leverett S. Lyon (recently recruited from the Brookings Institution), Henderson, and Edwards collaborated in support of what was to be known as Office Memorandum 228, issued on June 7, 1934. Its message was that codes should be revised to stimulate competition, not to suppress it. In particular, open price provisions could no longer require waiting periods and were to include explicit stipulations against price fixing.

This restatement of policy was an intellectual triumph of sorts. Its immediate practical impact was slight. Johnson, besieged by protests from business groups, interpreted the policy set out in Office Memorandum 228 as applying to codes to be negotiated in the future, but not to those already approved. As more than 90 percent of the industries that could potentially be affected by NRA had been codified by June 7, 1934, the proclaimed shift in policy was more semantic than real. What had been done could not readily be undone. Nevertheless, Office Memorandum 228 underscored the widening gap between policy and practice within NRA. And this, in turn, contributed to a further loss of esprit, both within the organization and outside it.[3] Johnson's public reference to economists as "kibitzers" (and the comments of Donald Richberg, his deputy, characterizing them as "dodos") did nothing to brace morale.[4]

By June 1934, Johnson might well have thought that Henderson and his fellow economists were in-house subversives. Henderson had proved himself to be an NRA loyalist, however, when the organization had been attacked by the National Recovery Review Board (more popularly known as the Darrow Board, in recognition of the noted trial lawyer who headed it). This investigative body had been put in place at the instigation of Senators William E. Borah (Montana) and Gerald P. Nye (South Dakota) who were persuaded that NRA was the captive of big businesses and out to crush smaller ones. The Darrow Board focused its attention on eight codes and reported that in all, save one, small enterprises had been "cruelly oppressed."[5] Henderson rallied to NRA's defense. As he wrote to Johnson: "This report is most difficult – it contains no statistical or factual evidence to be reviewed. ... FACTS AND FIGURES ARE NOT

3. Hawley, op. cit., pp. 86, 98ff.
4. As quoted by Charles Frederick Roos, *NRA Economic Planning* (Bloomington, Ind.: Principia Press, 1937), p. 62. Roos, who served in NRA's Research Division, reported on this experience: "Much new personnel was needed and it was difficult to find. In fact, economists throughout the world were ridiculing the NRA theory – even those employed by NRA freely criticized its policies – and as a result the whole class became persona non grata to the administrative officers." (Ibid., p. 62.)
5. Princeton's Frank Fetter, who had established an impressive track record in denouncing relaxations in the antitrust laws, served as a consultant to the Darrow Board.

AVAILABLE ANYWHERE ABOUT SMALL BUSINESSES [capitalization in the original]."[6] While Henderson denounced the Darrow Board's findings, he also seized this moment to inform Johnson of his personal credo:

> As you know, I have always felt that code provisions could be utilized to prevent and break monopolies, to induce competition, and to establish the broad rules of fair competition.[7]

Henderson expanded on this thought in a memorandum of June 27, 1934. The energy of the NRA, in his view, should be concentrated on stimulating increased productivity. This objective could be best served by "quiet persistent effort in revising codes so as to reduce prices" and thereby laying the base "for volume production ...."[8] Henderson sketched a selective approach to industrial revival and control. Some sectors of the economy, he expected, would require no separate codes and for them general federal legislation with respect to minimum wages and maximum hours for child labor would be sufficient. In others, extensive governmental participation in management would likely be needed (coal, oil, and lumber were cited as cases in point). Rethinking of strategy, he acknowledged, would require resolution of conflicts between NRA and the Federal Trade Commission, but he believed that reconciliation to be possible. In Henderson's words:

> Essentially this is a contest between an agency charged to prevent illicit trade combinations, and another agency with a mandate to bring industry into agreements, most of which negate competition in one form or another. Gradually it is becoming clear that the functions are not necessarily mutually opposed. NRA is needed to determine and assist in bringing about the concept of industrial action which will give positive gains, while the Trade Commission is needed to prevent antisocial activities of trade groups.[9]

2   NRA in interagency crossfires

Within the government, grievances registered against NRA in 1933 subsequently took on added force. The Federal Trade Commission continued to draw attention to the contradiction between its rulings and the NRA's treatment of basing point pricing in the steel industry's code. Ickes, as Public Works Administrator, reiterated his outrage at code-inflated prices for construction materials. Roosevelt responded to the latter complaint with an executive order permitting code members to sell to government at prices up to 15 percent below those posted. With this action, the federal government was branded as the "chief chiseler."

6. Henderson to General Hugh S. Johnson, "Special and Supplementary Report of Clarence Darrow and W. O. Thompson," May 18, 1934, Henderson Papers, FDRPL.
7. Ibid.
8. Henderson, "NRA," June 27, 1934, FDRPL.
9. Ibid.

On top of all this, the Department of Labor had begun to express discomfort. A survey of the first year of NRA's operations brought to light that workers were represented in only 37 of some 450 code authorities approved to that point. Not only was this held to be incompatible with the spirit of the program, but it also had unfortunate practical consequences. Labor representation, it was argued, was "essential" to ensure "access to dependable information concerning the actual operation of codes." As an official in the Department of Labor insisted, "It is probably safe to say that no one can ferret out a chiseler as well as an honest labor leader."[10]

One aspect of the impact of NRA on conditions of workers appeared to have come as a surprise – and a distressing one. Much of the initial rhetoric had advertised this experiment as assuring a fair deal for labor. By the spring of 1934, the available data indicated that one segment of the labor force had been disadvantaged by NRA's code machinery. A study prepared by an Interdepartmental Group in April 1934 reported that "many provisions in the codes have been, in effect, discriminatory against black workers." This result had come about in part through a specification of job categories that exempted many of the occupations in which black workers were most heavily represented from the maximum hour and minimum wage provisions of codes. In addition, a discriminatory element had been built into a "grandfather clause" (which had appeared in 18 approved codes) calling for minimum scales "for identical classes of labor based on wages received [on] July 15th, 1929." This meant that historically defined racial differentials in pay scales were perpetuated.[11]

Implications of the section of the National Industrial Recovery Act that encouraged collective bargaining had more sweeping significance for the prospects of black workers. As the report noted, some 26 unions still had constitutional or ritual restrictions to exclude black members. Even in the absence of formalized statements of eligibility, many unions also practiced flagrant discrimination. Organized labor, put simply, had discouraged blacks from entering its ranks. NRA's protection of the rights of employees "to organize and bargain collectively through representatives of their own choosing" effectively narrowed the employment opportunities open to them. Moreover, some of the interpretations of the National Labor Board – in particular, its judgment that workers who had been on strike should be rehired – imposed another hardship. Historically, employment as strike breakers had afforded black workers a point of entry into industries otherwise closed to them.[12]

3   Johnson and organizational redesign

With troubles pressing from a host of directions, Johnson advised Roosevelt in late June 1934 that the "time has come to take stock of NRA."

10. Rose Schneider, "Labor Representation on Code Authorities," n.d., FDRPL.
11. Report on Negro Labor of the Interdepartmental Group, April 18, 1934, FDRPL.
12. Ibid.

Code making was virtually completed, but decisions lay ahead about code administration and about the program's longer-term direction. He recommended the appointment of a Board of Directors with members drawn from the professions (economics, education, law, and engineering were mentioned specifically) and from the leadership of industry and labor. The board should function as a "High Court of Economic Relations" and be responsible – subject to the will of the president – for all NRA policy and administration. It was, however, imperative that the philosophical divide within the government be resolved. As Johnson stated the issue:

> This government must take a clean-cut decision between the theory of the Recovery Act – regulated competition to support and stabilize wage rates – or the theory of the Federal Trade Commission Acts – absolutely uncontrolled competition in spite of wage rates. The two ideas cannot exist side-by-side. ... At present N.R.A. has not the support of the F.T.C. and neither has it the full support of the Department of Justice.[13]

At this point, Johnson called upon Adolf A. Berle, Jr. for counsel. Berle, then a senior financial officer in the government of the City of New York, was the only member of the original Brains Trust who had not moved to Washington after Roosevelt's inauguration, though he had retained informal contacts with the administration's key policy makers. Berle's analysis of the situation could be read as offering comfort on one point: The theory underlying the NRA was sound. But he drew attention to two operational problems tending to give substance to charges that small businesses had been disadvantaged. The first concerned price policy. On the one hand, if prices were linked to the costs of the most efficient (and typically the larger) producers, the less efficient (and typically the smaller ones) would be driven out. On the other hand, if prices were set at levels sufficient to keep smaller firms going, the larger would reap abnormal profits that could be channeled into expanding their market share. Secondly, staffing of code authorities had tended to be weighted toward personnel drawn from the larger firms, which made it "easy for a small business for whom the going was hard to blame its difficulties on the National Recovery Act ...." Though small firms had some legitimate grievances, their most fundamental difficulties arose from the fact that, contrary to the thinking of the Brandeis group, their larger rivals were simply more cost-efficient.[14]

Meanwhile, dissatisfaction with Johnson's performance was already far advanced. His intemperance, both in language and in the consumption of alcohol, had taken a heavy toll on his earlier admirers. Bernard Baruch, for example, whose relationship with Johnson had a lot to do with his appointment in

---

13. Johnson to Roosevelt, June 26, 1934, FDRPL.
14. Berle, "Report to General Hugh S. Johnson: National Recovery Administration," n.d., Berle Papers, FDRPL.

the first place, advised the president on June 18, 1934: "The imperative problem is to establish a deliberative, responsible control of NRA. Present irresponsibility makes every business organization jittery and semi-hostile and generates increasing public distrust."[15]

By late summer, Johnson had managed to alienate virtually all his senior associates. His deputy, Richberg, reported to the president that the situation had become intolerable. "A team of horses," he wrote, "can't be driven in harness with a wild bull." In his view, "the people intimately concerned with this situation in Washington are struggling against inclinations to hysteria. Those responsible for keeping NRA going talk to me with tears in their eyes ...."[16] Tugwell, who had been asked by the president to canvass opinion within the bureaucracy, shared Richberg's appraisal of the situation. By this point, Tugwell was persuaded that NRA's price policies had decreased real purchasing power and constrained economic activity. This was the antithesis of his vision of high-volume production with lower prices.

While on the way back to private life, Johnson fired a parting shot. NRA, he told Roosevelt, needed to be reorganized around a recognition that it was "a new form of government – an economic government superimposed upon a political government." To work effectively, policy for the entire recovery program had to be coordinated. He regarded the existing state of affairs as totally unacceptable: "[W]e are rapidly approaching a condition where we [i.e., NRA] may be prosecuting a company for violating a code at the very moment when F.T.C. is prosecuting the same company for complying with it." NRA and the Department of Justice, he emphasized again, were working at cross purposes. When NRA sought punitive action against a code violator, it was obliged to request that legal proceedings be initiated by Justice's Anti-trust division where "the whole training and viewpoint" were alien to NRA's principles. As a result, NRA could not get prosecutions even "on the very strongest cases." Johnson's concluding recommendation to the president was that he "quietly reassemble" the old Brains Trust, with Richberg and Baruch added to the ranks of Moley, Tugwell, and Berle.[17]

Speaking to the nation by radio on September 30, 1934, Roosevelt reported that NRA was now entering "a period of preparation for legislation which will determine its permanent form." And he indicated that some of the organization's practices were eligible for review. In particular, he noted that "there may be a serious question as to the wisdom of many of those devices to control pro-

15. Memorandum prepared by Bernard Baruch and sent to Marvin McIntyre for transmission to the president, June 18, 1934, FDRPL. Baruch attributed the organizational disarray to "physical and mental fatigue of a man carrying an intolerable load for too long a period. This psychopathic condition of a man mentally ill from overstrain explodes into scandalous abuses of power."
16. Richberg to Roosevelt, September 4, 1934, FDRPL.
17. Johnson to Roosevelt, September 9, 1934, FDRPL.

duction, or to prevent destructive price cutting which many business organizations have insisted were necessary, or whether their effect may have been to prevent that volume of production which would make possible lower prices and increased employment."[18]

4   The search for fresh analytic underpinnings

By the late summer of 1934, NRA's operations satisfied virtually no one. Violations of code specifications had become commonplace. Though alleged "cheaters" might be exposed to some verbal abuse, there was a high likelihood that their activities would not otherwise be disciplined.

A redesign of what an optimal industrial policy might look like was drafted at this time by Gardiner C. Means (then the Economic Adviser on Finance in the Office of the Secretary of Agriculture). Means had been attracted to Washington at Tugwell's behest and the style of thinking of the two men was very much akin. One aspect of Means's background, however, set him apart from most other New Deal intellectuals: He had actually had some hands-on industrial experience. From 1922 to 1929, he had run his own textile manufacturing firm. Along the way, he developed an interest in economic research, which led him to pursue doctoral studies at Harvard and simultaneously to collaborate with Adolf A. Berle, Jr. in producing *The Modern Corporation and Private Property*. Means did the data grubbing for this study (which was presented as definitive documentation of the high degree of concentration in American industry and of the effective divorce between ownership and management in the corporate power structure). He had proposed to extend this line of investigation when preparing his Ph.D. dissertation, and with this end in view, developed a theoretical analysis of the implications of administered price making for overall resource allocation. Harvard's economics department was not disposed to give its imprimatur to this line of theorizing, but was willing to award him the Ph.D. for his empirical work.[19]

As Means appraised the situation in the late summer of 1934, the New Deal needed a coherent rationale to guide both the NRA and the AAA. In his judgment, the two programs could be justified on the same general grounds: They were responses to the failures of unregulated markets – inevitable under conditions of modern technology – to produce socially optimal results. Public intervention was thus essential. "The basic problem of both NRA and AAA," he wrote, "is ... to devise techniques of control for establishing the necessary elements of industrial policy. Until this is recognized as the basic function of NRA and AAA, the economic policies, not only of those two agencies but also

18. Roosevelt, Second Fireside Chat of 1934, September 30, 1934, PPA, Vol. III, p. 418.
19. For a discussion of this phase of Means's career, see Warren J. Samuels and Steven G. Medema, *Gardiner C. Means: Institutionalist and Post Keynesian* (Armonk, N.Y.: M. E. Sharpe, Inc., 1990).

of the whole administration, will continue to be contradictory and confused; once the true function of these two bodies has been recognized, the organization and policy implicit in this function will clarify much of the economic activity of the administration."[20]

Means reiterated a position that was common property to apostles of structuralist heterodoxy: The textbook model of atomistic competition bore no relation to reality. Empirical inspection of the behavior of prices and production in major sectors of the economy between 1929 and the spring of 1933, he maintained, indicated that various sectors had responded quite differently to circumstances of depression. In some, prices had been highly rigid and the burden of adjustment to reductions in demand had been absorbed by large cutbacks in output. In others, prices had fallen precipitously without significant curtailment in production. Producers of agricultural commodities – whose operations came closest during this period to the competitive conditions presupposed in the standard textbooks – had experienced a drop of 63 percent in wholesale prices while production had fallen only 6 percent. Statistics for the agricultural implements sector, by contrast, told quite a different story: Prices had fallen only 6 percent, but production had been curtailed by 80 percent.

The moral of this tale seemed to be self-evident. There was a significant asymmetry between the more concentrated sectors – in which prices were administered – and the more competitive ones – in which prices were established by the market. In a more refined version of this argument, Means developed an analysis of the frequency of price changes between 1926 and 1933 of some 747 items covered in the Bureau of Labor Statistics' wholesale price index. At the extremes, 125 items changed in price virtually every month over an eight-year span, while 95 items changed in price less than five times during this period.[21] These results seemed to add force to the conclusion that "the shift from market to administered prices ... [had] destroyed the functioning of the American economy and produced the pressures which culminated in the new economic agencies of government."[22]

A regime in which some prices were flexible and others not was prone to maladjustments. Aggregative economic instability, as well as the failure of unregulated markets to generate socially desirable allocative outcomes, could be understood in these terms. When businesses had power to administer prices, Means wrote:

20. Gardiner C. Means, "NRA and AAA and the Reorganization of Industrial Policy Making," August 29, 1934, FDRPL. Tugwell transmitted a copy of this memorandum to the White House and urged the president to give it his attention.
21. Means, *N.R.A., A.A.A., and the Making of Industrial Policy,* p. 2. Pagination hereafter refers to the version of this memorandum published as Senate Document 13, January 17, 1935.
22. Ibid., p. 8.

an initial drop in demand would result, not in price readjustment, but in maintained prices and curtailment of production, thus throwing workers and machines out of employment, reducing money income and spending power, and further reducing demand. The inflexible administered prices resulting from the shift from market to administration thus act as a disrupting factor in the economy and could cause an initial small drop in demand to become a national disaster.[23]

If such maladjustments were at the root of the problem, where then should one look for a solution? For Means, as for Tugwell, an attempt to atomize bigness to the point where competitive markets could protect the public interest was an exercise in futility. New thinking might usefully begin by recognizing Veblen's distinction between "business policy" and "industrial policy." People in business, when they could get away with it, had a natural tendency to suppress outputs in order to maximize profits. Industrial policy, on the other hand, had a different objective: "to accomplish what the market is supposed to accomplish, namely, a balance of the interests of the various groups which constitute industry so as to produce the most effective use of human and material resources." The essence of industrial policy was the making of the "right decisions," which Means defined as "those which will achieve the results the market has been supposed to produce." He added that "if the right decisions are made throughout all industries, the net effect will be the smooth functioning of the economic machine, the full use of human and material resources, and a balance of interests among individuals and groups."[24]

Restated in the terminology of a later era, Means's conception of the "right" price–quantity combinations were those that would be compatible with full employment of resources. But what mechanisms were available to ensure that the correct outcome would be achieved? He spoke more specifically about the approaches that were wrong than he did about those that were correct. By his lights, business decision making would obviously fail to do the job properly. Reliance on direct control by a central planning authority would also have hazards: Its operations would require too much dictatorial power to be congenial to American tastes. Means instead chose to invoke a conception of the "public interest" which, in his terms, could be regarded as the "balancing of conflicting interests in order that the results of economic activity will more nearly conform to the balance which the policy of laissez-faire was formerly expected to produce." To achieve this, government should ensure that a balance be struck between three parties with a stake in the economy's performance: (1) a business interest "primarily seeking more money income for less use of capital"; (2) a labor interest "primarily seeking more money wages for less work"; and (3) a consumer interest "primarily concerned with obtaining

23. Ibid., pp. 11–12.
24. Ibid., p. 14.

more or better goods and services for less money."[25] Means recognized that getting successful representation of the interests of consumers posed difficulties: Consumers, who were both many and scattered, were awkward to organize. In his view, this problem could usefully be addressed by utilizing skills found in organizations already in being, so long as those organizations were not held captive by a producers' perspective. Means had in mind "professional groups, engineers, chemists, etc., women's organizations." And he added: "Most importantly, the technicians are the logical representatives of the consumer interest, since their interest and skill are devoted to producing goods and not values."[26] There were overtones here of Veblen's faith in technicians as the rational resource allocators. Means's technicians, it would seem, were to perform a more modest, though still vital, function: They should lean against the business interest in high prices and low volume and insist on lower prices and higher volumes.

Means's pamphlet got a lot of play in Washington in late 1934 and 1935. Through the intervention of Senator Borah, it was elevated to the status of a state paper. On the strength of a resolution he sponsored, it was published as a Senate document in January 1935. Its message resonated well to those who needed to stiffen convictions that extraordinary policy initiatives remained valid at a time of disappointment with initiatives already taken. As a detailed blueprint for reforms to improve NRA and AAA performance, this statement still left a lot of questions unanswered.

5   Canvassing ways to implement a redesign

Within the bureaucracy, a number of schemes, which amounted to efforts to put flesh on Means's analytical skeleton, were soon explored. Most of the people involved had, like Means, been influenced by Veblen's writings. One of them – Isador Lubin, Commissioner of Labor Statistics – had received direct exposure to this teaching. At the University of Missouri in 1916–17, Lubin had been Veblen's student and had come to Washington as Veblen's statistical assistant when the latter joined the staff of the U.S. Food Administration during World War I. This proved not to be a happy episode for Veblen, and his employment was soon terminated. But it did give Lubin a taste for the kind of work on which he was to build a career. Government economists of Lubin's analytic persuasion converged around a central question in late 1934: What types of policy intervention might be contrived to press the industrial sector to adopt their recommendations on the desirability of high-volume production at lower prices?

This issue topped the agenda of an Interdepartmental Committee on the "Increase in Production and Employment" that was put in place in 1934. Lubin was a key participant, along with Louis Bean and Mordecai Ezekiel of the Department of Agriculture. Using the automobile industry as an example, com-

25. Ibid., p. 29.
26. Ibid., p. 34.

mittee members suggested that producers might be induced to develop a simplified low-cost car if government purchasing agents committed themselves to buy that product. Government might also exert leverage on an industry's decision making by offering attractive financing – through, say, a New Industries Bank – to firms that would undertake to develop standardized products along desired lines.[27] Some officials in the Department of Agriculture were then pressing to involve government still further in encouraging "coordinated" increases in production: government, they recommended, should guarantee producers against loss and undertake to be a buyer of last resort. Products thus acquired could be disposed of as relief in kind. These steps, however, should be taken only when "governmental authorities were satisfied that the program promised a real increase in employment; that the reductions in prices were consistent with the increased volume of business; and that a good part of the product would be sold at the new lower prices."[28]

This attempt to transfuse new blood into a planning strategy received largely negative reviews among NRA's economists. Henderson, for example, was not ready to conclude that market rivalry among producers had lost all relevance and that the interests of consumers could be protected only by still more elaborate administrative machinery. Price competition continued to have an important role to play, and it was up to the NRA strategists to devise ways to encourage it. In January 1935, Henderson reported on research findings showing that "particularly recently, ... where there has been price competition, production has been maintained, the flow of goods kept up and employment maintained." The "greatest question" facing NRA, in his view, was what should be done about the "increasing rigidity of prices in industries, particularly those in which the greatest reemployment can be expected." These rigidities should indeed be broken. But it did not follow, as Means had argued, that more visible hands were needed to establish prices and quantities. In Henderson's reading of matters, it was still possible that the socially desirable outcome could be achieved if the good offices of government were deployed to make the winds of market competition brisker.[29]

6   Rethinking industrial intervention for the longer term: The contributions of an academic consultant

In the absence of congressional action to extend its mandate, NRA's lease on life was due to expire in mid-June 1935. The prospect of hanging

27. Mordecai Ezekiel, Minutes of the Committee on Increase in Production and Employment, September 13, 1934, Henderson Papers, FDRPL.
28. Report of the Department of Agriculture to the Executive Council, October 2, 1934, Henderson Papers, FDRPL.
29. Henderson, Statement at the Public Hearing on Price Provisions in Codes of Fair Competition, January 9, 1935, NRA Records, NA.

served to concentrate a number of minds on the question of what, if anything, deserved to survive from this experiment.

In February 1935, Henderson engaged Columbia University's John Maurice Clark as a consultant to the Research and Planning Division when these matters were being pondered. This was an inspired choice. Industrial organization was Clark's professional specialty. No less important for the task at hand was Clark's intellectual style: He was undogmatic, fair-minded, willing to listen to new ideas and to appraise them judiciously.[30] Clark had already put on record some preliminary views about NRA. Writing in March 1934, he had argued that the act probably should be regarded "not as a means to stimulate immediate recovery, but rather as partly a measure to substitute work-sharing for relief, and partly a means of controlling the quality of a recovery already begun, with a view to putting it on a sounder and more enduring basis." He expressed general sympathy for NRA's attempt to raise labor's share of the national income, noting that this was "probably one of the things necessary to reasonable economic stability in the decades ahead." But he was also alert to potential dangers, particularly if the administrators succumbed to protecting inefficient producers and failed to undo the output-restricting provisions found in a number of the early codes.[31]

In his capacity as an informed outsider, Clark could provide a perspective that the insiders – concerned as they were with day-to-day crisis management – would find difficult to come by. In his view, NRA could validly offer strong rebuttals to a number of its critics. Those who had charged that business recovery would have been more rapid in its absence were mistaken. Clark was convinced that the business community, by 1933, had concluded that "this depression was not the ordinary business cycle" and doubted the "likelihood of automatic recovery of the usual sort." Confidence was lacking: "NRA could not destroy it, because it did not exist." Indeed in its earlier stages, NRA had

30. In his presidential address to the American Economic Association in December 1935, Clark was to display dimensions of this style:
    > Few would nowadays attempt to draw solutions ready-made from traditional theories. ... And the economist who does this is hardly less risky a guide than the one who follows the more popular course, throwing all received theories overboard and trying to work out every problem as a fresh and disconnected exercise. What is needed is a readiness to use accepted theories, and the methods by which they were derived, as tools of analysis, with a clear eye for the limitations of their applicability to the specific conditions of the problem at hand, and a readiness to make the theories over, if need be, on a basis of changed assumptions." (J. M. Clark, "Past Accomplishment and Present Prospects of American Economics," *American Economic Review,* March 1936, p. 9.)

31. Clark, "Economics and the National Recovery Administration," *American Economic Review,* March 1934, pp. 11–25.

provided a "strong psychological lift" to business.[32] Clark was also annoyed with critics who charged that NRA's interventions should be faulted because their possible effects had not been thoroughly analyzed before the fact. This position, he noted, implied policy paralysis "until the expert planners have solved all the doubtful questions beyond peradventure. ... [T]he process of feeling one's way experimentally seems to have a place ...."[33]

The experiment, moreover, was very much worth doing. The first stages of NRA had put a brake on what otherwise might have been a cumulative downward spiral and offered a "rational prospect of starting a chain of cumulative forces of expansion."[34] In addition, it had spurred a useful reconsideration of the appropriate role of government in the context of changing societal attitudes about acceptable forms of economic adjustment. As Clark saw this issue:

> One trouble with civilization is it can't stand for the cruel methods by which the jungle brought about certain necessary ends, especially the elimination of the "unfit," and it furnishes no clearly adequate substitute. Competition is getting civilized, in the above sense, with the resulting difficulties.[35]

But there would need to be clear thinking to distinguish policies that might legitimately blunt the harshness of a vigorously competitive order from those that sheltered the inefficient. Clark could support constraints on "extremes in price-cutting" in certain circumstances: e.g., in the cases of semidurable and durable goods, he argued that a "demoralized market" might lead buyers to postpone purchases, anticipating that prices would fall further; a price "floor" might then "stimulate revival of demand."[36] At the same time, government needed to make clear that it was not in the business of propping up the incompetent and that it would not sanction a general "loss-prevention" policy.

Clark's overview of NRA within an historical setting may have helped to bolster flagging morale. But this did not mean that he offered an uncritical defense of the status quo. Clark was obviously uncomfortable about the quasi-monopolistic features of some trade practice provisions and supported their elimination. He was aware of an argument that steps to purge them might provoke collapse of the entire code structure. With respect to that point, he held that "it would seem that the only final answer must come from trying the experiment and seeing how it works."[37]

Reflections of this sort were rendered moot by the action of the Supreme Court. In a unanimous decision announced on May 27, 1935, the Court struck

32. Clark to Blackwell Smith, Head of the Legal Department of NRA, "Preliminary Comments on the Brookings Study of NRA," n.d., Henderson Papers, FDRPL.
33. Ibid.
34. Clark to E. J. Working, February 23, 1935, Henderson Papers, FDRPL.
35. Clark to Henderson, February 2, 1935, Henderson Papers, FDRPL.
36. Clark to Henderson, February 23, 1935, Henderson Papers, FDRPL.
37. Clark to Blackwell Smith, loc. cit.

down the National Industrial Recovery Act, declaring that its code-making authority represented an unconstitutional delegation of legislative power and that its jurisdictional claims had impinged on intrastate commerce without constitutional warrant.

7   Groping for new moorings from a structuralist point of view

The Supreme Court's unanimous decision in the Schecter case left official Washington in disarray. In his diary entry of May 30, 1935, Tugwell commented that the national holiday being observed on that date was "quite appropriately being celebrated as a kind of memorial day for a good part of the New Deal."[38] The outcome did not come altogether as a surprise. Justice Louis D. Brandeis, who had maintained informal contacts with a fair number of intellectuals in the New Deal bureaucracy, had sent warning noises for some time about his determination to oppose what he understood as the collectivist trends in the administration's economic policy. Nor was Tugwell entirely dismayed: NRA's price policies (which mistakenly had put "bottoms on prices rather than tops" and tolerated restrictions on production) were indefensible.[39] It was still imperative to find ways – and better ones – to assert the principle of social control over industrial processes.

In this moment of perceived crisis, Tugwell's imaginative powers remained in healthy repair. He put before the president a scheme for an Industrial Adjustment Act, which he and Mordecai Ezekiel had drafted jointly. This proposal called for a levy on all industrial firms with the proviso that receipts be rebated to those signing "voluntary adjustment contracts," in which they agreed to comply with specified conditions on the type and volume of production, and accepted governmental recommendations on employment practices. Tugwell insisted that such arrangements "put a premium on the expansion of production on large volume and low price and at the same time protected competition where it is appropriate."[40] This scheme went nowhere. Tugwell's further suggestion that a constitutional amendment be drafted to liberate the executive branch from shackles imposed by the Supreme Court had a similar fate.

Some features of the NRA were reincarnated in subsequent legislation. The Connally Hot Oil Act and the Guffey Coal Act salvaged the equivalent of NRA code machinery in the crude oil and coal industries. In addition, the Wagner Labor Relations Act of 1935 gave statutory standing to rights of workers to bargain collectively, thus preserving a provision of the National Industrial Recovery Act of 1933. But comprehensive planning for the industrial sector was dead. Controversy over an appropriate industrial policy was to persist. As Tug-

38. Tugwell Diaries, May 30, 1935, FDRPL.
39. Ibid., May 31, 1935.
40. Ibid.

well then saw matters, "the issue [was] drawn very clearly ... between lawyers and those who take an economic view of the situation"[41] – by which he meant between lawyers of the Brandeis-Frankfurter persuasion and those who shared his economic view.

8   Further reactions to the demise of NRA

Tugwell and Ezekiel would not have won massive support among professional economists for a scheme to resurrect NRA on more secure constitutional foundations. Economists in the mainstream of orthodoxy rejoiced at the Supreme Court's decision. Even among those sympathetic to experimentation, there was a widespread recognition that NRA had been a flawed instrument. This venture into a form of planning had generated too many internal contradictions to be worth repeating. It was no use pretending that "codes of fair competition" meant anything more than legalized collusion. Thomas Blaisdell, whom Tugwell had brought to Washington from Columbia University, captured that mood. Testifying before a Senate Committee in his capacity as Director of the Consumers' Division of the National Emergency Council, Blaisdell reported that his studies of the workings of the Atlantic mackerel fishing code had produced some arresting – and not atypical – findings. As far as he could determine, the "only individuals who benefited were the mackerels themselves": The agreement among fishermen to restrict output in order to raise prices meant that fewer mackerel were caught![42]

Fisher was among those to applaud the collapse of NRA. His disgust with supply restriction as a depression remedy was by now a well-established matter of record. The uneasy coalition of 1933 between two types of price manipulators – monetarists and structural interventionists – had long since collapsed. There was no longer any point in disguising their fundamental incompatibility. By 1934, Fisher argued that Roosevelt should choose between the reflationists and the regimentalists. The president did not do so. Fisher continued to beat the drums for monetary stimuli (though specifics of his recommendations were to undergo some variations). With respect to one component of the First New Deal's alleged regimentalism, however, a choice was made for Roosevelt by the Supreme Court.

41. Tugwell Diaries, May 30, 1935.
42. Thomas Blaisdell, Testimony before the Senate Committee on Finance, 74:1, April 1, 1935, p. 841.

5

Rethinking the structuralist agenda (II): The fate of the Agricultural Adjustment Administration, 1934–36

When the Agricultural Adjustment Administration was created in May 1933, precisely what this novelty would amount to was not clear. The act conveyed to the Secretary of Agriculture extraordinary powers to raise farm prices. Counsels were divided, however, about the ways they should be exercised. Measures to raise demand (particularly through export promotion) had a formidable political constituency, particularly because their advocates preferred not to tamper with a farmer's decision about what and how much to produce. Techniques to restrict supply enjoyed no comparable popularity among the farm lobbies, though a substantial number of economists concerned with the plight of agriculture held them to be crucial to relief of farm distress. There were, however, two versions of supply management. One insisted that direct controls, via the domestic allotment method for shrinking outputs, were essential, at least in the short term. The other assigned priority to output shrinkage through governmental programs to retire acreages ill suited to tillage.

By the end of 1933, earlier uncertainties about which of the various strategies would take precedence were largely removed. The major in-house voice for market expansion (and ideally without production constraints), George N. Peek, had been replaced as Agricultural Adjustment Administrator by Chester Davis, who was more sympathetic to output controls. At the same time, the ways in which government intervened to reduce supply had given rise to complications that the planners had not anticipated. Nor should this have been a matter of surprise. The administrators of the First New Deal's farm policies were sailing in uncharted waters.

By one set of indices, outcomes associated with AAA's interventions gave grounds for satisfaction. Farm prices rose from their lows of 1932. Similarly, cash receipts of farmers registered a significant uptick (even though their costs

69

had also gone up). Government's cash payments to farmers who cooperated with recommendations to suppress output, contributed, of course, to the increase in cash receipts. But for the most part these subsidies represented a minor fraction of the annual increment in cash flowing into the farm sector. As planned, these income transfers were funded primarily from the special excise levied on processors. Though the processing tax was troublesome administratively and politically, this device enabled the administration to claim that its spending on farm programs was fiscally responsible.[1]

Supply restrictions, implemented through direct controls, made the running in the early going and the commodities subject to them swelled in number. At AAA's inception, seven types of farm output were defined as "basic" and thereby eligible for programmatic treatment. By August 1935, nine categories had been added.[2] The indirect method of supply restriction – i.e., systematic withdrawal of inferior land from production – did not disappear from the agenda completely, but its position was decidedly subordinate. That design for agricultural uplift, however, was to take on a fresh lease on life in 1936.

1   Improvisations, anomalies, and tensions in programmatic implementation

Supply restriction for the "basic" crops proved, in practice, to be more complex than it had seemed to be on the planners' drafting boards. With respect to some crops – cotton and tobacco were the most arresting cases in point – producer reluctance to "cooperate" on acreage restriction meant that the "voluntarist" component of the original design soon had to be compromised. It had been hoped that an overwhelming majority of the growers of crops in price-depressing surplus would endorse cutbacks. The incentives were in place: cash payments as rewards for reducing plantings (and in the case of cotton during the 1933 crop season, for ploughing under acreage already seeded). There was always the risk that some producers would choose to opt out and to enjoy the advantage of higher prices generated by the supply

1.

	Cash receipts of farmers ($ billions)	Benefit and rental payments ($ millions)	Farm price index (1909–14 = 100)
1932	4.7	—	65
1933	5.4	131	70
1934	6.8	466	90
1935	7.7	573	109
1936	8.7	287	114

[Murray R. Benedict, *Farm Policies of the United States, 1790–1950* (New York: Twentieth Century Fund, 1953), pp. 314–15.]

2. Originally, the outputs defined as "basic" were wheat, cotton, field corn, hogs, rice, tobacco, and milk and its products. Legislation in 1934 added rye, flax, barley, grain sorghums, cattle, peanuts, sugar beets, and sugar cane. Potatoes officially became "basic" in 1935.

curtailments of cooperators, while continuing to produce as usual. Free riders could obviously thwart the price-enhancing objectives of the exercise. In 1934, loopholes were effectively closed in the cotton and tobacco programs by subjecting growers to potentially heavy taxes when they sold their product. Those who complied with contractual restrictions, however, were issued tax-exemption certificates. Noncooperators, on the other hand, would have access to markets only on terms that the tax made unprofitable. In the wheat program, on the other hand, there was an unforeseen complication of a quite different order. Unprecedented drought conditions in the Midwest in 1934 and 1935 meant that nature was shrinking outputs dramatically. Accordingly, the planned restrictions on planting were considerably relaxed.

There were to be other unanticipated difficulties. Targeted increases in output prices, in a number of instances, proved to be more difficult to reach than had been believed to be the case ex ante. In the original design, it had been expected that benefits paid to growers to idle part of their lands and/or to destroy output would do the trick. These techniques, however, did not always deliver results to match expectations. To adjust for the discrepancies, another instrument was improvised: the nonrecourse loan. Under this scheme, which was used in cotton and to a lesser extent with wheat and corn, the government would advance to producers the value of their allowable outputs as determined by the target price. If the market price subsequently exceeded the price on which the loan had been calculated, the producer could retire the loan, reclaim the crop, and sell it through normal market channels at the higher price. If the grower chose not to exercise this option, the government was left holding the inventory.

This arrangement, which was to cast a long shadow over the subsequent evolution of American agricultural programs, did indeed put government in the business of setting price floors. But it also prompted some rethinking. The Department of the Treasury in 1935 drew attention to an anomaly in this situation, introducing arguments that would resonate for some decades ahead. The nonrecourse loan, it was noted, obliged the government to incur massive expenses in maintaining stockpiles and presented the "sickening prospect" that government would be obliged to hold ever increasing amounts of unsalable commodities. Would it not be wiser, a Treasury official asked in 1935, to allow the market price to reach its own level and to prop up farmers through direct income transfers? This scheme, it was noted, had a number of recommendations. It need cost the government no more to finance than the nonrecourse loan, and it would encourage greater sales of commodities then in surplus both at home and abroad. In addition, direct benefit payments had "the very decided advantage of seeming to be precisely what they are" – namely, government grants. When the same grants were disguised as loans, it was argued, "the beneficiaries are commonly unappreciative of the gratuity, regarding it as part of an ordinary business transaction, and are as apt to grumble as to praise."[3] Even so, the income transfer alternative never got beyond the idea stage. This outcome followed in no small measure from the fact that the beneficiaries of "disguised grants" had a political stake in camouflaging what the farm programs actually cost.

Within the agricultural bureaucracy, tensions surfaced as well over the balance to be struck between the conflicting interests of producers and consumers. Economists affiliated with AAA, like their counterparts in NRA, were at the forefront in reminding policy makers that service to the public interest meant that the welfare of consumers should not be ignored. There was, of course, no confusion about a central point: The primary purpose of agricultural legislation was to raise the prices farmers received. The Agricultural Adjustment Act of 1933 nonetheless stipulated that consumers should also be protected and, in that spirit, the Office of Consumers' Counsel had been created within AAA. There were to be some exposed live wires when it came to defining how that office should function.

In mid-1934 Gardiner C. Means, as Advisor on Finance to the Secretary of Agriculture, drew Wallace's attention to "major controversies [that] have arisen between two groups in A.A.A. (which I shall call respectively the commodities group and the consumer group)." The battlelines had been drawn over the extent to which the secretary's required approval of marketing agreements should be guided exclusively by their impact on the returns to growers. As a spokesperson for the consumer group, Means maintained that "the Secretary, since he is empowered to act in a way to affect the operations of the economic process, must use his power in the public interest which calls for an increase in farmers' income but in a manner most fair to other interested groups, namely the packers, the consumers and the workers involved in the industry."[4]

For his part, Tugwell was certainly aware of the divergent stakes of producers and consumers in the level of farm prices. He nonetheless held that it was "possible in many instances to raise the price of farm commodities without bringing a proportionate rise in the prices paid by consumers for the same commodities" because "total marketing charges remained relatively fixed."[5] The challenge was to control the spreads of processors and distributors to en-

3. George C. Haas to Secretary of the Treasury Henry Morgenthau, Jr., August 20, 1935, FDRPL. The scheme set out in this memorandum contained the essential features of the Brannan Plan, introduced by President Truman's Secretary of Agriculture nearly a decade and a half later.
4. Gardiner C. Means to Secretary Henry A. Wallace, July 5, 1934, Means Papers, FDRPL. The origins of Means's paper – *N.R.A., A.A.A., and Making of Industrial Policy* (discussed in Chapter 4) – can be traced to the mid-1934 debates within the Department of Agriculture between the consumer and commodities groups.
5. Tugwell, "Consumers and the New Deal" (an address delivered before the Consumers' League of Ohio, Cleveland, May 11, 1934), reprinted in Tugwell, *The Battle for Democracy* (New York: Columbia University Press, 1935), p. 284.

sure that they did not "continue to exact an undue share of the consumer's dollar."[6] He was squarely on the side of those who called for AAA's Consumers' Counsel to examine the terms of marketing agreements for the purpose of preventing abuses. During Peek's brief tenure as Agricultural Adjustment Administrator, proconsumer activism had been frustrated. When the Consumers' Counsel had argued vigorously that processors be required to open their books to public inspection as a quid pro quo for antitrust immunities, Peek had forcefully rejected this advice. Tugwell had hoped that Chester Davis, Peek's successor, would be more vigilant about monitoring the "spreads" in the marketing and distribution network, but Davis too came to regard the agency's consumer advocates as a thorn in the flesh.

The most explosive polarization within the AAA turned, however, on the impact of its operations on the distribution of income within the farming sector proper. The boiling point was reached over the cotton program, where it appeared that AAA had actively worsened the conditions of the neediest in the nation's farming population. Output restriction goals for cotton called for a major downsizing. In the 1920s, nearly half of U.S. cotton output had been sold abroad. Depression had battered those markets, and it was uncertain whether they could ever be recaptured. In the view of the agricultural planners, cotton's long-run prospects, given increasing competition from synthetic fibers, were bleak. Fundamental readjustments thus could not be avoided. The remaining question concerned how their burdens were to be distributed. The Southern agricultural pattern, in which the bulk of the cotton land was owned by white proprietors but tilled by black tenants, had a major bearing on the outcome.

In this environment, landlords had an economic incentive to establish a monopoly command over government benefits by displacing tenants who might otherwise stake a claim to an entitlement. Calvin B. Hoover, on leave from Duke University for service in AAA, drew attention to "these undesirable effects and hardships" flowing from the cotton program in a report prepared in early 1934.[7] AAA's regulations for cotton contracts had specified that landowners maintain the normal number of tenants and assign to them a proportionate share of benefit payments, but "enforcement of these provisions," Hoover noted, "[had] been inadequate." An interdepartmental study characterized the situation in mid-1934 more starkly: "The tenant in the South – and the Negro tenant in particular – is being separated from his means of earning a living."[8]

In early 1935, AAA's Legal Division attempted to address this problem by issuing an order (drafted by Alger Hiss and approved by Jerome Frank, the

6. Ibid.
7. Calvin B. Hoover, *Human Problems in Acreage Reduction in the South,* as quoted in a Report on the Negro in Agriculture Adopted by the Interdepartmental Group, June 1, 1934, FDRPL.
8. Report of the Agricultural Committee of the Inter-Departmental Group Concerned with the Special Problems of Negroes, June 1, 1934, FDRPL.

agency's General Counsel) requiring landlords in the South to retain tenants on the same land as a condition of eligibility for benefits in the coming contract season. This sparked a firestorm of protest from the Southern states, which led Davis to take drastic action. In his opinion, it was beyond the purpose of AAA to sponsor a "social revolution" in the South and he decided to clean house in the Legal Division. Frank and Hiss, as well as the Consumers' Counsel, Frederic C. Howe, were dismissed. Tugwell was outraged by this "purge," which he saw as "part of Davis' studied plan to rid the Department of all liberals and to give the reactionary farm leaders full control of policy, this meaning, of course, full satisfaction to all processors with whom we have dealings since most of the farm leaders are owned body and soul by the processors."[9] Meanwhile the situation on the ground had taken an ugly turn. Norman Thomas, the Socialist Party's once and future candidate for the presidency, drew Roosevelt's attention to the action of a group of armed planters who had prevented him and officials of the Southern Tenant Farmers Union from addressing a meeting of agricultural workers, most of whom were "colored," to have been held at a black church in Birdsong, Arkansas. Thomas called upon the president to demand an "open investigation of relief and eviction," asserting that "there is a complete disregard of spirit of AAA acreage reduction contracts … which makes it a weapon of tyranny and exploitation."[10]

By this point, Tugwell's disillusionment with AAA, as with NRA, was well advanced. Even before the blowup over Davis's personnel actions, he had come to believe that the use of processing taxes to retire individual acres had outlived its usefulness and that a change in policy was needed. And he lamented his inability to persuade Davis and Wallace to move. "An organization like the A.A.A.," he wrote, "gets used to doing a thing a certain way and resents any change in method. Then, too, the farm organizations have been taking some credit for the generous payments which are going to farmers and would hate to see them stopped."[11] It had become clear to him, as he later wrote, that the AAA benefited only about 20 percent of the total farm population, primarily the larger, commercially oriented farmers who were better off than most anyway. Little flowed to sharecroppers and other tenants or to farm laborers, and, in some instances, they were worse off. In his view, AAA had permitted processors of agricultural products and manufacturers of farm implements to do better than they deserved to.[12]

By early 1935, there appeared to be little prospect that Tugwell could regain significant influence within the regular agricultural bureaucracy. He had been the target of some unwelcome publicity in the spring of 1934 when the Su-

9. Tugwell Diaries, February 10, 1935, FDRPL.
10. Telegram from Norman Thomas to Roosevelt, March 15, 1935, FDRPL.
11. Tugwell Diaries, December 13, 1934, FDRPL.
12. Tugwell, *The Stricken Land: the Story of Puerto Rico* (Garden City, N.Y.: Doubleday, 1947), p. 24.

perintendent of Schools in Gary, Indiana, Dr. William A. Wirt, resurrected Tugwell's paper to the 1931 session of the American Economic Association (entitled "The Principle of Planning and the Institution of Laissez-faire") and used it to characterize him as a dangerous radical. In political circles, Tugwell was increasingly depicted as an impractical theoretician whose qualifications as an agricultural policy maker were suspect because he had never been a dirt farmer. When the Senate was considering Wallace's recommendation that Tugwell be promoted to the new position of Undersecretary of Agriculture, the Chairman of the Senate Agricultural Committee, "Cotton Ed" Smith (Democrat of South Carolina), asserted that this post should go to "one familiar with the lowly and despised occupation of farming instead of a professor" and that "the man who holds that job should be a graduate of God's University, the great out-doors."[13] Hugh S. Johnson, back in private life, joined the chorus, remarking that "Rex Tugwell knows as much about agriculture as Haile Selassie knows about Oshkosh, Wisconsin."[14]

2 Shifts in the status of land use planning doctrines

An atmosphere of "emergency" and the perceived need to produce fast results in the early days of the New Deal had shunted the land use planners to the sidings. Their design offered no promise of speedy results. Advocates of this type of supply management for the longer term remained on the premises, though their views were not in high fashion. In 1933 they managed to salvage a token program, amounting to some $25 million for land purchases, which was intended to reduce farm outputs by enough to offset increases made possible by the irrigation and reclamation projects sponsored by the Public Works Administration.

The land use planners aspired to do much more. Their enthusiasm stimulated a major study undertaken by the National Resources Board, released on December 1, 1934. The Land Section of this report – directed by L. C. Gray, with Wilson and Ezekiel as participants – advanced an arresting recommendation: A 15-year program of land purchase should be initiated with the objective of retiring some 75 million acres. If implemented, it was expected that acreage harvested for selected crops would be reduced from levels prevailing in 1929 by the following magnitudes: wheat, 23.6 percent; corn, 20.3 percent; cotton, 9.3 percent.[15] The authors articulated the rationale for these recommendations:

13. As quoted in Richard S. Kirkendall, *Social Scientists and Farm Politics in the Age of Roosevelt* (Columbia, Mo.: University of Missouri Press, 1966), p. 96.
14. As quoted in Bernard Sternsher, *Rexford Tugwell and the New Deal* (New Brunswick, N.J.: Rutgers University Press, 1964), p. 281.
15. National Resources Board, *A Report on National Planning and Public Works in Relation to Natural Resources and Including Land Use and Water Resources with Findings and Recommendations* (Washington, D.C.: U.S. Government Printing Office, 1934), pp. 175–83.

The huge waste of human and economic resources which has resulted from repeated attempts to farm land of poor agricultural quality
calls seriously in question the wisdom of a laissez-faire policy which
permits inferior land to be settled in response to the desires of interested promoters and local "booster" interests, without regard to the
capacity of the land to sustain a stable and profitable agriculture and
long-term requirements for expansion of the agricultural acreage.
There is a legitimate public concern in keeping settlers out of areas
where they cannot make a living and consequently will require re-
current provision for public relief; in discouraging sparse settlement
in the interest of social welfare and economy of governmental costs;
and, finally, in preventing overexpansion of the cultivated area, to facilitate the adjustment of farm production to demand.[16]

Echoes of the messages Ely and the Wisconsin school of agricultural economics had been sending for more than a decade came through loud and clear.

Planners of this persuasion argued with some vigor that their approach deserved more generous support. After all, it was at least arguable that outright
purchase would eventually cost the Treasury less than the alternative at hand:
the AAA's annual payments to farmers for temporary retirement of acreage.
Estimates based on data from 14 hard winter wheat counties in Kansas suggested, for example, that the cost to the government to reduce wheat plantings in a single year ranged from 17 to 36 percent of the sums necessary to
buy the land outright and withdraw it from cultivation permanently.[17] There
was no quarrel about the need to adjust production downward. But correct
strategy demanded that the shrinkage should be based on criteria of efficiency
in land use.[18]

The land use planners gained some reenforcement in early 1935 when Tugwell, dismayed with the outcomes generated by supply restriction of the domestic allotment variety, embraced their cause. While he retained the title of
Undersecretary of Agriculture, he had largely disengaged himself from AAA
as well as from the day-to-day operations of the department. His new crusade
focused on developing remedies for rural poverty, with particular attention to
the plight of farm families then on the relief rolls (some 900,000 of them) who
were linked to lands that could not provide them an acceptable standard of living. This part of the farm population had been totally bypassed by AAA interventions, and Tugwell believed that a program to address their circumstances
was overdue. Thus, the Resettlement Administration, to be headed by Tugwell,
was brought into being by executive order in May 1935. Much of the work of

16. Ibid., p. 184.
17. L. C. Gray, "Research Relating to Policies for Submarginal Areas," *Journal of
    Farm Economics,* April 1934, p. 301.
18. H. R. Tolley, "Agricultural Planning and Control: Discussion," *Journal of Farm
    Economics,* February 1935, p. 36.

this new agency was concerned with purchasing submarginal lands occupied by the rural poor who were then to be relocated to situations giving them a better chance to make it on their own. L. C. Gray, who had made rational land use his field of expertise, administered the land acquisition activities of the Resettlement Administration. Though this effort was handicapped by the lack of congressional appropriations earmarked for this purpose, enough funding was pieced together from various "emergency" programs to purchase nearly 10 million substandard acres by 1936.[19]

Land use planners had thus made some headway toward refocusing policy on the longer-term objectives of farm relief and reform. The thinking that had gone into that exercise came into its own in early 1936. The Supreme Court's decision in the Hoosac Mills Case undercut the linchpins of the Domestic Allotment formula for agricultural adjustment. The federal government was thereby precluded from negotiating contracts with farmers to curtail planting and from levying processing taxes to fund this activity. The initial strategy of direct controls to raise farm prices thus lay in ruins. Roosevelt recorded his reaction to this in a memorandum dictated on January 24, 1936:

> It has been well said by a prominent historian that fifty years from now the Supreme Court's AAA decision will, in all probability, be described somewhat as follows:
>
> (1) The decision virtually prohibits the President and the Congress from the right, under modern conditions, to intervene reasonably in the regulation of nation-wide commerce and nation-wide agriculture.
>
> (2) The Supreme Court arrived at this result by selecting from several possible techniques of constitutional interpretation a special technique. The objective of the Court's purpose was to make reasonableness in passing legislation a matter to be settled not by the views of the elected Senate and House of Representatives and not by the views of an elected President but rather by the private, social philosophy of a majority of nine appointed members of the Supreme Court itself.[20]

In light of the court's decision in January 1936, the Roosevelt administration could have decided to abandon agricultural planning altogether. This did not happen. Farm distress remained real and a return to old-fashioned laissez-faire was not an attractive political option in 1936. With one form of planning discredited, another would have to be found. The land use planners could fill the vacuum with a ready-made alternative. Their intellectual resources were swiftly deployed in the packaging of the Soil Conservation and Domestic Al-

19. Gray, "The Social and Economic Implications of the National Land Program," *Journal of Farm Economics,* May 1936, p. 266.
20. Roosevelt, Memorandum for AAA File (copy to Ray Moley), January 24, 1936, FDRPL.

lotment Act, signed into law on February 29, 1936. Planning survived, but in a new format and with a different rationale.

The imperative of rational use of the nation's land resources formed the centerpiece of the 1936 legislation. For immediate operational purposes, this was interpreted to mean that government should subsidize the reallocation of acreage from "soil-depleting" to "soil-conserving" crops by offering payments, to be financed out of general revenues, averaging roughly $10 per acre to farmers adopting the recommended practices. The goals of intervention were also reformulated. The Agricultural Adjustment Act of 1933 had set higher farm prices as the target. This language was now eliminated. The mandate given to administrators of the Soil Conservation and Domestic Allotment Act of 1936 was instead to raise the net income of farmers.[21]

There was more than a trivial element of opportunism about the form in which agricultural policy was hastily redesigned in early 1936. The Roosevelt administration was desperate to produce a program to aid farmers that could survive judicial scrutiny. This meant that objectionable features of the original AAA, such as direct controls in the interest of short-term price manipulation, had to be purged. It was expedient to draw on the insights of economists who emphasized indirect techniques for shrinking supply. The Roosevelt administration, whatever its rhetoric, was certainly not indifferent to the behavior of farm prices. It was no accident that those crops identified as soil-depleting – e.g., wheat, corn, cotton, tobacco – were subject to price-depressing surpluses, whereas the soil-conserving ones – grasses and legumes – were not.

Roosevelt urged farmers to take advantage of the financial assistance available to them for shifting "from the production of unneeded surpluses of soil-depleting crops to the production of needed soil-building crops." In mid-March 1936, he was advised by the Department of Agriculture that its surveys indicated that farmers were inclined instead to take advantage of AAA's demise by increasing plantings of "basic crops" formerly subject to direct controls. The president then warned that, should farmers "carry out their intentions as indicated in the Department of Agriculture reports, the consequent excessive production of such cash crops as cotton and wheat and tobacco might result once more in the wrecking of their prices and the mining of their soil."[22]

Though the timing of the tilt in agricultural planning that took place in 1936 was driven by constitutional considerations, a genuine departure from the original design had nonetheless occurred. At the outset, the principles guiding AAA, as was also the case with NRA, were oriented toward price manipulation orchestrated by visible hands. The resulting structural interventions in both the agricultural and industrial sectors had generated a fair number of dis-

---

21. Details on these points are elaborated in Murray R. Benedict, *Farm Policies of the United States, 1790–1950* (New York: The Twentieth Century Fund, 1953), especially Chapter 14.
22. Roosevelt, Statement for the Press, March 19, 1936, FDRPL.

appointments, and particularly for the nonmainstream economists who had been among their original sponsors.

With the collapse of AAA's original format, another component fell out of the policy mix of 1933. The Roosevelt administration was again in search of analytic moorings. With respect to agriculture, they were already in inventory in the analyses prepared by the land use planners. An interventionist twist – though one quite different from the direct control strategy of Domestic Allotment – could thus survive. The 1936 formulation of farm strategy, unlike its predecessor, was not to be predominantly preoccupied with a price orientation toward the behavior of the economy. On the contrary, its conceptualization was to be compatible with another view that income, rather than price, should be the principal category around which economic analysis and policy should be organized.

6

Rethinking macroeconomic strategies, 1934–36

The original designs for microeconomic policies affecting industry and agriculture had undergone considerable modification by 1936. There was to be mutation as well in the thinking available to the administration concerning factors conditioning the performance of the macroeconomic system. The active ingredient in the macroeconomic component of the policy mix of late 1933 was manipulation of the gold price. Fiscal policies were absent from the conceptualization of strategy, despite the fact that the administration tolerated deficits of unprecedented peacetime magnitude. This outcome was treated as an unintended and unwelcome by-product of the depression-induced erosion of the tax base and of the administration's humanitarian commitments to relieve the plight of the destitute.

By the time Roosevelt again faced the electorate in the campaign of 1936, his administration had yet to be at one with itself with respect to its macroeconomic posture. It had, however, long since abandoned the gold purchase program that had formed the *leitmotif* in the early going. The results of that experiment had been decidedly disappointing. The reflationary magic claimed for this alleged stimulant failed to make an appearance. When Roosevelt announced his decision to stabilize the gold content of the dollar on January 31, 1934, the price he then set – $35 per ounce – represented an increase of nearly 70 percent over the official gold price when his administration took office. But there was precious little to show for all this. In October 1933 (when active intervention in gold markets was begun), the wholesale price index stood at 71.2 (with a 1926 base = 100). In February 1934, the same index had reached 73.6.[1]

In the debates over monetary and fiscal policies between 1934 and 1936, familiar voices were to sing some variations on old tunes and, in a few instances,

1. *Statistical Abstract of the United States, 1938,* p. 306.

to transpose them into an entirely different key. In addition, some fresh voices sounded several unfamiliar themes.

1   Tactical adjustments in the reflationist position in 1934

Conceivably, the upshot of the administration's embrace of monetary heterodoxy in late 1933 might have shaken the confidence of its sponsors in the efficacy of gold price maneuvering, in particular, and of reflation as a recovery measure more generally. This did not happen. From the perspective of Fisher and Warren, shortcomings in policy execution, rather than flaws in the underlying model, were responsible for the outcome. Roosevelt had terminated the project prematurely and had stopped short of reducing the gold content of the dollar to the limit of the authority conveyed to him in the Thomas Amendment. In addition, he had failed to use other reflationary weapons that were potentially at his disposal.

Throughout the spring and summer of 1934, Fisher persisted in his efforts to persuade the White House to move reflation to the top of the policy agenda. With midterm elections approaching in November, Fisher insisted that prompt action would pay political dividends. As he wrote to a Roosevelt aide in mid-May:

> The one salvation of us all, including the President, is to get us out of the depression – and not "gradually" but at once and in the only way which has worked – monetary reflation. It would be wonderful if the President would tell the country that, of all the things he has tried, reflation has worked and will be resumed, that its suspension, as advised by so many (mostly "economic illiterates") has already proved harmful. … But the President, by assuming the initiative aggressively, could take the country again by storm, provided, as he went along, he actually reflated and got us out, or further out, of the depression before the election.[2]

Fisher followed this up with recommendations on specific techniques to promote monetary reflation, indicating his belief that his ideas were "practically identical with Warren's, certainly in principle."[3] At Roosevelt's request, Fisher put a complete itemization of his views directly before him in September 1934. He urged "an immediate raising of the price of gold to $41.34" (to the maximum allowed by law), adding that "this will help the farmer particularly." The so-called gold "profit" – the $2.75 billion increment in the nominal value of the nation's gold stock generated when the price was raised to $35 per ounce and a further gain of $1.75 billion in prospect from a $41.34 price

---

2. Fisher to M. H. McIntyre, Assistant Secretary to the President, May 12, 1934, FDRPL. In this communication, Fisher also volunteered to assist in preparing radio talks for presidential use "which would make all back-talk from Sprague and Warburg look silly, for they are wrong both as to facts and principles."
3. Fisher to Louis McH. Howe, Secretary to the President, May 18, 1934, FDRPL.

– should be put to work in support of reflation. This windfall should be used creatively as backing for a supplemental currency issue. The new notes should be designated as "yellowbacks" to distinguish them from greenbacks. Though Fisher was aware that there was always something suspect in the public mind about greenbacks, he nonetheless urged Roosevelt to announce that he was prepared, if necessary, to use his discretionary powers to issue $3 billion in greenbacks.[4]

As Fisher had long insisted, reflation should not be confused with inflation. Once the target of the 1926 price level had been reached, monetary stabilization should be the order of the day. In 1934, Fisher pressed again for congressional action that would write his version of monetary stabilization into the law of the land. In this iteration, he modified his earlier positions in two noteworthy respects. First, this version of a "Goldsborough Bill" called for the creation of an independent Monetary Authority (which would supersede the Federal Reserve Board). There was a familiar ring to the charge to this body: It would be required to "normalize" the general price level by replicating 1926 and thereafter to stabilize. Second, Fisher endorsed a new technique for keeping members of the Monetary Authority on course. If the price level deviated from the targeted norm by as much as 10 percent for three consecutive months, officers of the authority would be automatically removed.[5]

Fisher called upon the White House to endorse this legislation – to no avail – and a Goldsborough Bill, vintage 1934, went nowhere.[6] Congressional hearings on the proposed Monetary Authority nonetheless demonstrated that the intellectual chasm dividing Fisher from his more orthodox professional brethren was as wide as ever. O. M. W. Sprague, for example, saw matters differently:

> I think it is tolerably easy to keep prices from going up over 10 percent, but I think it is a far more difficult matter to maintain such sound conditions in the business of the country that you will escape some time from prices going down 10 percent or more. … If you get a disordered condition of production, prices and business activity are not responsive to moderate changes in monetary policy. I think that is where I differ most profoundly from Professor Fisher. He believes that the whole situation is far more readily responsive to monetary changes than I do.[7]

4. Fisher to Roosevelt, September 6, 1934, FDRPL. On this occasion, Fisher also re-iterated his support for stamped money.
5. Fisher, Hearings before the Subcommittee of the Committee on Banking and Currency, House of Representatives, 73:2, February 1, 1934, p. 78.
6. Fisher to Roosevelt, March 18, 1934, FDRPL.
7. O. M. W. Sprague, Hearings before the Subcommittee of the Committee on Banking and Currency, House of Representatives, 73:2, February 22, 1934, p. 329.

2   **Public works spending in designs for recovery strategy**

The notion that macroeconomic stabilization might usefully be promoted through countercyclical spending on public works was not new to Americans. Former President Hoover had played a formidable role in developing such a strategy as Secretary of Commerce in the 1920s and, as the nation's chief executive, he had deployed it in 1929 and 1930. Its promise, however, had not been fulfilled, in large part because Hoover had depended primarily (and unrealistically) on state and municipal governments to be the principal public sector spenders. In his scheme of things, the federal government's role centered on signaling to other governmental echelons when they should borrow and spend. He held it to be inappropriate for Washington to be a major spender in its own right. Were it to do so, it would usurp what properly belonged to the units of government closest to the people. In light of the condition of the economy when Hoover left office, compensatory public works spending appeared to have failed. Certainly Roosevelt did not find this strategy to be compelling. He had, to be sure, accepted the $3.3 billion appropriation for public works inserted into the National Industrial Recovery Act, but he had shown no disposition to make haste in spending it.

In mid-1934, a deficit-financed program of public works received renewed attention as a possible centerpiece for an active fiscal policy. Britain's John Maynard Keynes was in the vanguard of such advocacy. Through the intermediation of Felix Frankfurter of the Harvard Law School (who was then a visiting professor at the University of Oxford), Keynes had prepared the Open Letter to the President, which had received widespread publicity upon its release at the close of 1933. He struck a further blow for public works expenditure during a visit to the United States in May–June 1934, in which an hour with Roosevelt at the White House was fitted into his itinerary. The substance of his argument was set out in another Open Letter to the President, dated June 5, 1934, in which he called for loan expenditure of $400 million per month. This sum, he observed, "is not much more than 8 percent of the national income; yet it may, directly or indirectly, increase the national income by at least three or four times this amount. ... Most people greatly under-estimate the effect of a given emergency expenditure, because they overlook the Multiplier – the cumulative effect of increased individual incomes, because the expenditure of these incomes improves the incomes of a further set of recipients and so on."[8]

Keynes's intervention added prominence to a view that deficit financing in circumstances of depression should be pursued as a positive good, rather than merely tolerated as an unavoidable evil. It appears, however, that he had little impact on Roosevelt's thinking. (Keynes impressed the president as "a math-

8. John Maynard Keynes, "Open Letter to the President," transmitted to the White House, June 5, 1934, FDRPL.

ematician rather than a political economist.")[9] Keynes's American visit also
included a dinner in New York at which he presented, in embryonic form, the
theories of effective demand and of the multiplier that were later to receive extended treatment in *The General Theory*.[10]

As an example of properties of divergent macroeconomic perspectives at
this time, Fisher's reaction to Keynes's design is instructive. In the discussions
of monetary theory and policy in the 1920s, the two men had occupied much
common ground. By 1934, their ways had parted. Writing to his wife about
Keynes's presentation, Fisher observed: "His paper was interesting but to me
– and I think to everyone else – rather obscure and unconvincing. He was very
skillful in answering questions and objections but seemed to get nowhere."[11]
Fisher also offered instruction to Roosevelt on what he should absorb from
Keynes's message:

> I had a long talk with J. Maynard Keynes and find myself in sub-
> stantial agreement with him, but it should be noted that:
> (1) "loan expenditure" is really a *monetary* measure involving added (gov-
>   ernment) deposits and their use as purchasing power;
> (2) the quickest, cheapest and most beneficial loan expenditure is, it seems
>   to me, ... to lend to all those going concerns a year or more old, who
>   want it a dollar and a half per day per employee added to payroll for
>   one hundred consecutive days;
> (3) public works make the slowest, dearest, and usually least beneficial
>   form. It will require something of a wrench later to get millions of
>   workers out of jobs under government into their normal jobs in indus-
>   try. Under the plan I propose, most would be re-employed in their nor-
>   mal jobs to start with.[12]

Against this backdrop, the analytic divide between monetary and fiscal approaches to macroeconomics can be seen in sharper relief. Fisher's distance
from Keynes did not turn on the issue of deficit financing per se. Fisher offered no brief for balanced budgets in times of depression: To the contrary, he
held that deficits could provide a welcome stimulant, as long as they were financed by new money. Their impact should thus be understood as primarily
monetary, not fiscal. This line of argument suggested that it was at least conceivable that public works could be financed by deficits and still fail to stimulate spending. This could happen, for example, if governments covered increased spending by borrowing from the public, rather than from banks. In
their views on the relative merits of public works, Fisher and Keynes were

9. As quoted in Herbert Stein, *The Fiscal Revolution in America* (Chicago: University of Chicago Press, 1969), p. 150.
10. Those present at the New York dinner on June 6, 1934 included Irving Fisher, Wes-
    ley Mitchell, J. M. Clark, A. D. Gayer, Joseph Schumpeter, Alvin Hansen, Adolf
    Berle, Jr. [D. E. Moggridge, *Maynard Keynes: An Economist's Biography* (London
    and New York: Routledge, 1992), p. 584.]
11. Fisher to Margaret Hazard Fisher, June 7, 1934, YUA.
12. Fisher to Roosevelt, June 11, 1934, FDRPL.

separated for another reason. On principle, Fisher consistently opposed extraordinary efforts for job creation in the public sector. He held it to be far superior to spur expansion of private employment. On numerous occasions, he urged Roosevelt to endorse government loans and/or subsidies to private employers who agreed to enlarge their workforce.

3   Fiscal designs with native soil roots

Even before Keynes had put his case for loan expenditure before the American public, a local voice was beginning to attract attention to a similar perspective. Marriner S. Eccles – a Utah Mormon and self-made businessman-banker who lacked a college education – was an authentic American original. His influence was the greater for that. Though there was a singular convergence between the policies he pressed for and those recommended by Keynes, he was untutored in technical economic theory. In his memoirs, published in 1951, he observed: "The concepts I formulated, which have been called 'Keynesian,' were not abstracted from his books, which I had never read. My conceptions were based on naked-eye observation and experience in the intermountain region. Moreover, I have never read Keynes's writings except in small extracts up to this day."[13]

Eccles's economic thinking had clearly been molded in the crucible of depression. In company with fellow bankers, he had been engaged in a desperate struggle to forestall bank runs. Unlike many of his colleagues, Eccles succeeded in keeping his banks open, and not one of his depositors lost a penny. As he later recounted this episode:

> I began to wonder whether the conduct of bankers like myself in depression times was a wise one. Were we not contributing our bit to the worsening of matters by the mere act of trying to keep liquid under the economic pressures of deflation? By forcing the liquidation of loans and securities to meet the demands of depositors, were we not helping to drive prices down and thereby making it increasingly difficult for our debtors to pay back what they had borrowed from us?[14]

In 1931 and 1932 Eccles elaborated on these themes in a series of speeches delivered in Utah. Conventional views about the way out of depression, he argued, should be rejected. There was no foundation for the conclusion that the economic system would correct itself if left to its own devices. Nor should one anticipate that efforts to balance the federal budget – allegedly to restore investor confidence – would be successful. Deficits were the result, not the cause, of depressed national income. What was needed was more spending,

13. Marriner S. Eccles, *Beckoning Frontiers: Public and Personal Recollections,* Sidney Hyman, ed. (New York: Alfred A. Knopf, 1951), p. 132.
14. Ibid., p. 70.

not less. "The difficulty," as he diagnosed it in an address to the Utah State Bankers Convention in June 1932, was "that we were not sufficiently extravagant as a nation."[15] It was the task of government to direct its economic policies to guarantee opportunities to work for all who sought them.

A chance meeting with Stuart Chase, a nationally prominent publicist who had been invited to speak in Salt Lake City, was to bring Eccles to the notice of a wider audience. In the ensuing conversation in February 1933, Chase suggested that Eccles share his views about the requirements of the economic situation with Rexford Guy Tugwell, and the two met later that month in New York. Although Tugwell expressed surprise that a banker could be associated with such "radical" views, there was no immediate follow-up. In October 1933, however, Tugwell invited Eccles to visit Washington. By this time, Eccles had refined his position. As he expressed it that month in an address to the Utah Educational Association:

> The question is not how bankers and those who have idle money and credit can bring about recovery, but why they should do so, so long as there is no incentive offered in any field of profitable investment. A bank cannot finance the building of more factories and more rental properties and more homes when half of our productive property is idle for lack of consumption and a large percentage of our business properties are vacant, for want of paying tenants. The government, however, can spend money, because the government, unlike the bankers, has the power of taxation and the power to create money and does not have to depend on the profit motive. The only escape from a depression must be by increased spending. We must depend upon the government to save what we have of a price, profit, and credit system.[16]

Eccles's November 1933 visit in Washington was to lead to greater things. He was then offered a post as special assistant to the Secretary of the Treasury for monetary and credit affairs. He accepted, with the expectation that he would stay in Washington no longer than a year and a half. After the senior position on the Federal Reserve Board (then styled as "governor") fell vacant, Roosevelt appointed Eccles to this job in late 1934. Eccles took it on the condition that Roosevelt would support legislation to reorganize the system by strengthening the powers of the Board in Washington and weakening those of the Federal Reserve district banks.

From this base, Eccles became the point man within government in presenting a case for the wisdom of fiscal interventionism. "The Government," he maintained, "must be the compensatory agent in this economy; it must unbalance the budget during deflation and create surpluses in periods of

---

15. Eccles, as quoted in ibid., p. 83.
16. Eccles, as quoted in ibid., p. 130.

great business activity." He called on believers in the sanctity of balanced budgets to rethink their priorities: "Have we not yet learned that what we cannot afford is not the burden of carrying the national debt, but is an army of idle men and unutilized resources?" And he took on the traditionalists in the banking community by reminding them of their stake in deficit finance. "The bankers above all," he told them, "have been the beneficiaries of the Government's intervention. The Government alone could and did replenish the supply of deposits when individual borrowers were lacking and when banks had no other profitable outlet for their funds than the investment in Government securities."[17]

From late 1934 onwards, many of Eccles's speeches and memoranda were flavored with a touch of analytic seasoning provided by Lauchlin Currie, a young Harvard Ph.D., who had established his credentials as a critic of the Federal Reserve's post-1929 management of the money supply and as a supporter of New Deal spending programs. Currie had first come to the attention of official Washington in early 1934 when he had persuaded half a dozen of his junior faculty colleagues at Harvard to sign a letter to the president applauding his economic policy initiatives. The White House reacted warmly to this endorsement and released the letter to the press. The reception in Cambridge, Massachusetts, however, was chilly. The establishment figures in Harvard's Economics Department at the time were New Deal critics. Neither Currie nor any of his fellow "Young Turks" received a tenured appointment there.

Currie adapted quickly to the ways of Washington upon his arrival in the summer of 1934 with a Treasury Department assignment to study possible monetary reforms and their implications. This was, in effect, an extension of work he had already done in the preparation of *The Supply and Control of Money in the United States,* published in 1934. In this book, he had set out a trenchant critique of the institutional arrangements that had enabled the U.S. money supply to shrink so dramatically between 1929 and 1932 and had expressed sympathy for a scheme under which commercial banks would be obliged to hold 100 percent reserves against demand deposits. Currie and Eccles became acquainted early in Currie's Treasury sojourn. Eccles later invited Currie to accompany him to the Federal Reserve as a member of its research staff.[18]

It is a comment on the confusion of the times that two of the figures most conspicuous in championing an activist fiscal policy, led by deliberate deficits,

---

17. Eccles, Address to the American Bankers' Association Convention, November 14, 1935, FDRPL.
18. With respect to the Eccles-Currie collaboration, Currie was later to write: "Rarely have two people with such different judgments or aptitudes which complemented each other so well been so suddenly catapulted into a strategic spot at a critical moment which enabled them to make an impact." [Currie, as quoted in Roger J. Sandilands, *The Life and Political Economy of Lauchlin Currie* (Durham, N.C.: Duke University Press, 1990), p. 62.]

in the First New Deal were to be situated at the central bank where their official duties charged them to be preoccupied with monetary (rather than fiscal) policies. Similarly, there was an oddity about a primary concern of the nation's chief fiscal officer, the Secretary of the Treasury. Henry Morgenthau, Jr. was a consistent champion of monetary stimulants to recovery (as he had been, for example, when supporting Warren's gold doctrine) and was always ill at ease with deficits. But a rationale could be offered for the Eccles-Currie ventures into fiscal terrain from an operational base at the Federal Reserve. Both were convinced that increased government spending would have to be the recovery's prime mover and that such a program had an important monetary dimension in the accommodation of that additional spending. A key objective of the banking reforms they sought was to create structural conditions ensuring that that objective could be reached.

Currie also took it to be part of his brief to buttress the prodeficit spending position with statistical documentation. Toward this end, he (in company with Martin Krost of the research staff of the Federal Reserve) launched a pioneering line of investigation in 1935. Their target was to measure the "net income-increasing expenditures of the Federal government." This expression was taken to mean "all income received directly from Government agencies and from persons and institutions which are financing their expenditures by borrowing from Government agencies, minus all deductions from income paid over to the government as taxes, fees, etc." The results of this exercise were first circulated in November 1935, still in fairly rough form. Even so, the preliminary use of this technique suggested that the net stimulus to spending arising from government activities was not necessarily closely linked to the size of the federal deficit (as reported in accordance with the Treasury's accounting conventions). In three of the four calendar years investigated in this initial study, the magnitude of the net impact was substantially less than the officially reported deficit. This was a type of knowledge that could have been generated only by "insiders" with privileged access to information, and it invited a new way to look at fiscal policy.[19] And the look it supplied pointed to shortcomings in the New Deal's fiscal policies.

Fiscal activists thus had house room in the First New Deal. Their arguments nonetheless encountered stiff resistance. Though he accepted the inevitability of deficits in conditions of emergency, Roosevelt remained a fiscal conservative at heart. His first appointee as Director of the Budget, Lewis W. Douglas, served as the president's conscience on budgetary responsibility. Douglas was wont to remind him of the campaign pledge at Pittsburgh to match the "ordi-

19. Lauchlin Currie and Martin Krost, "Federal Income-Increasing Expenditures," circa November 1935, reprinted in *History of Political Economy,* Winter 1978, pp. 534–40. See also Byrd L. Jones, "Lauchlin Currie, Pump Priming, and the New Deal Fiscal Policy, 1934–1936," pp. 509–24, and commentary by Currie in the same issue.

nary" expenditures of government with receipts and to tolerate deficits only to the extent required to relieve distress. Though Douglas left no one in any doubt about his preference for a balanced overall budget, he readily gave his approval to generous relief outlays during the New Deal's first year. By mid-1934, however, his tolerance was strained to the breaking point. In his view, the administration's spending had destroyed the "confidence" essential to a solid recovery. He was particularly offended by the public works program, which he held to be ineffective and inefficient. On August 30, 1934, Douglas resigned.

4   Monetary designs in a new guise

The experience of a half-decade of depression stimulated some arrestingly fresh thinking about the adequacy of the nation's banking system in an economy under strain. Economic thinkers who disagreed sharply about other matters converged when concluding that the size of the nation's money supply was properly a governmental responsibility and that major institutional reforms were required to permit that responsibility to be appropriately discharged. It had long been recognized that demand deposits overwhelmed currency and coin as components of the money supply. And it was common knowledge as well that the volume of demand deposits was a by-product of the lending activities of commercial banks. In short, the bulk of the money supply was a creature of the profit-oriented activities of private bankers. Their decisions with respect to loans – whether to issue or renew them, whether to reject or recall them – were pivotal to the process of creating or destroying money. In the mid-1920s, following the Federal Reserve's discovery of the technique of open market operations, it was nonetheless widely understood that the central bank's instruments of control meant that the ultimate determination of the money supply was in the hands of public authorities, even though they might not use their powers wisely.

At least by 1934, it was far from clear that the Federal Reserve could effectively determine the money supply, even if it had a mind to do so. Its open market operations could, of course, augment the lending capacity of the commercial banks. But member banks were already saturated with excess reserves. Expanding them further offered no assurance that the primary objective – the expansion of private lending and spending – would be well served. It was self-evident that there was a missing ingredient: an adequate private demand for loans from creditworthy borrowers. At the same time, memories were also fresh about how commercial banks had shrunk demand deposits by contracting their lending activities after 1929.

How then could the primacy of public authority over the quantity of money be established? One answer readily suggested itself: The power of private interests to create or destroy money should be extinguished. This could be accomplished if commercial banks were required to hold 100 percent reserves against demand deposits. At a stroke, the capacity of private bankers to shrink or swell the money supply would be terminated.

This idea had been in circulation for some time, but it acquired new prominence in the context of the 1935 debates on the merits of fundamental reforms in the American banking system.[20] The doctrine of "100 percent money" entered American economic discourse in 1933 with the circulation of a mimeographed document known as the Chicago Plan, which was endorsed by seven economists associated with the University of Chicago.[21] In 1934, it appeared in published form in Henry Simons's *A Positive Program for Laissez-Faire: Some Proposals for a Liberal Economic Policy.*[22] Simons wrote as an outspoken critic of New Deal economic programs, and most particularly those associated with Tugwell. In his view, "the real enemies of liberty in this country are the naive advocates of managed economy or national planning," and he called for a return to the central principles of nineteenth-century liberalism which had been "subjected latterly to gross misrepresentation and to shallow satirical jibes in the 'new economics.'"[23]

The effective functioning of a proper competitive order presupposed, however, that governments maintained a stable monetary environment. This they had notoriously failed to do by allowing the behavior of banks to determine the money supply. Simons believed it unlikely that capitalism could "survive the political rigors of another depression," which seemed bound to come "unless the state does reassume and discharge with some wisdom its responsibility for controlling the circulating medium."[24] Hence, Simons concluded, nothing short of a radical restructuring of commercial banking – one that stripped banks of the power to generate fluctuations in the money supply – would do.

Under a new regime, banks accepting deposits payable on demand would become secure warehouses of funds. Risk-free checking facilities would be maintained, and the bank would charge for this service. Lending and borrowing activities would continue, but they would be channeled through financial institutions organized as investment trusts, which would be the intermediaries between savers and investors. Simons emphasized two fundamental differences between the proposed system and the regime of fractional reserve commercial banking: (1) The linkage of lending and money creation would be broken, and (2) no financial liabilities would be eligible for repayment on call.

---

20. Frederick Soddy, a Nobel Prize-winning chemist at the University of Oxford, had sparked the contemporary discussion with a pamphlet calling for 100 percent reserves in 1926.
21. The original sponsors were Henry C. Simons, Aaron Director, Garfield V. Cox, Lloyd W. Mints, Henry Schultz, Paul Douglas, and A. G. Hart.
22. This essay originally appeared as a Public Policy Pamphlet issued by the University of Chicago Press. It was reprinted in Henry C. Simons, *Economic Policy for a Free Society* (Chicago: University of Chicago Press, 1948). Pagination refers to this version.
23. Simons, op. cit., pp. 41, 42.
24. Ibid., p. 56.

Meanwhile the supply of money would be the exclusive jurisdiction of a governmental body – Simons proposed that it be called the National Monetary Authority – and its responsibilities would be unambiguously stipulated. In the system he sought "the rules of the game as to money are definite, intelligible, and inflexible. They are intended to avoid both the 'rulelessness' of the present system and the establishment of any system based on discretionary management. 'Managed currency,' without fixed rules of management, appears to me as one of the most dangerous forms of 'planning.'"[25] How then should the appropriate rule be specified? Simons could accept one based on fixing the quantity of money or of total turnover (the money supply times velocity) on the one hand, or one based on "stabilizing some index of commodity prices" on the other.[26] The crucial point was that the ultimate rule guiding the National Monetary Authority would be totally insulated from political tinkering.

Independently and more or less simultaneously, Currie had arrived at broadly similar conclusions concerning the inherent instability of fractional reserve banking and the need to correct it. From the point of view of the public, he saw distinct advantages to the 100 percent scheme over and above its attractiveness in giving government undiluted control over the money supply. If the government sought, for example, to maintain a stable price level in an economy experiencing normal growth in real output, an increment in the money stock of some 2 to 4 percent annually would probably be required. Government could supply it by financing some of its current expenditures with newly created money. Thus the tax-paying public would eventually be better off.[27] Currie's recommendations for policy, however, were poles removed from those advanced by Simons. Currie was adamantly opposed to the adoption of an inflexible rule to govern the actions of a monetary authority. He held instead that "no government can delegate to an independent body such a supremely important factor for good or ill as the control of the monetary system."[28]

By the autumn of 1934, Irving Fisher had assimilated the 100 percent money doctrine into his crusade for reflation.[29] When doing so, he acknowledged his intellectual indebtedness to Simons and Currie, who had first exposed him to this line of thinking. Once having embraced this proposal, Fisher, with characteristic zeal, lobbied aggressively for its adoption. In his statement of the case, he was to enlarge on a number of features of the basic scheme.

25. Ibid., p. 63.
26. Ibid., p. 64.
27. Lauchlin Currie, *The Supply and Control of Money in the United States* (Cambridge, Mass.: Harvard University Press, 1934), pp. 151–6.
28. Ibid., p. 155.
29. Fisher endorsed this idea publicly in *The Wall Street Journal* on October 9, 1934. He had earlier placed it before Roosevelt when meeting with him at Hyde Park in September 1934.

In Fisher's version, central control over the money supply would be exercised by a body designated as the Currency Commission. Its initial function would be to buy up enough of the securities of commercial banks to provide them with sufficient cash to back fully all their demand deposit liabilities. In the conditions of 1934 and 1935, he argued, this maneuver could be executed rather painlessly. At that time, government securities were abnormally heavily represented in the portfolios of commercial banks. The Currency Commission could readily convert these assets into cash. This meant, of course, that the banks would no longer earn interest – then amounting to about $300 million per year – on their holdings of government debt. Banks, however, could more than overcome this loss by levying a modest service charge on checking accounts. Fisher was later to suggest that an assessment of $1 per month would be more than ample for this purpose.

Once complete liquidity against demand deposits had been achieved, the Currency Commission's task would be to buy still more securities – whether held by financial institutions or by the public – in a volume sufficient to reflate the price level to a prescribed point. Once the target had been achieved, the Commission would thereafter buy and sell securities to stabilize the price level. Fisher noted, however, that "buying would predominate in the long run, because the growth of the country and its business would continually require more money in order to sustain a given price level."[30]

Fisher saw virtually no end to the advantages that adoption of this scheme would bring. Deposit insurance – at least against demand deposits – would now be redundant and banks could be relieved of their costs. The survival prospects of small banks would be improved with their solvency assured. Indeed, Fisher argued, 100 percent money was in the long-term interests of bankers themselves, even though he expected them to oppose this proposition. The 100 percent system, he argued:

> might afford the banks the only escape from nationalization. For if,
> in another decade, we should have another depression like the one
> we have just been passing though, the banks would probably find
> themselves permanently in the hands of the Government. It would
> be better for the banks to give up gracefully their usurped function
> of minting money (in the form of bank notes and checkbook
> money) and be content to conduct their strictly banking business,
> unmolested and uninterfered with by boom and depressions – so
> largely of their own making.[31]

As far as the general public was concerned, the benefits would be widespread. Everyone stood to gain, Fisher insisted, from a system in which eco-

---

30. Fisher, *100% Money: Designed to Keep Checking Banks 100% Liquid; to Prevent Inflation and Deflation; Largely to Cure or Prevent Depressions; and to Wipe Out Much of the National Debt* (New York: Adelphi Company, rev. ed., 1936), p. 100.
31. Ibid., p. 203.

nomic fluctuations were dampened. The taxpayer would be particularly blessed. Through its normal operations, the Currency Commission would gradually absorb the bulk of the national debt. This meant, in effect, that Treasury financing would be largely interest-free. As a bookkeeping matter, the Treasury would continue to pay interest on the Currency Commission's holdings of its obligations, but these funds would then be returned to the Treasury. Fisher even entertained the possibility, which he held to be "at least conceivable," that the "Government's main receipts would eventually come from the Currency Commission."[32] If that day arrived, what would happen? He suggested that "the money could, if desired, be used to reduce taxation and, in time, if we wish to imagine so extreme a result, to abolish all Federal taxes." But suppose that Currency Commission surpluses continued after all taxes had been wiped out. A social dividend might then be declared: "[I]n effect, money would be given by the people to the people, to supply the needs of growing business and prevent the fall of the price level which such growth would otherwise cause."[33]

5   Reform and the Banking Act of 1935

Fisher's indefatigable campaign for 100 percent money notwithstanding, this proposal failed to win converts among officials within the administration who would have a say in administration-initiated recommendations for legislation. From the perspective of the structuralist school of New Deal economists, this scheme – and all others aimed at controlling the general price level, for that matter – missed the critical point. For Means and Tugwell, for example, the economy's problems were created by imbalances in the structure of relative prices, rather than by the behavior of the general price level. They agreed that money mattered. But the task of monetary policy should not be conceptualized in the Fisher mode. Instead monetary policy should be designed "to bring prices at the more flexible end of the scale back into line with the inflexible prices. This does not mean raising the price level in the sense that all prices should rise together but rather a restoring of the price structure." This called for selective reflation, not general reflation. Achievement of the desired balance, however, required some form of control over prices in the sector in which they were administered.[34] In this spirit,

---

32. Ibid., p. 208.
33. Ibid., pp. 208–9.
34. Means to Tugwell, September 8, 1934, FDRPL. Tugwell readily appreciated the implications of this argument and passed it along to the president with his enthusiastic endorsement. "The relation of money volume to price in an economy of partly rigid and partly flexible prices," he observed, "has a bearing of the utmost importance on your future economic policy. If together with this currency action we could (1) proceed under anti-trust laws against unauthorized price fixers and (2) have a series of authorizations for government control of monopolies (businesses which are capable of fix-

Means took exception to Fisher's attachment to the 1926 price level as a benchmark for monetary policy. Again he supported disaggregation along sectoral lines. In his words:

> I believe the use of indexes of production for rigid priced commodities and of prices for the flexible commodities would be preferable. Flexible prices and production should be kept in line with the inflexible prices and production.[35]

Eccles's position had a more significant bearing on the practical prospects for 100 percent money. While he was sympathetic to Fisher's desires to see the economy stimulated, he preferred incremental reforms within the existing framework to a wholesale scrapping of the Federal Reserve in favor of a Currency Commission. His packaging of the Banking Act of 1935 was intended to serve three purposes. First, it was to change the composition of the governing body by displacing the two *ex officio* members – the Secretary of the Treasury and the Comptroller of the Currency – and restyling the Federal Reserve Board as the Board of Governors of the Federal Reserve System. Second, it was to restructure the Open Market Committee by placing its decisive weight with the Board of Governors in Washington by reducing the voting strength of Federal Reserve district banks. Third, it was to increase the power of the central Board over the determination of discount rates and to widen its discretionary latitude over required reserve ratios. Eccles distanced himself from a legislative prescription that Fisher and others endorsed, i.e., a stipulation that the Board's policy should be directed toward some price level target (such as 1926). But he did express discomfort with the language in the original act indicating that the Federal Reserve should "accommodate" the needs of trade. In his view, this was procyclical, rather than countercyclical. He preferred a mandate to the system that it "shall exert such powers as it has toward promoting business stability and moderating fluctuations in production, employment, and prices."[36]

In the end, Eccles got the essentials of what he wanted, but not without a fight. Professional opinion among economists and alleged monetary "experts" was sharply divided about the merits of the bill. James P. Warburg, a New York banker and sometime consultant to the administration in 1933, was outspokenly hostile. He rejected the theory underlying the structure of the bill, which he characterized as Curried Keynes, "for it is in fact a large half-cooked lump of J. Maynard Keynes – the well-known British economist whose theories find more support in this country than in his own – liberally seasoned with a sauce prepared by Prof. Laughlin [sic] Currie."[37] Princeton's Edwin W. Kemmerer,

ing their own prices) we should be on the right track." (Tugwell to Roosevelt, September 8, 1934, FDRPL.)

35. Means to Wallace, January 23, 1935, FDRPL.
36. Eccles, Testimony before the Subcommittee of the Committee on Banking and Currency, U.S. Senate, 74:1, May 10, 1935, p. 290.

the international "money doctor" whose faith in the gold standard remained un-shaken, warned of dangerous consequences flowing from political pressures that would be applied to a Board with enhanced powers. And "political pres-sures," he maintained, were "usually exercised in the direction of cheap money. ... The opinion of the masses is almost never in favor of deflation or even in favor of restricting a dangerous boom while it is still in a stage in which it can be controlled."[38] Though O. M. W. Sprague had joined Kemmerer and 60 ad-ditional members of an Economists' National Committee on Monetary Policy in declaring that no legislation affecting the Federal Reserve was needed, he gave a more charitable reading to Eccles's bill. A trend toward centralization in central banking was observable throughout the world. Even so, he believed that it was a mistake to "give the Reserve Board more power unless you can make certain that it will possess greater independence than in the past."[39]

Fisher, by contrast, was dismayed that the Banking Act of 1935 had not been drawn more ambitiously. He faulted it on two counts. First, it failed to give the Board a clear legislative directive, such as the restoration of the 1926 price level and thereafter stabilization. Second, it conveyed to the Board all too much discretion in the setting of required reserves. As he put it:

> Instead of allowing Mr. Eccles, irresponsibly, without any guidance, to raise or lower the reserve requirements of the 15,000 banks in the country, according to whatever rules he and his associates may es-tablish, instead of doing that ... it seems to me much better to raise the reserve requirements at once to 100 percent ....[40]

6   Redefining the role of government as a provider of economic security: The Social Security Act of 1935

The first Roosevelt administration did not achieve an intellectual equilibrium with respect to a macroeconomic strategy to reach full employ-ment. It was, however, imaginatively creative in its longer-term planning to position government to support the livelihoods of those most vulnerable to downturns in the economy. There had never been any doubt about the presi-dent's willingness to allocate federal resources to relieve the plight of the des-titute. New ground had been broken: Standard American practice had held that this job properly belonged to private charities and to state and local govern-ments. Even though the entry of the federal government into the direct relief

37. James P. Warburg, Testimony before the Subcommittee of the Committee on Bank-ing and Currency, U.S. Senate, 74:1, April 24, 1935, p. 74.
38. Edwin W. Kemmerer, Testimony before the Subcommittee on Banking and Cur-rency, U.S. Senate, 74:1, May 10, 1935, p. 338.
39. O. M. W. Sprague, Testimony before the Subcommittee of the Committee on Banking and Currency, U.S. Senate, 74:1, May 3, 1935, p. 229.
40. Fisher, Testimony before the Committee on Banking and Currency, House of Rep-resentatives, 74:1, March 22, 1935, p. 521.

business had been essential, there was still something distasteful about this activity. The administration was prepared to be receptive to fresh thinking about ways in which government could help the needy in a manner that would be less damaging to human dignity.

There was nothing particularly new about the concept of governmentally sponsored programs of unemployment insurance. In one form or another, most of the industrialized nations of Europe had put such a system in place. The United States had been a laggard, largely for reasons related to strictures in American federalism. Unemployment insurance schemes – financed by assessments on employers – had, in fact, been under discussion by a number of state governments for some time. But it was difficult for any individual state to launch out on its own: Unilateral action would place its businesses at a competitive disadvantage vis-à-vis rivals in other states. Nonetheless, the state of Wisconsin took an initiative in 1932 when it enacted an unemployment insurance plan that would become operational in mid-1934. Wisconsin's pioneering role in this matter was very much in the spirit of the brand of institutional economics that John R. Commons had long disseminated at the state's university. Commons was unequivocal in his reasons for regarding unemployment compensation as superior to direct relief. The latter, he observed, was "based on *needs* and require[d] case-work investigators to visit families and study their budgets, which is the most obnoxious of all interferences in the private life of individuals and families. ... But unemployment insurance gives a *right* to a definite sum of money which the recipient can spend as he wishes" (emphases in the original).[41]

In mid-1934, Roosevelt determined that it was timely to mount a systematic investigation of the part the federal government could play in promoting the "greater economic security" of individuals. It was not surprising that a Wisconsin product and a Commons disciple, Edwin E. Witte, should have been chosen as the executive director of a special committee formed for this purpose. There was a fair amount of elasticity in the charge to this group: Should it elect to do so, it could bring proposals for governmentally sponsored schemes for old age pensions and for compulsory health insurance within its purview. It was the judgment of the economists associated with this exercise, however, that top priority should be assigned to developing unemployment insurance on a nationwide scale.

The staff orchestrated by Witte generated a plan for comprehensive unemployment insurance that offered promise of surviving a test of its constitutionality. The proposal put forward called on the federal government to levy a payroll tax on all major employers at a rate that would be standardized throughout the country. Ninety percent of that obligation, however, could be

41. John R. Commons to John B. Andrews, American Association for Labor Legislation, November 19, 1934, Social Security Administration Records, NA.

offset by payments to unemployment insurance programs operated by state governments. (The remaining 10 percent was to be set aside to cover administrative expenses at both federal and state levels.) While the federal government would specify certain minimum standards, state governments would have considerable latitude in working out the programmatic details. This recommendation, which was presented to Congress in January 1935, gave the states an incentive to act, but it stopped short of a federal prescription about the precise form that action should take.[42] The University of Minnesota's Alvin H. Hansen, who was then serving as an advisor to the Trade Agreement Section of the State Department, also participated in this project. When testifying in its support before congressional committees, he extolled the virtues of federal-state cooperation envisioned in this approach to unemployment insurance.[43] Hansen further spoke to the manner in which funds accumulated as unemployment insurance reserves should be managed. He held centralized management to be imperative and that it should be performed by an arm of the federal government. Unless coordinated with overall credit policy, he argued, the accumulation (or decumulation) of unemployment reserves might well have an undesirable procyclical effect.[44]

In the 1935 discussion of economic security, economists and the Congress diverged in their assessments of priorities. Unemployment insurance had little political resonance, but old age insurance decidedly did. Public attitudes (especially among senior citizens) had been conditioned by Dr. Francis E. Townsend's plan for speedy recovery. In his view of the world, prosperity would be guaranteed if government provided a pension of $200 per month to every person aged 60 or over, on the condition that recipients withdrew from the labor force and spent every penny of this transfer payment within a month of receipt. Witte argued with some vehemence that this plan was bizarre: Its proposed financing would impose unsustainable tax burdens and would involve a gift of "more than half of the national income ... to the less than 9 percent of the people who are over 60 years of age."[45] Townsend, on the other hand, insisted that the country should embark on a "new experiment ... which

42. A thorough survey of this legislative history is contained in Edwin E. Witte, *The Development of the Social Security Act* (Madison, Wis.: The University of Wisconsin Press, 1963).

43. Alvin H. Hansen, Testimony before the Committee on Ways and Means, House of Representatives, 74:1, January 28, 1935, pp. 372–84.

44. Hansen had earlier given this matter systematic study. [Alvin H. Hansen, Merrill G. Murray, Russell A. Stevenson, and Bryce M. Stewart, *A Program for Unemployment Insurance and Relief in the United States,* (Minneapolis, Minn.: The University of Minnesota Press, 1934).]

45. Witte, "Why the Townsend Old-Age Revolving Pension Plan is Impossible," as reproduced in Hearings before the Committee on Ways and Means, House of Representatives, 74:1, February 4, 1935, pp. 894–6.

has not had the blessing of the so-called 'economists'. ... I say to you gentle-men," he informed a congressional committee, "that every time an economist says this proposal is 'lunacy' the people react by sending additional thousands of letters to their representatives in Congress saying, in effect, that the denun-ciation of the economists is another reason why they insist that their Con-gressmen and Senators vote for the ... bill."[46]

Thanks in large measure to the impression the Townsend movement left on some sensitive political nerves, legislation providing for some form of old age insurance was placed higher on the congressional agenda than would oth-erwise have been the case. What emerged was a social security plan funded by matched contributions from employer and employee. Payments into this fund were scheduled to begin with the payrolls of January 1937, but dis-bursements to old age pensioners would not begin until 1942. In the months during which the Social Security Bill was negotiated through the congres-sional pipeline, Roosevelt had insisted that old age insurance and unemploy-ment insurance were inseparable. Had he not done so, provision for the latter would probably not have been included in the legislation he signed into law in August 1935. Along the way, proposals for health insurance, which had been seriously contemplated in the early going, had been jettisoned as politi-cally premature.

7   Stock taking in the run-up to the campaign of 1936

The American electoral cycle obliges the citizenry and its elected of-ficials to evaluate where they have come from and where they are going every four years. There were mixed messages in the macroeconomic numbers com-piled by the Roosevelt administration during its first term. Contemporary mea-sures of the money value of the "national income produced" registered a gain of more than 50 percent over the low point of 1932. But this result fell far short of an ideal recovery: The figure recorded for 1936 amounted to only a shade more than 78 percent of the one achieved in 1929.[47]

46. Dr. Francis E. Townsend, Testimony before the Committee on Ways and Means, House of Representatives, February 1, 1935, in ibid., p. 678.
47. Contemporary estimates, as published in the *Statistical Abstract of the United States, 1938,* p. 302, are as follows:

	National income produced ($ billions)	Percent of 1929
1929	81.1	100
1930	68.3	84.2
1931	58.8	66.3
1932	40.0	49.3
1933	42.3	52.1
1934	50.1	61.7
1935	55.2	68.0
1936	63.5	78.2

With respect to the administration's achievements on the reemployment front, the picture was also cloudy. Contemporaries had imperfect data at their disposal concerning the condition of the labor force. Latter-day estimates indicate that the ranks of the unemployed fell from roughly 12,830,000 (or 24.9 percent of the labor force) in 1933 to approximately 9,030,000 (representing an unemployment rate of 16.9 percent) in 1936.[48] Other types of data, however, provided a window on the condition of the labor market to those studying it at the time. For example, the U.S. Employment Service reported total placements of 5,091,000 in 1936. Jobs in the private sector accounted for less than 30 percent of the total; the bulk of the placements were made in "public works and government service, the Works Progress Administration and relief."[49]

Many observers at the time were particularly alert to other numbers that spoke to the outcomes of New Deal policies. Champions of reflation who sought a return to the 1926 price level were disappointed that the wholesale price index (1926 = 100) stood at 80.8 for 1936, virtually unchanged from 1935. Nevertheless they could draw some satisfaction from the knowledge that these results marked a distinct improvement over the 1933 reading of the wholesale price index at 65.9.[50] The numbers with the highest political sensitivity were those pertaining to the budgetary outcomes. Roosevelt's 1932 campaign pledge to produce a balanced budget (apart from expenditures deemed essential for relief) had become something of an albatross. With the aid of some creative decision making about categories to which expenditures were assigned – i.e., whether to "general" vs. "recovery and relief" – the Treasury's bookkeeping for the first two fiscal years for which the administration was responsible indicated that the pledge had been honored.[51] This strategy was blown off course in the 1936 fiscal year. In February 1936, Congress mandated the payout of the second half of the World War I Veterans' Bonus by overriding Roosevelt's veto. (The first half had been distributed in 1931 through the Congressional override of Hoover's veto.) With these transfers (which came to nearly $1.8 billion in fiscal year 1936) treated as "general expenditures," there was red ink in both components of the New Deal's "double budget." But the electorate could not reasonably hold the president accountable for congressional behavior of which he disapproved.

48. As reported in the *Economic Report of the President* (Washington, D.C.: U.S. Government Printing Office, 1962), p. 230.
49. *Statistical Abstract of the United States, 1938,* p. 342.
50. Ibid., p. 306.
51. For fiscal year 1934 (July 1, 1933–June 30, 1934), receipts exceeded "general expenditures" by $13 million, while total expenditures amounted to roughly $7.1 billion (of which slightly more than $4 billion was counted as "recovery and relief"). In fiscal year 1935, an excess of receipts over "general expenditures" was reported in the amount of $81 million; total expenditures approached $7.4 billion, with more than $3.6 billion classified as "recovery and relief." (Ibid., pp. 171–3.)

Nevertheless Roosevelt perceived himself to be politically vulnerable on the deficit issue. And he allocated more time addressing it during the campaign than he did to any other economic issue. It is readily understandable why it was chosen as the central theme of his address at Pittsburgh, the site of his fiscal responsibility commitment in 1932. As he argued in 1936, "The only way to keep the Government out of the red is to keep the people out of the red. And so we had to balance the budget of the American people before we could balance the budget of the national Government. ... To balance our budget in 1933 or 1934 or 1935 would have been a crime against the American people." But, with the growth in incomes set in motion by New Deal policies, it was reasonable to project growth in revenues to match spending, and without any increase in tax rates.[52]

All this was couched within a framework that presupposed that budgetary outcomes were driven by the behavior of the national income. There was no suggestion here that fiscal results could also influence the determination of income itself. Roosevelt's formulation of the problem contained an element of electoral expediency, but his words also had the ring of conviction. The macroeconomic component of the policy mix of late 1933 had been an intentional commitment to an aggressive approach to raising the gold price. When that policy was abandoned, no deliberately formulated macroeconomic strategy replaced it. To be sure, ideas aplenty competed for attention. Some fresh twists on monetary manipulation received a hearing but left no mark on policy. Some innovative thinking about the potential role of fiscal policy was also underway. Roosevelt, however, had no disposition to embrace fiscal activism as the macroeconomic ingredient of an "official model." Deficit financing, despite its continuation, was not his option of choice. His critics regarded its magnitude – in the period 1934–36, the federal deficit ran in the range of 4½ to 5½ percent of GNP – as recklessly extreme. Nonetheless, as later scholarship has shown, the New Deal's deficits, unintended though they were, were still not all that stimulative.[53]

When Roosevelt presented himself for reelection in 1936, the public was entitled to award his first administration less than full marks for the results of its recovery efforts. Full employment was still a distant dream, and the gap be-

52. Roosevelt, Campaign Address at Pittsburgh, Pa., October 1, 1936, PPA, Vol. V (1936), pp. 402–4, 408.
53. E. Carey Brown's estimates of fiscal thrust – in which the net shift in aggregate demand arising from governmental taxing and spending is measured as a percentage of full employment GNP – indicate that federal fiscal operations were only weakly expansionary throughout the 1930s. During the Roosevelt years, their most potent impact – amounting to a positive net shift in aggregate demand of 2.5 percent – occurred in 1936. This could be explained primarily by the Veterans' Bonus payments, which Roosevelt opposed. (E. Carey Brown, "Fiscal Policy in the 'Thirties: A Reappraisal," *American Economic Review,* December 1956, pp. 857–79.)

tween potential and actual income and output remained huge. Moreover, he had not articulated a coherent strategy for addressing these problems. But the electorate had a lot more than that on which to form a judgment. The administration had salvaged a banking system when it was on the verge of collapse. It had been daring in its initiatives to bring relief to the destitute. Not least, its legislative programs had produced reforms that would permanently alter the terms on which economic life in America would be conducted. The Social Security Act was to bring some measure of economic security to older Americans, and it institutionalized benefit entitlements to the unemployed as well. Also notable were the Securities and Exchange Act (which held financial intermediaries to higher standards), the National Labor Relations Act (which brought a different climate to collective bargaining), the Tennessee Valley Authority (which stimulated a dramatic uplift in one of the nation's more depressed regions).

Roosevelt subtitled the 1935 volume of his public papers "The Court Disapproves." The subtitle he chose for the 1936 volume was "The People Approve." Indeed they did. Only the voters in Maine and Vermont denied him a clean sweep in the electoral college.

7

Shock tremors and their repercussions, 1937–38

The contrast between the mood of the first hundred days in 1933 and that prevailing in the opening months of the second Roosevelt administration in 1937 could not have been more striking. The former case was dominated by an atmosphere of crisis calling for immediate responses to conditions of economic emergency. In 1937, on the other hand, the economy – though still containing all too many idle workers and machines – appeared to be on a sustained recovery trajectory and seemed no longer to require high-priority attention. The agenda at the start of Roosevelt's second term was dominated instead by his proposals for governmental reorganization, notably plans to restructure the executive and judicial branches, including a politically inflammable proposition to enlarge the Supreme Court from 9 to 15 members.

In the economic environment of early 1937, Roosevelt believed that he was standing on solid ground when insisting that a genuinely balanced budget (as conventionally understood) was achievable in the fiscal year beginning on July 1, 1937. "The programs inaugurated during the last four years to combat the depression and to initiate many new reforms," he wrote in his Budget Message to the Congress in January 1937, "have cost large sums of money, but the benefits obtained from them are far outweighing all their costs. We shall soon be reaping the full benefits of those programs and shall have at the same time a balanced Budget that will also include provision for redemption of the public debt."[1] Roosevelt was in earnest about reaching the elusive goal in fiscal year 1938. Toward that end, he called on departments and agencies to shave spending by no less than 10 percent of their appropriations for that period and urged emergency lend-

1. Roosevelt, Annual Budget Message to the Congress, January 7, 1937, PPA, Vol. V, p. 642.

ing agencies (such as the Reconstruction Finance Corporation) to liquidate assets and to convey the proceeds to the Treasury. Plans to phase down spending on public works and work relief formed part of this program as well.

At the Federal Reserve, contingency preparations were being made for the day when the central bank's dominant concern would be inflation fighting. It was believed that the Board's capacity to restrain lending by commercial banks would be compromised were the latter to be allowed to hold abnormally large sums as excess reserves, as was the case in 1936 and early 1937. Accordingly, the Board of Governors acted to increase its leverage by using authority acquired in the Banking Act of 1935, which enabled it to double the required reserve ratios. Board action was taken in two steps: (1) Required reserve ratios were raised half the distance toward the legal maximum in August 1936; (2) increases to the full limit allowed by law were ordered in the spring of 1937. All this was perceived as precautionary, not as a retreat from cheap money. Eccles insisted that "the supply of money to finance increased production at low rates [was] ample."[2] Nor was Washington officialdom alone in its optimistic reading of the course of the economy. Fisher, for example, indicated in early 1937 that he had "a hunch that we have about reached the point where no further 'reflation' should be permitted."[3] By midyear, he was persuaded that defenses against inflation should be put in place.[4]

Indeed, possible storm clouds were identified in the upward pressures on prices observable in certain sectors, particularly those producing materials for the construction industry (such as steel, copper, lumber). It was certainly conceivable that these phenomena would not only be inflationary but could put a brake on capital spending needed to sustain the recovery's momentum. Writing in March 1937, Leon Henderson (then serving as a consulting economist with the Works Progress Administration) noted that wholesale prices had risen almost 10 percent since September 1936, and he perceived a "real danger of runaway prices." In the absence of "firm action," he argued, "the expected boom may never materialize." Henderson concluded that "government obviously should avoid programs, such as armament, private ship building, and large pub-

---

2. Eccles, Statement with Reference to His Position on Credit and Monetary Policies, March 15, 1937, FDRPL. After the full increase in reserve requirements became effective on May 1, 1937, Eccles estimated that the volume of demand deposits and currency in circulation would exceed the 1928 and 1929 peak by $2 billion.
3. Fisher to Gardiner C. Means, January 11, 1937, YUA.
4. Fisher set out his thinking at this time in a letter to the sometime NRA Administrator, General Hugh S. Johnson: "... I and my assistant have been working on ... what to do about gold in the future since it must inevitably be reduced in value and should be reduced in price. Otherwise we shall suffer from great inflation. Of course, I agree with you that raising the price of gold was a life saver but the time has come now, or is about to come, when it must be lowered." (Fisher to General Hugh S. Johnson, July 27, 1937, YUA.)

lic works projects which intensify the demand for basic commodities like steel and copper." It should also attack industries exercising price-raising market power with some creative procompetitive tilting: e.g., aggressive antitrust surveillance, tariff reductions, preferential RFC lending to small competitors, publicity campaigns.[5] By late August, Henderson, though remaining a bit anxious about the impact of higher commodity prices, still anticipated that there was "a greater than even chance" of "a new burst of vigor in recovery" in the months ahead.[6] Meanwhile the procompetitive position that he and like-minded administration economists supported had suffered at least one setback.[7]

Optimists about the economy's prospects were dealt a rude blow in the second half of 1937. The downturn in the economy that began in August was, in fact, more precipitous than the one immediately following the crash of October 1929. The Federal Reserve's index of industrial production declined by more than a third between August 1937 and May 1938; by the same measure, the scale of decline in manufacturing output in the year 1930 from the high point in 1929 was roughly 20 percent.[8] The 1937–38 episode also produced sharp drops in payrolls and employment, as well as in profits and in stock market values.

1   Interpretative perspectives on the recession of 1937–38: Modulations in the voices of 1933

The 1937–38 recession presented a formidable challenge to economic analysis, even more so than had the crash of October 1929. In the earlier instance, the upper turning point had occurred when the economy was operating at a high level of capacity utilization. A cyclical adjustment might then have been regarded as part of the normal order of things. Events of the late summer of 1937 were something totally different: Collapse had set in

5. Leon Henderson, "Boom and Bust," March 29, 1937, FDRPL.
6. Leon Henderson, August 31, 1937, FDRPL.
7. The Miller-Tydings Bill – which was drafted to give the sanction of the federal government to state legislation authorizing resale price-maintenance agreements between wholesalers and retailers – provides another reminder that the American polity can produce outcomes that are at variance with the policy objective of the executive branch. The administration's economists were united in opposing this legislation. M. L. Wilson, for example, then Undersecretary of Agriculture, pointed out that it would generate a "wider average spread between farm and retail prices" and prompt severe "public resentment against rising retail prices" (Wilson to Roosevelt, July 26, 1937, FDRPL). Officials at the Treasury and the Federal Trade Commission were also outspokenly opposed. Yet the Miller-Tydings Bill became the law of the land through a legislative maneuver: It was attached as a rider to a bill that the administration supported, one dealing with taxation in the District of Columbia.
8. *Statistical Abstracts of the United States,* passim. With the monthly average 1923–25 = 100, the index in August 1937 stood at 117 and at 73 in May 1938. The monthly average for 1929 was 118 and for 1930, 95.

when the economy was still far short of full employment. The economy's performance at this time did not mesh with anyone's prior conception of how it ought to behave.

To virtually all contemporary observers, the 1937 downturn came as a surprise. Explanations offered, ex post, usually – but not always – were informed by perspectives already in place. Nor should this be wondered at. When the unexpected happens, there is a natural human tendency to "round up the usual suspects." Thus, critics of the administration were inclined to treat the recession as a damning indictment of its policies, as testimony to the bankruptcy of deficit financing, or as a reaction to the mischief of tax policies that "harassed" business (such as the controversial undistributed corporate profits tax enacted in 1936). Roosevelt's attempt to "pack" the Supreme Court, with its negative fallout on public confidence, could also be identified as the villain of the piece. Alternatively, the Federal Reserve could be faulted for its decisions in raising reserve requirements which, it could be argued, had a deflationary impact, notwithstanding the Board's protestations to the contrary.[9] Within the bureaucracy, the events of 1937 also gave fresh ammunition to those who wanted the "administered price-makers" to be disciplined, though differences remained over how this could best be done.

Many who had offered interpretations of the economy in 1933 were to do so again in 1937–38. There were some noteworthy discontinuities, as well as continuities, in their readings of these crises. A number of the champions of heterodox thinking who had contributed to the policy strategies of 1933 were still in good voice. No longer, however, was there an audience for important components of their earlier messages. No nostalgia for NRA code making or for gold price manipulations was in evidence. Even so, there were lingering attributes of the mind-sets of structuralism and monetarism, vintage 1933, but what they had to offer had mutated by 1937–38.

Two of the pioneering structuralists in the Roosevelt entourage, Tugwell and Berle (both then in private life), were in character when perceiving the events of the autumn of 1937 as an opportunity to reconstruct the industrial

9. Two latter-day commentators, Milton Friedman and Anna Jacobson Schwartz, have assigned major responsibility for the 1937–38 recession to the Federal Reserve's decision to double required reserve ratios. Their account rests on the assumption that excess reserves, which the Board held to be needlessly excessive, were, in fact, desired as liquidity cushions in circumstances of depression. Hence, the Federal Reserve's actions in shrinking them led banks to constrain lending activities. [Milton Friedman and Anna Jacobson Schwartz, *A Monetary History of the United States* (Princeton, N.J.: Princeton University Press, 1963).] It is worth noting, however, that Fisher – a contemporary observer, whose analytic perspective had something in common with the one Friedman was later to articulate – did not draw this conclusion. As Fisher saw matters, problems arose not because the Board raised reserve requirements, but because it could not raise them to 100 percent!

order. In that spirit, they convened a gathering of business and labor leaders in New York to explore prospects for cooperation. And there were big names on their list: John L. Lewis, President of the United Mine Workers; Philip Murray, President of the United Steel Workers; Owen D. Young, Chairman of the General Electric Company; Thomas W. Lamont of the Morgan investment banking house. At the first meeting of this group on December 23, 1937, its members agreed "without reservation … that the present disunity in industrial, financial, and political circles could not continue" and that "one object of national policy should be to bring about a harmonious agreement, so far as possible." It was agreed as well that a "proposed wide program of anti-trust prosecutions offered very little hope of anything."[10] An echo or two of themes that had resonated around the National Recovery Administration could be heard: The superiority of "harmony" over "competition and conflict." But something had dropped out of the earlier battle cry calling for coordination and control. Coordination remained, but control did not. Writing to Roosevelt, Tugwell reported enthusiastically about these proceedings, noting his belief that the group would "find grounds for agreement which will surprise you by their conciliatory tone and real content."[11]

When the findings of this informal group of concerned citizens were presented to Roosevelt in early 1938, it was indeed apparent that thinking about industrial recovery had moved considerable distance beyond the structuralist position of 1933. In the first instance, the group emphasized the primary importance of "measures to raise the national income." Within this framework, the "problem of capital markets" was held to be "of prime importance," but there should be no rerun of the 1933 solution to this problem. The group's report treated this matter as follows:

> Five years ago the Government was obliged, in order to meet the extraordinary circumstances then prevailing, to preempt in effect and in large measure the capital markets, and to furnish upon an extensive scale capital funds which theretofore had flowed from private investment sources. Now, however, with prudent curtailment of current government expenditures for public works, the constant need for expenditures in the capital goods industry – if the national income is not to suffer seriously – must be met through normal investment processes.[12]

10. Adolf A. Berle, Jr., Minute of a Conference between Mr. John L. Lewis, Mr. Thomas W. Lamont, Mr. Owen Young, Mr. Charles Taussig, Mr. Rexford G. Tugwell, Mr. Lee Tresman, Mr. Philip Murray and A. A. B., Jr., December 23, 1937, Berle Papers, FDRPL.
11. Tugwell to Roosevelt, December 23, 1937, FDRPL.
12. Memorandum to Roosevelt signed by Berle, Lamont, Lewis, Murray, Young, and Charles W. Taussig, February 16, 1938, FDRPL. This document was the written follow-up to a White House meeting held on January 14, 1938.

In an earlier incarnation, the Columbia Brains Trusters would not have used a macroeconomic orientation as a point of departure, nor would they have endorsed the efficacy of private capital markets so confidently. They would, however, have felt comfortable with another part of the group's recommendations: i.e., the proposed creation of a "council of twenty-five, representing say six major groups: Government, Agriculture, Industry, Labor, Transportation, Finance and Capital Markets." The council's purpose was to "secure an accord" on measures designed to raise the national income. Overtones of organizational schemes drafted in 1934 – ones that had been intended to provide the NRA idea with a new lease on life – were unmistakable here.

Modulation was detectable as well in views articulated from a monetarist perspective. In 1937, no serious thought was given to a replay of the Warren doctrine on the gold price as the crucial policy variable. Though Fisher had lent some sympathetic support to that position in 1933–34, he had long since moved beyond it. Events of 1937, as he saw them, validated the wisdom of his latter-day recommendations on monetary reform. The deflationary forces in evidence would have been forestalled under a regime of 100 percent reserves. Banks would be unable to destroy checkbook money by selling government bonds, as they were then doing. In October 1937, he characterized the situation for Roosevelt as follows:

> This reverses the process by which, largely, you have been creating more purchasing power by selling bonds to banks for new checkbook money. ... [W]e are now threatened by the same sort of deflation as followed 1929. ... The chief difference is that Government bonds now play the role then played by private debts. *Under our present laws there is nothing dependable to prevent this new deflation from proceeding far beyond the old deflation* [emphasis in the original].[13]

For Fisher, the moral of the tale was self-evident. Legislation mandating 100 percent reserves should be enacted at the earliest possible moment. And there should be no delay, he told the president in December 1937, in moving the Treasury and the Federal Reserve to take measures to increase the circulating medium. "A quick recovery," he wrote, "is entirely feasible and ought to help toward some of the needed permanent reforms."[14]

A voice heard from overseas in 1933 also reacted to the recession of 1937–38. In the earlier instance, Keynes's commentary, which endorsed deficit spending on public works and threw cold water on the gold purchase program, took the form of an open letter to the president. In February 1938, on the other hand, his communication with Roosevelt was marked "private and personal." There was continuity in the analytic substance of his mes-

---

13. Fisher to Roosevelt, October 24, 1937, YUA.
14. Fisher to Roosevelt, December 20, 1937, YUA.

sage: "[P]ublic works and other investments aided by Government funds or guarantees" had been pivotal in promoting the recovery experienced up to mid-1937, but their curtailment had aborted the momentum of recovery. Keynes attributed this policy mistake to "an error of optimism" and argued that it was urgent that this error be corrected by measures to swell capital spending. He identified housing, public utilities, and railroads as particularly ripe for major injections of investment. But would private capital spending be forthcoming in the desired volume? Clearly government could control investment in these sectors if it chose to nationalize them, a possibility he held to be unlikely in the American context. Otherwise, Keynes counseled, Roosevelt should make "real peace" with business. This was not the note he had struck in 1933.[15]

2   The emergence of fresh thinking on government as a macroeconomic stabilizer: The contributions of Lauchlin B. Currie and Alvin H. Hansen

The recession of 1937–38 was indeed a wake-up call to economists in both the bureaucracy and the academy. Within the government, probings for an explanation of the turn of events gave new prominence to a statistical series measuring the "net contribution of government to spending," which Currie and Krost had been compiling. Their data indicated that the "net Federal government contribution to community expenditure" had turned negative in August 1937 for the first time since 1931.[16] In 1936, by contrast, governmental fiscal activities had been sharply stimulative. The reasons for this abrupt turnaround were not far to seek. Government had provided a major stimulant to 1936 purchasing power through the final payout of the Veterans' Bonus, but this was a nonrepeatable transaction and there was nothing to replace it in 1937. Meanwhile the payment of payroll taxes into the Social Security Trust Fund had begun. These collections withdrew income from the potential expenditure stream; that income would not

15. Keynes to Roosevelt, February 1, 1938, FDRPL. Keynes's mastery of English prose was abundantly on display on this occasion:

> Business men have a different set of delusions from politicians; and need, therefore, different handling. They are, however, much milder than politicians, at the same time, allured and terrified by the glare of publicity, easily persuaded to be 'patriots,' perplexed, bemused, indeed terrified, yet only too anxious to take a cheerful view, vain perhaps but very unsure of themselves, pathetically responsive to a kind word. You could do anything you liked with them, if you would treat them (even the big ones), not as wolves and tigers, but as domestic animals by nature, even though they have been badly brought up and not trained as you would wish. ... If you work them into the surly, obstinate, terrified mood, of which domestic animals, wrongly handled, are so capable, the nation's burdens will not get carried to market.

16. Leon Henderson, for example, drew attention to the Currie statistical series in a memorandum to Hopkins, October 12, 1937, FDRPL.

be replenished until the start of payments to Social Security beneficiaries, which was not scheduled until 1942. In light of these findings, the recession no longer seemed so mysterious. Primary responsibility could be assigned to an unfortunate shift in fiscal operations between 1936 and 1937.

In late 1937 and early 1938, Currie was diligent in his efforts to educate governmental insiders on the significance of this insight.[17] It had long been recognized that fluctuation in the level of national income was a potent determinant of the budgetary outcome. Now the facts seemed to demonstrate that changes in tax receipts and government spending, other than those caused by cyclical fluctuations, were potent determinants of aggregate income. This conclusion synchronized with the analysis Keynes had presented in *The General Theory* in 1936. Currie was familiar with this work and welcomed its intellectual reinforcement to a position he had reached independently. But he also took issue with Keynes on a number of points. As Currie wrote in a review of *The General Theory,* prepared in 1937:

> Here, perhaps, at last, is the answer to an economist's prayer – the key that will enable him to make accurate interpretations and predictions. Such expectations, I am afraid, are doomed to disappointment. Certain aspects of our big problem are illuminated here and there, but all too often we find that familiar things are being described in unfamiliar language, that concepts cannot be given statistical meaning and that precision and definiteness are being purchased at the expense of reality.

Currie found it a "peculiarity of Keynes's work that he appears always to think of an increase in income as being generated by an increase in investment and never by an increase in consumption." Nor did he find Keynes's conception of the multiplier to be convincing.[18]

Though there were affinities between the Keynesian perspective and Currie's design, what he had to offer was nonetheless a home-grown product and it would have been available had there been no *General Theory*. There can be little question that the indigenous quality of his arguments, based on American data and expressed in an American idiom, enhanced prospects for their ultimate acceptability in official Washington. Keynes's appeal to Roosevelt of February 1, 1938, it is worth recalling, received only perfunctory attention.[19]

17. Currie elaborated the argument at considerable length in a memorandum entitled "Causes of the Recession," April 1, 1938. This document has been published in *History of Political Economy,* Fall 1980, pp. 316–35.
18. Currie, "Some Theoretical and Practical Implications of J. M. Keynes' General Theory," *The Economic Doctrines of John Maynard Keynes* (New York: National Industrial Conference Board, 1938), pp. 15, 18, 21.
19. On Roosevelt's instruction, Secretary of the Treasury Morgenthau, whose hostility to Keynesian-style spending policies was undisguised, drafted the response to Keynes for the President's signature. Morgenthau's reply ignored Keynes's views

The postmortem on the 1937 recession marked a turning point in the "fiscal revolution" in American economic thinking. The capacity of the "new" line of analysis to account for the observable facts enhanced its credibility. And it was crucial in winning converts to a Keynesian style of thinking, not the least of whom had expressed major reservations about the message of *The General Theory*. The intellectual odyssey of Alvin H. Hansen, who was shortly to become the leading American apostle of Keynesian doctrine, is especially noteworthy in this context.

Hansen had reacted negatively to *The General Theory* when it first appeared. He wrote two reviews of the book, one for a general audience, the other for a professional one. He informed readers of the *Yale Review* that Keynes had now "abandoned ... the imposing edifice" he had built in the *Treatise on Money,* alleging that it had become untenable in light of "the damaging attack of its critics" (of whom Hansen had been one). He added: "It is reasonably safe to predict that Keynes's new book will, so far as his theoretical apparatus is concerned, fare little better than did the *Treatise.*"[20] Hansen covered this ground again, though at greater length, in a review essay prepared for the *Journal of Political Economy.* In its concluding paragraph, he observed: "The book under review is not a landmark in the sense that it lays a foundation for a 'new economics.' ... The book is more a symptom of economic trends than a foundation stone upon which a science can be built."[21] (These sentences were deleted when Hansen reprinted this review in a collection of essays published in 1938.)[22]

Hansen's reaction to *The General Theory* in 1936 was of a piece with doctrines he had espoused for the better part of a decade. In his early commentary on the depression, for example, he had written as a champion of neoclassical orthodoxy. Lapses from full employment, for example, could be traced primarily to inflexibility in wage making. Policies of wage maintenance, in face of unemployment, were "inimical to recovery" and accelerated spending on public works would aggravate the problem if it forestalled a downward adjustment in wage rates and thus "work[ed] counter to the forces making for cost reduction."[23] Nor had Hansen been swayed when Keynes presented the analytic skeleton of *The General Theory* to American economists at a New York meeting in June 1934. In Hansen's view at the time, Keynes's multiplier was "really a transactions velocity of money concept" and his analysis of

on government spending. [John Morton Blum, *From the Morgenthau Diaries: Years of Crisis, 1928–1938* (Boston: Houghton Mifflin, 1959), pp. 402–5.]

20. Alvin H. Hansen, "Under-employment Equilibrium," *Yale Review,* June 1936, pp. 828–30.

21. Hansen, "Mr. Keynes on Underemployment Equilibrium," *Journal of Political Economy,* October 1936, p. 34.

22. See Hansen, *Full Recovery or Stagnation?* (New York: Norton, 1938), p. 34.

23. Hansen, *Economic Stabilization in an Unbalanced World* (New York: Harcourt Brace, 1932), pp. 189, 366.

"leakages" from the expenditure stream, of which the most important was saving, was "nothing more or less than our old friend a change in income veloci
ty."[24] He cautioned J. M. Clark – who had attended the session with Keynes in
New York and was then at work on a study of "The Economics of Planned
Public Works" for the New Deal's National Resources Board – to be skeptical
of this approach. After reviewing Clark's report in draft, Hansen observed: "I
have the impression that your analysis still follows too much along the Keynes
lines. ... It is always Keynes' defect to be far too mechanical."[25]

The recession of 1937 was to be a conversion experience for Hansen. Writing in November of that year, before the full depth of the recession could be appreciated, he began to rethink his position on the behavior of the macroecono-
my. The partial recovery of 1933 through early 1937, he argued, had been a
consumption-led revival. In his view, a normal cyclical upswing would have
been spurred by fresh waves of investment spending fed by technological innovation. In the mid-1930s, this had not happened. Increased consumption
spending had set the pace and, in accordance with the acceleration principle,
some additional capital formation had followed. But the expansion of 1933–37
was still vulnerable because "a recovery based on consumption cannot stand
still." As soon as consumption flattened out, net investment would cease and
this, in turn, would lead to subsequent reductions in income and employment.[26]

This line of argument suggested that Hansen was near the point of embracing the Keynesian account of income determination, but he was not yet all the
way there. His analysis was developed within the framework of the accelera-
tor, an idea which had been common property for two decades. He remained
skeptical of the Keynesian multiplier. Even so, the furrow he was then ploughing increased his receptiveness to interventionist fiscal policies as a macroeconomic stimulant. The revival through 1936 may have been consumption-
led, but the increase in consumption had largely been nourished by
governmental deficits. The risk in late 1937, as he viewed the situation, was
that withdrawal of this "prop" to spending might touch off a major recession.
He referred to data indicating that the net contribution of government to consumer spending had undergone a "dramatic reversal" – "from a plus of three
billion dollars" in 1936 (largely accounted for by the final payout of the Veterans Bonus) "to a minus of 400 million dollars" in 1937 (an outcome reflecting the impoundment of funds collected through the newly instituted Social
Security tax).[27] If a "considerable recession" was to be avoided, then con-

24. Hansen to J. M. Clark, August 8, 1934, Alvin H. Hansen Papers, Pusey Library,
    Harvard University.
25. Ibid.
26. Hansen, "The Consequences of Reducing Expenditures" (a paper presented at the
    Annual Meeting of the Academy of Political Science, November 10, 1937), *Pro-
    ceedings of the Academy of Political Science,* January 1938, pp. 64–5.
27. Ibid., p. 66.

sumption would need to rise autonomously – a prospect he held to be unlikely – "or else investment must be pried loose from the narrow limits imposed by the immediate requirements of the existing volume of consumption."[28] The latter outcome would be difficult to achieve, in part for reasons that had long been imbedded in his thinking: A "forbiddingly high level of costs" – owing to a mix of governmental policies, monopolistic practices in pricing, and labor practices that increased wage rates – deterred new capital formation. Minimizing rigidities in the price system was still part of Hansen's conception of the route to full employment. But on this point there was a modulation in tone. In November 1937 he maintained that "the all-important desiderata are total income and employment." Hansen now feared that a problem of "secular stagnation" might well "over-shadow that of the business cycle" in the years immediately ahead. Accordingly, "governmental expenditures took on a new significance."[29] In particular, spending on public works should be viewed in a different light. He anticipated that "public expenditures may come to be used increasingly as a means for directing the flow of savings into real investment," adding that "it may not be amiss to note that the modern network of highways, unlike the old, is publicly financed and publicly owned."[30]

Though a note of tentativeness ran through all this, Hansen had clearly moved well beyond the analysis he had earlier offered and had assimilated the Keynesian conceptions of the macroeconomic aggregates. But the form of this accommodation still had a flavor of the vintage Hansen. Since the days of his earliest writings on business cycles in the 1920s, he had emphasized the long-term dynamic factors underlying economic change. From the vantage point of late 1937, the prospects for a fresh burst of expansion from technological change and population growth seemed slight. It was thus appropriate to rethink the role of government as a stimulator. Moreover, the flow of events during the next year added urgency to that undertaking. The recession deepened in 1938, just as Hansen had suggested it might in his analysis in the preceding November. The weakening of the economy thus strengthened confidence in the validity of a new perspective on the role of fiscal policy in macroeconomic management.

3   The U-turn of April 1938

Roosevelt was slow to respond to the onset of recession in August 1937. There was no denying its reality. He took note of it in his Budget Message to the Congress, transmitted in January 1938, in connection with its impact on the expected revenues. A shortfall from the receipts that had been anticipated was inevitable. Thus, he had decided to recommend a curtailment of spending on public works. With that reduction on the expenditure side, total federal outlays would be lower in fiscal year 1939 than in the preceding one.

28. Ibid., p. 66.
29. Ibid., pp. 71, 72.
30. Ibid., p. 72.

With a tinge of regret, he reported that the drop in estimated tax receipts precluded achievement of budget balance in the fiscal year beginning on July 1, 1938, but there was some satisfaction to be drawn from the projection that the magnitude of the deficit would be smaller than it had been in the year before.[31]

Within Roosevelt's official family, programs for action were being formulated and the one with highest public visibility was promoted by those disposed to trace most of the economy's ills to the market power of business concentrations. At times, the president gave aid and comfort to advocates of this position. In October 1937, for example, he directed the Head of the Justice Department's Anti-trust Division, Robert H. Jackson, to inquire into the "important facts bearing upon the success or failure of our present anti-monopoly laws, and the necessity for revision or amendment."[32] Jackson was to embark soon thereafter on a public speaking campaign, aided by the speech-writing skills of antimonopolists, such as Thomas Corcoran and Benjamin Cohen. The burden of his argument was that monopolists had produced the slump and that their power should be aggressively attacked.[33]

Roosevelt, however, had made no commitments to this point of view. In early January 1938, he implied that the recession might have been avoided if industries were permitted to "make a more intelligent group estimate as to the purchasing power of the country and inventories of the particular article necessary for the immediate future." The legality of such information sharing, he noted, was questionable under the antitrust laws. He added: "I would very much favor making it a completely legal thing to do: to meet around a table to find out, with the help of the Government, what the demands are, what the purchasing power of the country is, what the inventories are." All this conjured up images of NRA warmed over, though Roosevelt told his audience that he was not advocating its "immediate reenactment."[34]

In mid-February 1938, presidential ambivalence was again in evidence. Roosevelt then read to reporters a four-page statement on the administration's economic policy, indicating that it had been prepared by senior officials. (The language, however, was largely the handiwork of Gardiner C. Means, then based at the National Resources Committee.)[35] There were echoes in this document of themes familiar from 1933 with the emphasis on a price orientation

31. Roosevelt, The Annual Budget Message, January 3, 1938, PPA, Vol. VII (1938), pp. 14–30.
32. Roosevelt to Robert H. Jackson, October 22, 1937, FDRPL.
33. For details on this episode, see Ellis W. Hawley, *The New Deal and the Problem of Monopoly* (Princeton, N.J.: Princeton University Press, 1966), Part IV.
34. Roosevelt, Press Conference, January 4, 1938, PPA, Vol. VII (1938), pp. 33–4.
35. Roosevelt attributed the statement to Henry Morgenthau, Jr., Secretary of the Treasury; Henry A. Wallace, Secretary of Agriculture; Frances Perkins, Secretary of Labor; Marriner Eccles, Chairman of the Board of Governors of the Federal Reserve System; and "economists of various executive departments."

toward policy. A "moderate rise in the general price level" was called for, though the word "reflation" was not used. But the price rise should be selective and aimed at the restoration of sectoral "balance." The phrase "administered prices" was avoided, but the idea was there. Industries "not subject to highly competitive market forces" – ones that had "maintained prices and curtailed output" – were urged to "seek the restoration of profits through increased rather than through restricted output." Price rises should be confined to "industries, such as agriculture, that operate at a high level of capacity even when business activity is at low levels."[36] All this suggested that Roosevelt's thinking had not yet transcended the analytic categories of 1933.

By April 1938, with unemployment rising and relief rolls expanding, Roosevelt was under mounting pressure to pursue a different strategy. Members of his inner circle who had absorbed the lessons of Currie's findings on the turnaround in the "net contribution of government to spending" were clear in their own minds about what it should be: a stronger dose of deficit spending to enhance purchasing power. But the president's aversion to deliberate deficits presented a formidable obstacle. Up to this point, he could always say that he had been obliged to tolerate deficits but had not chosen them. Could Roosevelt be persuaded to make a U-turn?

The point men in this phase of "the struggle for the soul of FDR"[37] were Leon Henderson (then with the Works Progress Administration), Harry Hopkins (WPA Administrator), and Beardsley Ruml (then Treasurer of Macy's Department Store and an advisor to the National Resources Committee). In April 1938, they presented the case for deficit spending in homely fashion, rather than in its more technical form. There was nothing radical, they argued, about the engagement of the federal government in the creation of purchasing power; to the contrary, this practice was deeply rooted in the American tradition. The federal government, they pointed out, had long been in this business, notably through the alienation of the national domain to private ownership via land grants. With the closing of the frontier, this technique was no longer available. In modern conditions, government was obliged to support purchasing power through its own spending.[38]

Over the objections of the Secretary of the Treasury, Roosevelt sent a message to Congress on April 14, 1938 calling for more than $3 billion worth of spending or lending in the immediate future for relief, public works, housing, and assistance to state and local governments. For the first time, the administration committed itself to a calculated strategy of fiscal stimulation. This pro-

36. Roosevelt, Press Conference, February 18, 1938, PPA, Vol. VII (1938), pp. 113–20.
37. This apt phrase was coined by Herbert Stein, *The Fiscal Revolution in America* (Chicago: University of Chicago Press, 1969).
38. The memorandum, undated and untitled, in which this argument is set out is in the Hopkins Papers, FDRPL.

gram was explicitly designed to raise aggregate income, and it was announced without apologies for the deficits it entailed.[39] At the same time, the Federal Reserve lowered required reserve ratios and some $1.4 billion in idle gold was desterilized.

This was indeed a new departure. An income orientation toward macroeconomic policy, with fiscal activism as a key ingredient, was coming into clearer focus. But equilibrium was not yet in sight with respect to the administration's posture toward industrial concentrations and their price-making power. On this matter, Roosevelt chose to temporize by substituting investigative studies for action. In a "Monopoly Message" to the Congress of April 29, 1938, Roosevelt proposed an appropriation of $500,000 to fund an exhaustive inquiry into the concentration of economic power. This was to be the origin of the Temporary National Economic Committee, charged with this assignment, which was to generate some 30 volumes of testimony and 43 technical monographs before its demise in 1941.

39. When explaining this change of course to the nation, Roosevelt invoked some imagery supplied to him by Henderson and Hopkins. In a radio address, he observed:
> In the first century of our republic we were short of capital, short of workers, and short of industrial production; but we were rich in free land, free timber and free mineral wealth. The Federal Government rightly assumed the duty of promoting business and relieving depression by giving subsidies of land and other resources. Thus, from our earliest days we have had a tradition of substantial government help to our system of free enterprise. ... It is following tradition as well as necessity, if Government strives to put idle money and idle men to work ...

[Roosevelt, Fireside Chat on Present Economic Conditions and Measures Being Taken to Improve Them, April 14, 1938, PPA, Vol. VII (1938), p. 243.]

8

Toward a new "official model," 1939–40

Roosevelt's decision to embark unapologetically on a "spend-lend" program in April 1938 appeared to signal that the administration had come to terms with an Americanized version of Keynesian aggregate demand management. This orientation toward macroeconomic policy making was solidified in early 1939. With a nudge from Marriner Eccles, the president urged a number of his cabinet officers to assist in selling "compensatory fiscal policy" to the public. As he put it:

> We must present our case to the country. ... For instance the Secretary of the Treasury could explain the soundness of the case. The Secretary of Commerce could do it with the aid of the more liberal members of the Business Advisory Council. The Secretary of Agriculture could do it with the objective of education of agricultural interests. The Secretary of the Interior could speak on the same subject from the angle of conserving material and human resources. ... Economic soundness of the policy is already recognized by many economists and business men in this country ....[1]

Meanwhile another vehicle for economic education was moving on a different track. The Temporary National Economic Committee (TNEC), with its charge to investigate the concentration of economic power, was off and running. Given its makeup, there was considerable uncertainty about what

---

1. Roosevelt to the Secretary of the Treasury, the Postmaster General, the Secretary of the Interior, the Secretary of Agriculture, the Secretary of Commerce, and the Secretary of Labor, January 21, 1939, FDRPL. The president cribbed some phrases from Eccles who recommended this strategy. (Eccles to Roosevelt, January 11, 1939, FDRPL.)

116

its activities would ultimately amount to. This body was, after all, an institutional hybrid. Half of its members were drawn from the Congress (three from the Senate, three from the House of Representatives), and six were appointed to represent executive departments and agencies. Before the fact, it was not clear whether they would be able to find common ground. In the view of TNEC's executive secretary, Leon Henderson (who was by now an old hand in bureaucratic in-fighting), the committee's task was to amass the evidence before framing conclusions.[2]

1 Widening the beachheads for the "new" macroeconomics

The success of the president's plan for conditioning the electorate to the soundness of fiscal activism turned, in part, on the government's ability to recruit economists who could aid in projecting this message. Harry Hopkins – who had already shown his colors when persuading Roosevelt to make the U-turn of April 1938 – was to play a key role in ensuring that economists sympathetic to Keynesian-style thinking received a hospitable reception in Washington. In late December 1938, Roosevelt named Hopkins to the post of Secretary of Commerce.

On the face of it, Hopkins would seem to have been an unlikely choice to head a department that historically had been expected to reflect the business viewpoint. Hopkins lacked the usual credentials for the job. He had never met a payroll; on the contrary, as a relief administrator, he had specialized in dispensing handouts. Nevertheless, he regarded direct relief as repugnant and insulting to human dignity, even though, in some circumstances, a dole was unavoidable. The real remedy for worklessness was work. By the time he took up his assignment at the Commerce Department, Hopkins was convinced that action, informed by the macroeconomic insights then emerging, held the key to reemployment.

Hopkins aspired to make the Department of Commerce a focal point for the analysis and dissemination of the "new" economic knowledge. Since the days when Herbert Hoover had occupied the post of secretary, the department had played a role as an economic "educator," but now its mission was redefined. Hoover's conception had been preoccupied with the collection and publication of current market intelligence – for example, data on production, sales,

2. The composition of the Temporary National Economic Committee was as follows: Senate members: Joseph O'Mahoney (Democrat of Wyoming), chairman; William E. Borah (Progressive Republican of Idaho); William King (Democrat of Utah); House members: Hatton W. Sumners (Democrat of Texas); B. Carrol Reece (Republican of Tennessee); Edward C. Eicher (Democrat of Iowa); representatives of executive departments and agencies: Thurman Arnold (Justice); Herman Oliphant (Treasury); Isador Lubin (Labor); William Douglas (Securities and Exchange Commission); Garland Ferguson (Federal Trade Commission); Richard Patterson (Commerce).

changes in inventories – to enhance the rationality of business decisions. Hopkins's vision of economic intelligence emphasized instead analyses of the macroeconomic variables determining the behavior of aggregate income. The department's national income accountants already had in hand much of the material required for this work. What was needed was a richer understanding of its significance.[3]

Among Washington economists of the new breed in 1939, the standard view was that a national income of $80 billion to $85 billion was necessary to achieve a high level of employment. Numbers of this order of magnitude were in circulation not only at the Department of Commerce but also at the Federal Reserve Board and at the National Resources Committee. There could be no doubt that the economy was operating far short of this target at the time Hopkins assumed his new duties. As Robert Nathan (then styled as the chief of the National Income Section of the department's Division of Economic Research) informed him, preliminary estimates indicated a national income of $61 billion to $62 billion for 1938, a step down from $69.8 billion in 1937.[4] There was clearly work to be done.

But although Hopkins and his associates recognized the importance of fiscal measures, they were also persuaded that government alone could not fill the spending gap. It was thus important to create an environment in which capital spending in the private sector would be substantially increased. This meant that government needed to establish better rapport with the business community.[5]

Hopkins devised a three-part approach to this issue. The first component involved expansion and elaboration of the department's studies of the behavior of the national income. Although the department had pioneered in the regular official preparation of national income accounts, its work to date had been concentrated on estimating aggregate income by industrial source and type of payment, supplemented by studies of income that individuals received by type of payment and by analysis of individual incomes by state. As Nathan pointed out to the secretary in June 1939, this material, valuable though it was, left many important questions unanswered. Nathan assigned priority to developing a capability to break down the national product into categories of output (pro-

---

3. The change in approach was signaled in an internal Commerce Department memorandum of April 10, 1939, titled "Policy and Program." It was argued therein that priority should be assigned to "the interpretation of information assembled by the Department and to its prompt dissemination," rather than to "the publication and wholesale distribution of a multitude of items whose place is really in a reference or handbook." (Department of Commerce Records, NA.)

4. Robert R. Nathan to Hopkins, "The National Income in 1938," January 20, 1939, Hopkins Papers, FDRPL.

5. The attention given to this point at this time, although not necessarily inspired directly by Keynes, is consistent with views Keynes had transmitted to Roosevelt in February 1938. See Chapter 7, Section 1.

ducers' goods, durable consumers' goods, perishable consumers' goods, services), to identify flows and sources of savings, and to measure the size distribution of income. Reliable data of this type, he emphasized, would enrich understanding of the behavior of aggregate consumption, saving, and investment.[6] Shortly thereafter, Nathan's jurisdiction was enlarged and his title upgraded to chief of the National Income Division. A major step in the direction of creating new knowledge about the behavior of the Keynesian macroeconomic variables was thus taken.

A second prong of the Hopkins strategy called for a major strengthening in the department's analytic capabilities, and for that purpose he created a Division of Industrial Economics. To staff it, he wanted economists sympathetic to the new macroeconomic way of thinking. This initiative, however, had controversial aspects. As the Undersecretary, Edward J. Noble (formerly chairman of Life Savers Corporation), noted: "There is a very widespread impression among businessmen that economists are very theoretical and often impractical." Noble recommended an "infusion of genuine business experience," adding that he saw "no reason why we should not use a good many young men from the graduate schools of business and other men who have something more than a passing acquaintance with economic theory."[7] As matters worked out, the lineup of the Division of Industrial Economics included a mix of theorists and practical men, although the former were clearly dominant. The person selected to head it, Richard V. Gilbert of Harvard, had already come into prominence as coauthor of one of the first American manifestos proclaiming Keynesian demand management, spurred by expansionary fiscal policy, as the solution to the nation's problems.[8] Others recruited to the new division included Gerhard Colm, a German immigrant brought to Washington from the New School for Social Research; V. Lewis Bassie, a junior colleague of Currie's on the research staff of the Federal Reserve Board; Walter Salant, one of the unidentified contributors to *An Economic Program for American Democracy;* Donald Humphrey, formerly on the research staff of

6. Nathan to Hopkins, "Proposed Expansion in the Work of the Department of Commerce in National Income and Related Fields," June 15, 1939, Hopkins Papers, FDRPL.
7. Edward J. Noble to Hopkins, July 20, 1939, Hopkins Papers, FDRPL.
8. This document, titled *An Economic Program for American Democracy* (New York: Vanguard Press, 1938), was billed as the product of the discussions of seven Harvard and Tufts economists. The collaborators identified were Richard V. Gilbert, George H. Hildebrand, Jr., Arthur W. Stuart, Maxine Yaple Sweezy, Paul M. Sweezy, Lorie Tarshis, and John D. Wilson. Walter Salant, Emile Despres, and Alan Sweezy also participated, but in their capacities as government employees, they elected to remain anonymous. Alan Sweezy, "The Keynesians and Government Policy, 1933–1939," *American Economic Review Papers and Proceedings,* May 1972, pp. 116–33.

the Works Progress Administration; and Roderick Riley, a former research assistant to Senator La Follette.[9]

Hopkins thus provided a nest in the Department of Commerce for economists of the new persuasion, but their job involved more than packaging macroeconomic data in novel forms and interpreting their significance for policy making. They were also expected to develop a liaison with business and to encourage private investment. This was the third ingredient of the strategy. Various mechanisms of communication were available. A familiar one was the department's monthly publication, *The Survey of Current Business,* which began to present data in formats that highlighted the determinants of macroeconomic activity: i.e., the magnitudes of business capital spending, aggregate consumer outlays, inventory accumulation, and the net contribution of government to spending. This publication helped to educate the business community to a new way of perceiving both the performance of the economy and its prospects. But another mechanism was called into play as well: a revitalized Business Advisory Council. This organization, structured as an informal consultative body, had been in place for a number of years and had been conceived as a channel through which business leaders could communicate their views or grievances to government. Hopkins also saw it as a two-way street through which economists on his staff could enlighten members of the business community on the insights of macroeconomics. It is perhaps no accident that a substantial number of the members of Hopkins's Business Advisory Council were later to be associated with the Committee on Economic Development, a business-sponsored organization that championed compensatory fiscal policies.[10]

2   Unsettled business with industrial policy: TNEC and the role of Thurman Arnold

TNEC's inception was marked by a lack of precision with respect to its objectives and procedures. Indeed, a number of contemporary observers detected method in this ambiguity: An open-ended study meant that decisions about the direction of industrial policy could be put on hold.[11] Members of the

---

9. Willard L. Thorp to Hopkins, August 17, 1939, Hopkins Papers, FDRPL.
10. Among them were Henry Dennison, Ralph Flanders, and Lincoln Filene. Of the 20 original trustees of the Committee on Economic Development in 1942, 14 had served or were serving on the Business Advisory Council. [Robert M. Collins, *The Business Response to Keynes, 1929–1964* (New York: Columbia University Press, 1981), p. 84.]
11. Raymond Moley of the original Brains Trust – who, as a journalist, had become a Roosevelt critic – perceived the president's motivation in such fashion. As he saw the matter, TNEC "merely relieved Roosevelt, for the moment, from the nagging of subordinates who, whatever the differences in their own economic philosophies, recognized that an administration which was of two minds on this all-important question would contradict itself into disaster. It merely put off the adoption of a

committee, however, did not lack for procedural or conceptual guidance. Berle, for example, urged them to eschew preconceptions, by which he meant, in the first instance, that they should suppress any temptation to "idealize" small business. On the contrary, the facts about the impact of large-scale enterprise needed to be systematically examined. There were more than trace elements of the thinking of 1932–33 in his fear of a pro-Brandeisian tilt to TNEC. Berle maintained that its report should "develop the areas in which *all control forms* namely, competition, regulation and direct production [i.e., production by government enterprises] are used."[12] Henderson, as TNEC's executive secretary, put the emphasis a bit differently. In his view, government's job was to be a rule maker and umpire. It had fallen "way, way behind" in the performance of these functions and "as a result numerous practices, not necessary either for profit-making or for efficiency, had grown up and become a part of the business psychology." He saw it to be TNEC's function "to do a fearless but complete job of examination of these practices before any intelligent policy could be recommended."[13] On the other hand, one member of TNEC, Thurman Arnold (appointed to head the Justice Department's Antitrust Division in March 1938), saw no need to wait for a report before pursuing an active industrial policy. From his vantage point, legislation already on the books was adequate; it only needed to be enforced.

Arnold brought unprecedented vigor to his assignment as head of Justice's Anti-trust Division. During his five-year tenure (1938–43), he initiated nearly half of the proceedings brought under the Sherman Act in the first 53 years of its history. In the process, he increased the division's professional staff by more than five-fold.[14] This was all the more remarkable in light of his background. In 1937, while a member of the faculty of the Yale Law School, he had proclaimed the futility of antitrust legislation. His best-seller, *The Folklore of Capitalism,* was a spoof written in a style reminiscent of Veblen at his satirical best. As Arnold then put it, the antitrust laws should be regarded as "the answer of a society which unconsciously felt the need of

    guiding economic philosophy." [Moley, *After Seven Years* (New York: Harper and Brothers, 1939), p. 376.]

12. Berle, Memorandum of Suggestions: Investigation of Business Organization and Practices, July 12, 1938, FDRPL. When transmitting a copy of this document to the White House, Berle indicated that he had prepared it at the request of Thurman Arnold (representing the Justice Department on TNEC) and Jerome Frank (alternate member of TNEC for the Securities and Exchange Commission). (Berle to Stephen Early, White House Press Secretary, July 15, 1938, FDRPL.)

13. Henderson, Diary, November 15, 1938, FDRPL. In his diary entry, Henderson was reporting on a conversation with TNEC Chairman O'Mahoney concerning the desired outcome of the investigation.

14. Corwin D. Edwards, "Thurman Arnold and the Antitrust Laws," *Political Science Quarterly,* September 1943, p. 339.

great organizations, and at the same time had to deny them a place in the moral and logical ideology of the social structure. They were part of the struggle of a creed of rugged individualism to adapt itself to what was becoming a highly organized society." Their significance, however, was largely symbolic, but the symbols had "promote[d] the growth of great industrial organizations by deflecting the attack on them into purely moral and ceremonial channels." Moreover, Arnold held that "if the antitrust philosophy had not been developed, it is doubtful if the great organization could have achieved such an acceptable place in a climate of opinion in which rugged individualism was the chief ideal." Unfortunately, the "economic meaninglessness [of the antitrust laws] never quite penetrated the thick priestly incense which hung over the nation like a pillar of fire by night and a cloud of smoke by day."[15]

Given the views Arnold had articulated in 1937, his credentials for appointment as an Assistant Attorney-General with responsibility for antitrust enforcement were not self-evident. It should not be wondered at that Idaho's Senator Borah should be skeptical on this point. (In *The Folklore of Capitalism,* Arnold's prose had made a target of Borah's enthusiasm for antitrust enforcement: "Men like Senator Borah founded political careers on the continuance of such crusades, which were entirely futile but enormously picturesque, and which paid big dividends in terms of personal prestige.")[16] Pressed by Borah to clarify his views, Arnold explained to a subcommittee of the Senate Judiciary Committee that his writings referred to "what the antitrust laws had been during the period of great mergers in the 1920s" and that he was prepared to give them new meaning, once in office.[17]

Arnold did indeed bring fresh vitality to antitrust enforcement. His strategy was distinctly different from a Brandeisian approach to trust busting: The emphasis, he wrote, should be placed "not on the evil of size but the evils of industries which are not efficient or do not pass efficiency on to consumers."[18] Pressuring producers better to serve consumers, however, touched concerns that extended beyond those of microeconomic efficiency. Arnold also insisted that market power in price making should be attacked because it shrank production and generated unemployment.

Arnold was particularly innovative in his choice of techniques for antitrust enforcement. He relied far more heavily than had any of his predecessors on

15. Thurman Arnold, *The Folklore of Capitalism* (New Haven, Ct.: Yale University Press, 1937), pp. 96, 211, 212, 228.
16. Ibid., p. 217.
17. As quoted by Wilson D. Miscamble, "Thurman Arnold Goes to Washington: a Look at Antitrust Policy in the Later New Deal," *Business History Review,* Spring 1982, p. 9.
18. Arnold, *The Bottlenecks of Business* (New York: Reynal and Hitchcock, 1940), pp. 3–4.

the use of criminal prosecutions for perceived antitrust violations. But he was prepared to bargain with alleged offenders by substituting a consent decree, under the terms of which defendants would be obliged to change their behavior, for continued criminal proceedings. This procedure grabbed headlines. It also got results, even though some in the business community regarded it as legalized blackmail.

Arnold developed something of a reputation as a grandstander, an attribute that did not endear him to all his TNEC colleagues. Henderson, for example, had "an uneasiness" about the consent decree policy. He also criticized Arnold's "contempt for processes of analysis and fact-finding as a basis for recommendation."[19] Even so, in light of the high public visibility that Arnold enjoyed, would it not be reasonable to conclude that Arnold's approach to antitrust had been assimilated into a new "official model"? The bulk of the evidence suggests that it would be incorrect to do so. Roosevelt and Arnold were never close. Roosevelt had appointed him sight unseen to fill a vacancy before the monopoly issue had acquired high prominence. The president tolerated Arnold's activities – at least until mobilization for war signaled the importance of business–government cooperation – but he did not embrace them. Wilson D. Miscamble's findings on this point are perceptive:

> Forced to make decisions in April 1938, Roosevelt had chosen to couple public spending with a vague attack on monopoly. Having made this decision, he could hardly restrain Arnold who quite unexpectedly developed a comprehensive antitrust program. Roosevelt had to content himself by leaving Arnold to his own devices, which, in fact, contributed to Arnold's great success by allowing him autonomy in the antitrust field.[20]

3   Adjusting the focus of the TNEC investigation

The Temporary National Economic Committee had been created with a mandate to inquire into "the concentration of economic power." The usual understanding of the scope of this topic would seem to differentiate it from the macroeconomic orientation of the "new economics." In mid-1939, however, the TNEC hearings were reshaped to provide a pulpit from which Americanized Keynesian doctrine could be preached. Roosevelt, at the instigation of Henderson, offered a rationale for this adjustment in focus. It was a proper function of the committee, the president asserted, "to ascertain why a large part of our vast reservoir of money and savings have remained idle in stagnant pools" and to determine why "the dollars which the American people save each year are not yet finding their way back into productive enterprise in suf-

19. Henderson, Diary, January 30, 1939, FDRPL.
20. Miscamble, loc. cit., p. 14.

ficient volume to keep our economic machine turning over at the rate required to bring about full employment."[21]

Harvard's Alvin Hansen was the lead-off witness in this phase of TNEC's work. Armed with graphs and charts, he seized the opportunity to put Keynesian-style aggregative categories to work in his diagnosis of the state of the economy. When so doing, he deployed a set of arguments he had first presented in his presidential address to the American Economic Association in December 1938, in which he had offered a full-blown statement of the "stagnation thesis." The central problem was to generate "a volume of investment expenditures adequate to fill the gap between consumption expenditures and that level of income which could be reached were all factors employed." Reaching that goal, however, was increasingly difficult in view of the depressing effect on investment opportunities brought by stagnating population size and by the closing of the frontier. It was thus the task of economic policy to enlarge aggregate demand through measures designed to increase the propensity to consume and through an expanded program of public expenditures. The alternative was a future of "sick recoveries which die in their infancy and depressions which feed on themselves and leave a hard and seemingly immovable core of unemployment."[22]

Hansen enlarged on these themes in his testimony before the TNEC. In May 1939, he registered his "growing conviction that the combined effect of declining population growth, together with the failure of any really important innovations of a magnitude sufficient to absorb large capital outlays, weigh very heavily as an explanation of the failure of the recent recovery to reach full employment." The moral of the tale seemed to be clear: "Considering the current investment outlet deficiencies compared with the decade of the twenties …, it appears very doubtful that we can solve our problem of full employment by relying exclusively on private investment. Private investment … will have to be supplemented and, indeed, stimulated by public investment on a considerable scale."[23] To aid in driving that point home, Currie presented his estimates of "offsets to savings." As savings were withdrawals from the income stream, the economy was doomed to a chronic state of underemployment unless these withdrawals were "offset" by capital spending by business, outlays for residential housing construction, lending abroad, or loan-financed expenditures by government. As a shortfall in the private sector's capital spending was expected, government's role as a spender would be crucial. Under questioning, Hansen and Currie acknowledged that tax reduction

21. Roosevelt to Senator Joseph C. O'Mahoney, Chairman, TNEC, May 16, 1939, FDRPL.
22. Hansen, "Economic Progress and Declining Population Growth," *American Economic Review,* March 1939, pp. 4, 5.
23. Hansen, Testimony before the Temporary National Economic Committee, May 16, 1939, pp. 3514, 3546.

might pay dividends in stimulating private spending. But their central argument held that government could better manipulate aggregate demand by other means.

The Hansen-Currie line of analysis amounted to a domesticated Keynesian perspective on the performance of the economy. The TNEC also took testimony from a veteran of the original Brains Trust who had assimilated the Keynesian account of the role of investment in national income determination. Berle, however, gave a different twist to the policy implications of this finding. His sympathies for planning were in good repair when he recommended that the government underwrite a "capital credit banking system." This exercise, for all practical purposes, would put the state in the investment banking business. As Berle read matters, the private capital market had effectively been closed since 1931, a view he shared with Thomas Lamont, the New York investment banker in the briefly resuscitated Brains Trust inspired by the 1937–38 recession. Berle accepted the Keynesian proposition that recovery depended on capital outlays to absorb a high-employment level of saving. He stood back, however, from concluding that this situation required that the expenditure gap be closed primarily by governmental spending. He held it to be far superior – and certainly more compatible with the American tradition – if government spurred investment by acting as a catalyst to lending. This could be accomplished through the instrumentality of publicly sponsored capital credit banks "whose business it should be to provide capital for those enterprises which need it, when they need it; and it should make that capital equally available to the Government or to local units for public work, when public enterprise went into action, or to private enterprise when private enterprise, either new or old, needed the assistance."[24]

Berle stressed the novel features of this projected institution, emphasizing that it should not be a "passive mechanism which can be availed of" but rather an "active group" that took "responsibility for filling certain needs of the community, and for finding the means and the men who can fill those needs, and for putting at their resources the capital necessary to do so." This vision was certainly not intended as a replica of the conventional investment bank. The new institution should be enabled to fund worthwhile projects in ways that made it easy for the borrower: i.e., it should be empowered to abandon an inflexible interest rate in favor of allowing a firm to pay a lower rate in bad years and a higher rate in good ones. In addition, it should aim to open up a "new layer of enterprise, which is not now comprehended in the private profit field." Thus, construction spending for "necessary nonprofit enterprises," such as hospitals, might be financed at an interest rate of zero. Obviously, no commercially oriented lender would touch such a proposition. Public (or semipublic) capital credit banks, however, ought to do so because

24. A. A. Berle, Jr., A Banking System for Capital and Capital Credit: Memorandum before the Temporary National Economic Committee, May 23, 1939, FDRPL.

the effects on the economy, via the Keynesian multiplier, would be no different from private capital spending of the same magnitude.[25]

Presumably, Berle's new breed of public-spirited bankers could find sufficient "offsets to saving" to achieve full employment. Their charge, after all, was to direct the allocation of capital. A residual of the 1932–33 planning mentality thus resurfaced, even though part of Berle's 1939 position bore the markings of the "new" macroeconomic style.

4   Adaptations and resistances to the "new economics": Divergent responses by members of the First New Deal's "structuralist" camp

By 1938–39, a fair number of the more prominent champions of the "structural maladjustment" reading of the Great Depression had long since ceased to walk in Washington's corridors of power. What many of them had offered with high confidence in 1933 had come to look rather shop-worn. Certainly the expectations associated with the early days of NRA (and, to a lesser extent, of AAA) had failed to be borne out in reality. Nevertheless, a number of economists who had been conspicuously identified with the structuralist doctrine in the early going continued to occupy influential official positions. Some found it easier to make peace with the new mode of aggregative economic thinking than did others.

The career of Gardiner C. Means in the later 1930s is instructive on this point. In 1935, he had shifted his base from the Department of Agriculture to the National Resources Committee (formerly styled as the National Resources Board and subsequently restyled as the National Resources Planning Board). As head of its industrial research group, he took it to be his task to lay the analytic foundations for a fresh round of planning exercises. The studies he produced from this post replayed familiar themes: the bankruptcy of laissez-faire and the malevolent influence of administered price making on the functioning of the American economy. At least to his satisfaction, these conclusions were abundantly documented statistically in his drafts of a major study, entitled *The Structure of the American Economy,* which was ultimately published in 1939.

The final version of this document did not appear in the form Means would have preferred. He had hoped to persuade his superiors at the National Resources Committee that structural maladjustment in the pattern of relative prices was responsible for the depression and its persistence and that bold measures to address the output-suppressing propensities of producers with market power were essential. This line of argument clashed head-on with the macroeconomic diagnoses of "Curried Keynesianism" then being forcefully articulated. This conceptual dissonance bred tensions between Means and Currie (who served as a member of the advisory group assigned to review Means's work). Operating within the new analytic framework, Currie was preoccupied

25. Ibid.

with the problem of generating sufficient spending to lift the economy to full employment. From this perspective, oversaving was the obstacle to be overcome, and it should be attacked by fiscal policies designed to raise aggregate demand. Means, on the other hand, continued to insist that the real villain was "insensitive prices." In his reading, the appearance of an oversaving problem was in reality a "by-product of price inflexibility." Thus, for example, a lowering of prices in the capital goods sector (where administered price making was held to be prevalent) would stimulate investment and provide a channel through which additional savings could be absorbed.[26]

Though Means had maintained intertemporal consistency, he was clearly out of step with the new analytic fashion, a fact brought home to him by economists of the new breed who evaluated his findings. At their insistence, publication of the *Structure* study was acceptable only when his claims were moderated and presented on the responsibility of the primary investigator, but without formal NRC endorsement of his results. To add insult to injury, the NRC – over Means's protest – sponsored an additional study, which appeared in 1940 as *The Structure Report: Part II*. This document was packaged as a critique of Means's 1939 report and included an essay by Alvin Hansen in which the "administered price" thesis was treated dismissively and in which the case for aggregate demand management was set out.[27]

Accommodation to an aggregative analytic style tended to come much more easily to a number of the agricultural economists who had championed structuralist doctrine, vintage 1933. Transition to an income orientation toward analysis and policy, as opposed to a price orientation, was not difficult at all for those among them who had attached high priority to supply management through rational land use planning. Short-run price behavior had never been at the forefront of their thinking: Instead they had looked to structural adjustments that would alter the context for market behavior over the longer term. The scale of the land retirement program had been a source of disappointment; actual land purchases fell far short of the targets the National Resources Board had recommended in 1934.[28] From the administration's point of view, however, struc-

26. Documentation on these episodes is contained in the Minutes of the Industrial Committee of the National Resources Committee, June 1938–June 1939, FDRPL and Means's Comments on Currie, May 1939, Gardiner C. Means Papers, FDRPL.
27. See Means, *The Structure of American Economy, Part I: Basic Characteristics,* National Resources Committee, 1939, and National Resources Planning Board, *The Structure of the American Economy, Part II: Toward Full Use of Resources,* 1940.
28. At the same time, the size of this operation was not trivial. By early 1939, more than 6.4 million acres in the Great Plains and Intermountain regions had been acquired or brought under contract since the beginning of the New Deal. This was the equivalent of two-thirds of the combined area of the states of Massachusetts, Connecticut, and Rhode Island. The goal established in 1934 had called for the purchase of 5 million acres per year over a 15-year span. (L. C. Gray, "Federal Pur-

turalists of the land use planning variety had earned their keep by packaging an agricultural program on short notice in 1936, the one designed to substitute soil-enriching crops for soil-depleting ones. It soon became part of their larger message that many of the solutions for farmers' problems should be sought outside agriculture, with emphasis on full employment to be pursued with primary reliance on the tools of fiscal and monetary policy. While macroeconomic expansion would increase the demand for farm products in general, farmers producing outputs with a positive income elasticity of demand, such as meat producers, would be particularly well-positioned to benefit. In such an environment, the desired conversion of tilled land to pasture would be accelerated.

On this point, the intellectual journey of Mordecai Ezekiel is particularly illuminating. In his approach to agricultural policy during the First New Deal, he had been both an architect of AAA's direct controls and an advocate of an aggressive program of land retirement. His leanings toward direct intervention to correct structural imbalances again came to the fore in 1935–36 in his advocacy of a post-NRA plan for an industrial adjustment board along the lines Tugwell had endorsed.[29] By mid-1938, he had begun to distance himself from that perspective. In the Means-Currie debates within NRC, Ezekiel sided with Currie.[30] By the time he testified before the Temporary National Economic Committee in February 1941, he had fully embraced the Keynesian perspective on aggregate demand management – both as necessary for full employment and for raising the standards of farm families.[31]

5   Indigenized Keynesianism at center stage

Within the Roosevelt administration, an American version of Keynesian doctrine had been internalized by a significant cadre of government

chase and Administration of Submarginal Land in the Great Plains," *Journal of Farm Economics,* February 1939, pp. 126–7.)

29. See Mordecai Ezekiel, *$2500 a Year: From Scarcity to Abundance* (New York: Harcourt, Brace and Co., 1936).
30. In June 1938, for example, Ezekiel put on record his judgment that Currie had developed an "exceedingly significant" point: i.e., that "it is probably hopeless to expect to maintain prices sufficiently flexible so that periods of depression can be cured by readjustment in prices" and that "other means of checking depressions, such as compensatory public fiscal policy, will have to be relied upon." He added that this point "was ignored entirely" in Means's statement of the problem. Ezekiel to Thomas Blaisdell, National Resources Committee, June 14, 1938, Means Papers, FDRPL.
31. This is apparent in Ezekiel's presentation to the Temporary National Economic Committee, February 24, 1941, Ezekiel Papers, FDRPL. Two years earlier he had not quite reached that point. Though he held expansion in the industrial sector to be essential to agricultural uplift, he then assigned more weight to governmental targeting of expanded industrial production (with government acting as a buyer of last resort) than to the stimulus of fiscal policy. [Ezekiel, *Jobs for All through Industrial Expansion* (New York: Alfred A. Knopf, 1939).]

economists by 1940. And it promised to provide the design for the macroeconomic component of a new "official model." There was, however, a remaining competitor: the monetarist approach to theory and policy championed most ardently by Irving Fisher.

Fisher's efforts to win converts had been unceasing. Nor was he alone in pressing for adoption of 100 percent money and the creation of a Monetary Authority charged to maintain a dollar of constant purchasing power through its control of the money supply. By 1939, his collaborators in drafting "A Program for Monetary Reform" with these features were Paul H. Douglas (University of Chicago), Frank D. Graham (Princeton University), Earl J. Hamilton (Duke University), Willford I. King (New York University), and Charles R. Whittlesey (Princeton University). Collectively, they petitioned the nation's academic economists to endorse this proposal. They managed to recruit some followers in the academic community and to line up the support of a number of members of Congress. Within the executive branch of the Roosevelt administration, on the other hand, the monetarist design for macroeconomic management was a nonstarter.[32]

With Currie's appointment to the White House staff in mid-1939 to the newly created post of economic adviser to the president, the locus of the New Deal's analytic center of gravity was clear. Currie's commitment to the priority of Keynesian-style fiscal activism was by then complete. He drew all the threads together in a lengthy Memorandum on Full Employment, which he placed before Roosevelt in mid-March 1940. He then wrote:

> I have come to suspect that you are somewhat bothered by the apparent conflict between the humanitarian and social aims of the New Deal and the dictates of "sound economics." I feel convinced that in place of conflict there is really complete harmony and for that reason only the New Deal can solve the economic problem. ... After having had to interview and read the outpourings of numberless cranks and crack-pots, I feel a little abashed at coming forward and saying, "I know the answer." I trust, however, that you will make a distinction![33]

The resolution of the "apparent conflict," Currie observed, rested on "the line of investigation I initiated at the Reserve Board and which is today being carried on by the brilliant group of young economists in Harry Hopkins' office. ... The basic analysis is that of J. M. Keynes."[34]

Though he acknowledged a debt to Keynes, Currie's argument was less than pure Keynes. The apparatus for the analysis of the components of aggregate

---

32. Characteristically, Fisher kept Roosevelt fully apprised of the details of "A Program for Monetary Reform" and of his lobbying efforts on its behalf. The president's acknowledgments were politely noncommittal.
33. Currie to Roosevelt, "Memorandum on Full Employment," March 18, 1940, FDRPL.
34. Ibid.

demand was deployed, a Keynesian consumption function was explained, and an investment-income multiplier introduced. Standard conclusions of Keynes's analysis were derived: that the achievement of full employment depended on a volume of nonconsumption spending sufficient to absorb the savings generated at a full-employment level of income and that the dimensions of this problem would be magnified as income rose and the ratio of savings to income increased.

But the primary remedy Currie offered for a deficiency in aggregate demand was not the one that Keynes had emphasized. Currie downplayed deficit spending on public works in his recommendations for action. There was still a place for such public investment – financed, if possible, outside the budget – but it should not play the major role. Further increases in the national debt would touch politically sensitive nerves in the American context and should be constrained. The main weight in the strategy Currie proposed to the president was assigned to government programs to shift the consumption function upward. The objective was to achieve a "high-consumption and low-saving" economy. This goal could be reached by combining a "truly progressive" tax system with redistributive transfer payments and enlarged public outlays for health, education, and welfare. Thus the "humanitarian and social aims of the New Deal" could be reconciled with "sound economics."[35]

A Keynesian style of thinking was well rooted in the bureaucracy by the time this analysis was produced. But there were also some temporary setbacks for economists of the new breed. Hopkins's Division of Industrial Economics, which had begun with such promise, was terminated in mid-1940, when Congress balked at further funding of its operations. Congressional ire had been aroused by a comment comparing people in business with savages in *An Economic Program for American Democracy,* the book Gilbert had written with several others while still at Harvard.[36] This crisis was short-lived. Veterans of the defunct Division of Industrial Economics were quickly reabsorbed elsewhere in government. Some, including Gerhard Colm, joined the recently reorganized Bureau of the Budget. Others, including Gilbert and Walter Salant, moved to the newly created Office of Price Administration.

Though there were some bumps along the way, proponents of a new design for the role of government in the management of aggregate demand had arrived near the commanding heights of economic policy making by 1940.

35. Ibid.
36. The passage that gave offense read as follows: "The truth is that the businessman, caught in the toils of events he does not understand, is merely seeking to lay the blame on something he thinks he does understand, just as the savage in the face of the mysterious forces of nature seeks to make them more intelligible by inventing a host of gods and devils. But business is afflicted with a disease far more serious than government intervention in economic affairs." (Richard V. Gilbert et al., *An Economic Program for American Democracy,* p. 90.)

The form in which they articulated their arguments was conditioned by the American political and economic environment. This model had originally been conceptualized to address the problems of an underemployed economy. It was soon to be deployed for a purpose quite different from the one for which it had been intended: the formulation of economic policy for a nation fully mobilized for war.

9

Designs for the management of an economy at war

The fall of France in May 1940 was to be a wake-up call in official Washington. To that point, those concerned with shaping U.S. economic policy had taken little note of events in Europe. The task of moving the domestic economy toward full employment remained their primary concern. The Nazi blitzkrieg in continental Western Europe moved the issue of an American defense program to a much higher position on the national agenda.

In the summer of 1940, it came easily to contemporaries to compare their situation with the one the nation had faced in World War I. In the judgment of a number of economists within the bureaucracy, economic mobilization in the 1940s ought to be an easier task than it had been in 1917–18. By contrast with the earlier episode, expertise that economists could provide was readily at hand: The mushrooming of the New Deal agencies had already positioned them within government. Moreover, the professional experiences of many of them during the 1930s suggested that the nation could expect qualitative improvement in the advice they offered. The tools of the "new" macroeconomics, it appeared, could usefully be redeployed to shape fiscal policies to restrain private spending to magnitudes compatible with the targets set for a defense build-up. But that was not all. Economists well placed in the official establishment by 1940 believed that the 1933–35 experience with the NRA had taught useful lessons about how a new round of industrial mobilization should be organized. In their reading, many of NRA's mistakes could be traced to misguided attempts on the part of its key operatives to replicate the apparatus of the War Industries Board of 1917–18. Certainly the thinking of General Hugh S. Johnson as National Recovery Administrator – himself a veteran of the War Industries Board and protégé of Bernard Baruch, the board's chairman – was cast in that mold.

132

Nevertheless, a reincarnation of the World War I pattern of industrial control – in which individual industries effectively dominated decision making on pricing and production (as they had done in the days of NRA) – could not be dismissed out of hand. The version of an Industrial Mobilization Plan promoted at the War and Navy Departments was essentially a codification of World War I operations. This kind of planning, as Lauchlin Currie informed the president in May 1940, was "hopelessly antiquated." Its "suggested economic controls of prices and production similarly [were] based almost exclusively on the first World War experience, with little study or recognition of the vast new developments in price and other economic controls during the subsequent 20 years, both in various New Deal agencies and in other countries."[1] Mordecai Ezekiel was no less outspoken in his denunciation of the existing Industrial Mobilization Plan. It made "little use," he also observed, "either of the experience accumulated, or of the administrative mechanisms developed, by the New Deal during the past decade." He further maintained that "its flat adoption would involve the danger of sacrificing many of the most important advances of the New Deal, including the Wagner Labor Act and the Wages and Hours Act, and of handing economic control right back to the same big business interests that dominated under Hoover."[2]

War and the threat of war did indeed bring new challenges to economic policy making. In such conditions, there was no ambiguity about what its goals should be: Overriding priority should properly be assigned to maximizing the "fund" of resources available to the state to defend the national interest. In the American context, there was a subsidiary stipulation as well: Maximization of this "fund" should be accomplished with minimal elevation in the general price level. Some adjustments in relative prices should, of course, be expected as a part of the signaling for resource reallocation. But, to the fullest extent possible, a shift of resources to the state (at the expense of the private sector) via the devices of inflation should be avoided. In principle, this technique for asserting the state's claim on goods and services was always available. As a

---

1. Lauchlin Currie to Roosevelt, Comments on Our Industrial War Plans, May 20, 1940, FDRPL. Currie further warned that estimates of potential military requirements and supplies had largely been prepared by Army officers without specialized statistical training. "Many parts of our most precious war plans," he wrote, "carefully guarded as valuable secrets by the Joint Army-Navy Munitions Board, consist of nothing more profound than a student's exercise, worked up in a few hours or days as a problem in a brief Army Industrial College course. The entire set of estimates and calculations needs to be overhauled by a group of professional statisticians, experienced in the analysis of agricultural and industrial data, and highly proficient in methods of statistical and economic analysis and forecasting."
2. Mordecai Ezekiel, Suggestions for Strengthening Our Industrial War Plans, May 15, 1940, Richard Gilbert Papers, FDRPL.

preemptive buyer, government could always price civilians out of the market. American economists, however, were at one when insisting that government should do its best to put the brakes on inflation.

Though clarity of purpose was inherent in the economics of mobilization, consensus among economists on how shared goals should be reached did not necessarily follow. In the early stages of the accelerated defense effort in 1940–41, divergent recommendations on appropriate tactics were in evidence. There was, however, an element of predictability in the thrust of some of them. Thurman Arnold, for example, maintained that vigorous antitrust enforcement was a vital part of an effective national defense program. In the first instance, his work and that of his colleagues aimed "to prevent restrictions of production, particularly conspiracies which are blocking the defense effort." In addition, he held that this activity was "indispensable" to attempts to contain upward pressures on prices. As he put the case to Roosevelt, the antitrust laws provided the "only legal remedy … [to] combinations to raise prices, or to maintain artificially high prices."[3] Similarly, Irving Fisher's advice to Roosevelt stemmed from a well rooted perspective. "The success of our armament program," he wrote in June 1940, "may … depend to a large degree on our ability to prevent inflationary price rises. The crucial question before the country seems now whether we shall be able to do this without instituting the rigorous controls to which Germany had to resort."[4] Nor was it surprising that Fisher should persist in urging the president to support the Program for Monetary Reform calling for 100 percent money. When transmitting yet another version of this scheme to the White House in early 1941, Fisher expressed his hope that Roosevelt would "prepare in advance" for the "money problem [which] is bound to recur as it regularly does with great wars. …"[5] The ideas that were to attract the bulk of the attention of economists in the pre-Pearl Harbor phase of mobilization, however, were those associated with policies promoted by advocates of the "new" macroeconomics and its critics.

1   Divergent perspectives on the nature of an inflationary "gap" in 1940–41

Well before Pearl Harbor, Americans sympathetic to the macroeconomic perspective set out in *The General Theory* were acquainted with Keynes's views on the way this "model" could be adapted to guide wartime economic policy. He had presented his thought on economic mobilization in the British context in a monograph entitled *How to Pay for the War,* published in 1940. This document had called for stringent fiscal constraints, through tax increases and compulsory savings, to reduce private demand. Rationing and

3. Thurman Arnold to Roosevelt, May 17, 1941, FDRPL.
4. Fisher to Roosevelt, June 16, 1940, FDRPL.
5. Fisher to Roosevelt, January 27, 1941, FDRPL.

control over prices and wages also formed part of this program. But, Keynes had insisted, the effectiveness of such measures of direct control ultimately depended on shrinking private purchasing power through fiscal interventions.[6] His analytic frame in 1940 was of a piece with the one he had built in 1936. In both instances, the objective of policy should be to manipulate the values of the macroeconomic expenditure categories: consumption, investment, government spending. Only the character of the problem to be solved had changed. In an underemployed economy, the objective was to close the "gap" between actual effective demand and the volume of spending needed to reach and sustain full employment. By contrast, the goal of policy in a fully mobilized economy was one of suppressing excessive effective demand.

Members of Washington's cadre of economists had an opportunity to explore Keynes's thinking at first hand in the late spring and early summer of 1941. Keynes was then in the United States as a member of the British delegation negotiating lend-lease arrangements with American officials. The trip included meetings with a number of American colleagues, including Lauchlin Currie, Alvin Hansen, Leon Henderson, Gerhard Colm, in addition to Richard Gilbert, Walter Salant, and Donald Humphrey. The focus of their conversations was the threat of inflationary pressures arising from the American defense build-up. In the discussion of this issue, Keynes found himself at odds with a number of his American followers.

The predominant opinion among Washington's "new school" economists in mid-1941 was that the United States could still have both guns and butter. Richard Gilbert had articulated this view forcefully a year earlier, when a serious American preparedness program had been launched, by maintaining that the economy still suffered altogether too much from unemployment and idle capacity and that the stimulus to demand from debt-financed defense spending posed no threat.[7]

By mid-1941, Gilbert conceded that there was some inflationary danger, but argued that it could be contained with a control over prices and inventory accumulations, supplemented by a scheme of allocation priorities for commodities in short supply.[8] For Keynes's benefit, Walter Salant summarized the thinking of the American Keynesians:

> We do not say that the expansive effects of the defense program
> upon income will die out before full utilization of all capacity is
> reached. If there is a "gap" at the point of full utilization (or in

6. Keynes, *How to Pay for the War: a Radical Plan for the Chancellor of the Exchequer* (New York: Harcourt Brace, 1940).
7. Richard Gilbert, "National Defense and Fiscal Policy," June 1940, as reported by Joseph P. Lash, *Dealers and Dreamers* (New York: Doubleday, 1988), pp. 400–1.
8. As reported by Gerhard Colm in his summary of a meeting of American economists with Keynes on July 23, 1941; see Colm to J. Weldon Jones, "Discussion of Anti-inflationary Measures," July 24, 1941, Records of the Bureau of the Budget, NA.

practice somewhat before that point is reached), we are perfectly willing to take whatever special measures are necessary to close it. But we are strongly opposed to taking those measures long before full utilization is reached. Such a policy would retard further expansion. ... If the choice were between a 50 percent rise of prices and several hundred thousand unemployed, no doubt we would regard the latter as the preferable alternative. I think, however, that the actual alternatives for 1942 are closer to a 15 percent rise of prices or 6 million unemployed. Faced with that choice we would prefer the former alternative.[9]

The Americans, who were not yet at war, still saw the achievement of full employment as the overriding priority. Keynes, on the other hand, believed that the Americans had failed to take the threat of excessive effective demand seriously enough. He registered his disappointment in correspondence with Columbia University's J. M. Clark:

I agree with what you say about the danger of a "school," even when it is one's own. There is great danger in quantitative forecasts which are based exclusively on statistics relating to situations that are by no means parallel. I have tried to persuade Gilbert and Humphrey and Salant that they should be more cautious. I have also tried to persuade them that they have tended to neglect certain theoretical considerations which are important in the interests of simplifying their statistical task.[10]

Some of Washington's economists, however, were inclined to read Keynes's displeasure with their position as reflecting a different priority: namely, positioning the U.S. economy to be of maximum support to the British war effort.

But a more technical issue underlay this intrafamilial disagreement. Salant and Gilbert had appropriated tools from the conceptual kits of *The General Theory* in preparing their estimates of the likelihood of inflationary pressures. Their procedure involved three steps: (1) estimating the volume of investment spending and net government spending expected in a future period; (2) forecasting the level of income associated with these magnitudes, taking into account multiplier and acceleration effects; and (3) calculating aggregate consumption on the basis of a presumed value for the marginal propensity to consume.

To be sure, this was the Keynesian way of approaching the problem, but Keynes had two quibbles with the results produced in the mid-1941 American exercise – hence, the "cautions" that he urged. The first concerned what he read as an implicit assumption of perfect elasticity in the supply of nondurable con-

---

9. Walter S. Salant to Keynes, June 12, 1941, as reproduced in *The Collected Writings of John Maynard Keynes*, XXIII, Donald Moggridge, ed. (London: Macmillan, 1979), p. 186.

10. Keynes to Professor J. M. Clark, July 26, 1941, in *The Collected Writings of John Maynard Keynes*, XXIII, p. 192.

sumer goods (which he regarded as unrealistic, as was no doubt so in the United Kingdom). The second turned on the presumed value of the marginal propensity to consume (which he feared was too low). Salant estimated that only 39 percent of the anticipated increment in national income for 1942 would be allocated to consumption. In support of this calculation, he argued that it was consistent with historical values for the marginal propensity to consume: In other words, the underlying consumption function was normally taken to have stable and predictable properties. This was the basis for the initial approximation. The "normal" consumption–income relationships were then adjusted to take account of special factors expected to prevail in 1942. Salant identified three such factors: (1) increases in consumption were expected to lag behind increases in income; (2) some shortages of consumers' durable goods were anticipated, and they were expected to lower the marginal propensity to consume (on the ground that frustrated spending on durables would not be fully reallocated to the purchase of nondurables); and (3) the effects of increased tax rates, which would reduce the consumption share of pretax household income, were estimated. Keynes applauded the way in which "various disturbing factors" were built into the analysis, but his doubts were not fully put to rest. As he wrote to Salant in July 1941: "Whether your assumptions about the marginal propensity to consume are correct is another matter which experience will test."[11]

Considerable scope for argument thus remained about how solidly based the findings on the size of the inflationary gap really were. At least there was consensus that this problem should be at the top of the research agenda. And, as not infrequently happens in Washington, bureaucratic in-fighting provided an extra stimulus to discussion. In the first phase of inflationary gap analysis, economists associated with the Office of Price Administration set the pace. Competitors for leadership soon appeared. Economists at the Bureau of the Budget, for example, perceived "gap analysis" as an opportunity to enhance their organization's status. As Gardiner Means (who had migrated to the Bureau of the Budget in 1940) saw matters in August 1941, the experts in the operating agencies had better access to the resources needed to analyze specific tax and price control measures. In one field, he observed, "the other agencies have made such little progress that the Bureau could easily place itself in a position of practical authority, namely the determination of the 'gap' which needs to be closed by policy adjustment." It was important, he then argued, that the deflationary effect to be sought through fiscal measures be determined with reasonable precision. Otherwise, "as in 1937, it would be possible to produce too much as well as not enough deflationary effect."[12] Means subsequently

11. Salant to Keynes, July 15, 1941 and Keynes to Salant, July 24, 1942, in *The Collected Writings*, XXIII, pp. 188–90.
12. Gardiner C. Means to J. Weldon Jones, "The Gap Problem and Bureau Leadership in Developing Fiscal Policy," August 14, 1941, Records of the Bureau of the Budget, NA.

proposed that the problem should be approached by estimating the "hypothetical discrepancy" between saving and investment at the targeted future level of national income.[13] This line of argument also presupposed that consumption and saving functions would be well behaved.

There was to be a friction at the Bureau of the Budget, however, over the proper interpretation of observable price behavior in 1940 and 1941. Means's reading was shaped by the structuralist residue in his thought. The rise in wholesale prices between August 1940 and May 1941, he maintained, had been "selective": They had risen by 28.6 percent for the "most competitive" group of commodities, by 17.3 percent in the "competitive" group, but by only 1.3 percent in the group most heavily dominated by administered price making. He concluded from these findings that "wholesale prices are in general in better balance than before the current war." In other words, producers in the flexible price sector were at last catching up with those in the administered price sector, and depression-induced distortions in the structure of relative prices were being repaired. Such complacency was at odds with the perspective of Keynesians who sought to build defenses against inflationary pressures on the general price level. Persuaded that "effective teamwork" with colleagues in the Bureau of the Budget was no longer possible, Means left government before Pearl Harbor.[14]

Yet another department of government, the Treasury, had an obvious stake in the analysis of counterinflationary strategies. But there, under the leadership of Secretary Morgenthau, anything that smacked of Keynesianism was immediately suspect. As an aid to organizing its thinking on counterinflationary strategies, the Treasury drew on a study, begun in June 1941, by Carl Shoup of Columbia University, assisted by Milton Friedman and Ruth Mack. Shoup was nominally the senior member of the team, but Friedman developed the technique of analysis. This group was charged to consider the magnitude of tax increases necessary to prevent inflation. Its preliminary findings were presented to the Treasury in October 1941.[15]

This study was distinctly different, both in method and in conclusions, from other attempts then underway to calculate the magnitude of the "gap."

13. Means, "Statistical Bases for Anti-inflation Policy," August 15, 1941, Records of the Bureau of the Budget, NA.
14. This clash is revealed in the correspondence, particularly the exchanges between Means and Gerhard Colm, concerning the preparation of the Quarterly Report of the Bureau of the Budget's Fiscal Division of July 31, 1941, Means Papers, FDRPL.
15. The preliminary mimeographed report, completed on October 15, 1941, was titled "Amount of Taxes Needed in June, 1942, to Avert Inflation." An expanded version of this study later appeared in book form as Carl Shoup, Milton Friedman, and Ruth P. Mack, *Taxing to Prevent Inflation: Techniques for Estimating Revenue Requirements* (New York: Columbia University Press, 1943).

Friedman, the architect of its methodology, wanted to start from the data to which a reasonable degree of confidence could be assigned: for example, observable consumption spending in the base period and prospective increases in defense spending (based on projections supplied by the military authorities). Insofar as possible, he sought to avoid working with multiplier concepts, the coefficients of which he regarded as highly problematic at best. Various assumptions were introduced about possible growth in real GNP during the next period. These magnitudes were then compared with projected increases in claims arising from the defense budget. Four possible combinations were considered, but in none of them could the increased claims for defense be satisfied from the increment in real output. It followed that the private sector's share of the total product would need to shrink. To accomplish this result without an increase in prices, private spending would obviously have to be reduced. If tax measures were used for this purpose, however, the increase in tax revenues would have to exceed the value of resources diverted from civilian to military purposes. This conclusion could be derived from the fact that a reduction of private disposable income by one dollar would not reduce private spending by the same amount because part of what was taxed away would otherwise have been saved. By how much then should taxes rise to avert inflation by mid-1942? The authors offered not one answer, but four, ranging from $4.6 billion to $8.4 billion.[16] In their view, it would be unscientific to claim greater precision. Nevertheless, they regarded this experiment as a constructive contribution. The framework it provided for organizing thinking about tax policy was a decided improvement over untutored intuition and "guesses of what Congress or the public at large would be willing to accept."[17]

The differences between these approaches to inflation containment were publicly aired in exchanges between Salant and Friedman at the December 1941 meetings of the Econometric Society. Salant criticized the Shoup-Friedman-Mack study because it failed to measure secondary effects of changes in spending and because "it does not deal with the curves that correspond to the consumer disposable income of the base period." The OPA method, on the other hand, was built around a "logically complete system of interdependent quantitative relations" designed to provide forecasts of the components of aggregate demand in a future period.[18]

From Friedman's perspective, what the Keynesians had to offer was less fact than fiction. He preferred to concentrate on the observables: Only they could actually be measured. The attempt to specify future consumption–income relationships, for example, was an exercise in speculation. Much de-

16. Ibid., p. 67.
17. Ibid., p. 75.
18. Walter S. Salant, "The Inflationary Gap: Meaning and Significance for Policy Making," *American Economic Review,* June 1942, pp. 308–20.

pended on how income was redistributed in the movement from one aggregate income level to another. A variety of possibilities could be entertained; for example, a shift in the income distribution between profit and wage incomes would certainly alter the marginal propensity to consume. Friedman concluded that "at the present stage of our knowledge of the functioning of the economic system, estimating the gap is a presumptuous undertaking." In December 1941, he cautioned those who might "suppose that a new technique has been developed for guiding public policy in peacetime. ... Gap analysis has added nothing to our understanding of economic change."[19]

Friedman's skepticism was informed, at least in part, by his experience as an economist in government. Between 1935 and 1937, he had cut his professional teeth as a technical adviser to the National Resources Committee, which had conducted studies of household consumption behavior. Subsequently, he had worked with Simon Kuznets in research on the income and expenditure patterns of professionals. As an empirical investigator into the raw material on which calculations of the aggregate consumption function were based, he was sensitized to the fallibility of the data and to the hazards of forecasts that presupposed high predictability in spending behavior.

2 Charting directions for microeconomic intervention, 1940–41

Roosevelt took the first steps toward creating the machinery to administer price controls in late May 1940 when he established an Advisory Commission on National Defense and appointed Leon Henderson as the Commissioner for Price Stabilization. Henderson's credentials as a New Deal faithful by this time were well validated. He brought to this new assignment the accumulated experience of an insider in the operations of both the NRA and the TNEC.

In company with others in the hierarchy of official economists, Henderson was persuaded that economic planning for preparedness should not be a replay of the earlier War Industries Board. On a number of points, he sharply differentiated his position from the one to which Bernard Baruch remained committed. Baruch insisted that an effective control system needed to be comprehensive, covering the prices of all goods and services as well as wage rates. To the contrary, Henderson held that administrative attention should be selective, with price ceilings placed only on commodities "where a price advance seemed unlikely to result in a material increase in production, and where the price advance might contribute significantly to price spiraling, inflation and profiteering." Nor in 1940–41 did he believe that the price of labor should be within his jurisdiction. It was hoped that responsible wage

19. Milton Friedman, "Discussion of the Inflationary Gap," *American Economic Review,* June 1942, pp. 319, 320.

making would follow from a selective control program's success in constraining increases in the cost of living and in suppressing unreasonable profits. Henderson and Baruch parted company as well in their approaches to price making in vital industries characterized by substantial differences in the cost patterns of various producers. In World War I, it had been typical administrative practice to establish a price that would yield a normal return to the high-cost producer; that meant, in turn, that low-cost producers reaped abnormally high returns. Henderson proposed instead to keep the high-cost firms going through subsidies, a solution that would bring both lower transaction prices and lower industrywide profits.[20] This strategy had a further implication: Economists, not businesspersons, would be at the forefront in decision making with respect to prices.

This point of view was further elaborated by John Kenneth Galbraith, a 32-year-old economist then in Washington while on leave from Princeton University. Given the condition of the American economy in early 1941, he argued that supply bottlenecks in key sectors could be expected well before full employment was reached. The inflationary potential they contained was not a matter that could be effectively treated through restrictive macroeconomic measures. Instead the bottleneck cases should be addressed head-on. He proposed three lines of specific intervention. In the first instance, steps should be taken to expand capacity in sectors in which shortages could be anticipated. Secondly, direct controls should be imposed when supply conditions were highly inelastic, and this promised to "check inflation without hampering expansion or curbing the consumption of commodities or services which are plentiful." Thirdly, an inflation control effort should attempt to constrain particular categories of consumer spending. For example, demand for consumer durables – products that competed directly with defense requirements for raw materials and plant capacity – should be reined in. A ban on installment credit for such purchases would contribute toward that end.[21]

Henderson and Galbraith were to collaborate in giving operational meaning to this "model" of selective price control. When they joined forces in late April 1941, they lacked full authority to produce the results they wanted. Arnold, at Justice's Anti-trust Division, was technically correct when informing Roosevelt in May 1941 that his office possessed "the only legal remedy ... [to] combinations to raise prices, or to maintain artificially high prices." Henderson's office

20. Leon Henderson and Donald M. Nelson, "Prices, Profits, and Government," *Harvard Business Review,* Summer 1941, pp. 389–403. Nelson, formerly a vice-president of the Sears-Roebuck Company, was to lead the War Production Board.

21. John Kenneth Galbraith, "The Selection and Timing of Inflation Controls," *The Review of Economic Statistics,* May 1941, pp. 82–5. At the behest of Currie, who maintained that "we need a good Keynesian," Galbraith had been recruited to Washington in midsummer 1940. [Peggy Lamson, *Speaking of Galbraith: a Personal Portrait* (New York: Ticknor and Fields, 1991), Chapter 4.]

as Commissioner for Price Stabilization, to which Galbraith had been added as head of the Price Division, was the creature of an executive order. As such, it could issue price "schedules" (i.e., recommended maximum prices), and some 38 such schedules had been announced by October 27, 1941.[22] But this amounted to no more than moral suasion. In the absence of Congressional authorization, powers to discipline noncompliance were lacking.

The Emergency Price Control Bill, which Roosevelt sent to Congress on July 30, 1941, was drafted to give some teeth to an Office of Price Administration. Henderson was the star witness during the course of its review by congressional committees. He appealed for the authority to penalize "that old familiar person, called in the N.R.A., the chiseler." But there now was a difference: "[T]his time he is on the other side – not cutting prices, but raising prices."[23] The controls sought, he insisted, would continue to be exercised selectively; he expected that ceilings on 75 to 100 of the principal commodities and fabrications would be sufficient. Nevertheless, the bill had been drafted to convey powers to control all commodities "because you never know when you will get a special situation."[24]

The learning accumulated from NRA (and even more significantly from TNEC), Henderson maintained, equipped his office to administer price controls fairly and effectively. TNEC, for example, had generated a wealth of data on the cost structures of individual industries. This information was invaluable to those engaged in deciding whether subsidies to high-cost producers were in the public interest and, if so, in what amount. He lamented that the insights into industrial behavior revealed by TNEC's investigations had not been available earlier. In the days when he had worn an NRA hat, he observed that "he could have done so much better if [he] had had the things that we got in the T.N.E.C."[25]

TNEC's findings were important to the price control exercise in yet another respect. This documentation provided some historical benchmarks on "normal" rates of return by industries. A price fixer could thus stand on firmer ground when determining whether a ceiling needed adjustment because profits associated with it were excessive (or conceivably inadequate). Even so, the question of what constituted a "fair" profit remained a thorny one. As he had done in NRA days, Henderson called on John Maurice Clark for counsel. In Clark's view, economists were "substantially unanimous that price controls are neces-

22. Hearings before the Committee on Banking and Currency, House of Representatives, 77:1, pp. 853–4. The list of 38 was dominated by raw materials: e.g., scrap of aluminum, zinc, iron and steel, nickel, brass, copper; pig iron, copper, ethyl alcohol, wood alcohol, glycerin, etc.
23. Henderson, Testimony before the Committee on Banking and Currency, House of Representatives, 77:1, August 5, 1941, p. 24.
24. Henderson, ibid., September 17, 1941, p. 838.
25. Henderson, ibid., August 11, 1941, p. 436.

sary ... in a defense emergency of the present magnitude." But judgments about the "reasonableness" of rates of return, he pointed out, should not be invariably tied to "customary standards." Profits in some sectors in the past, after all, might well have been artificially elevated by elements of monopoly for which there was no justification. Clark further spoke forcefully about how decisions should not be made: He did not wish "to allow businesses or businessmen, singly or as a group, to be the judges in this matter, with powers to make returns 'reasonable' according to their own views."[26] This position was squarely at odds with Baruch's preference for allowing industries largely to police themselves.

The economists at OPA were at one in embracing the view Clark had articulated with respect to the locus of authority in a regime of price fixing. Their ranks were to grow quickly. Galbraith, as OPA's chief operating officer, hastily assembled a professional staff, recruited both from the universities and from depression-related agencies that were in the process of winding down.[27] Not surprisingly, this phenomenon raised a number of congressional eyebrows. Nor was it unreasonable that this should have been so. The powers requested in the Emergency Price Control Bill had no peacetime precedent. It was no trifling matter to contemplate suspending price making via the market for price fixing via alleged "experts," few of whom could claim hands-on business experience.

There was an arresting contrast between the congressional response to this presidential request and the reaction of legislators to Roosevelt's appeal for extraordinary authority to influence price making some eight years before. The AAA and NRA bills had essentially been shouted through in the spring of 1933 with only cursory inspection. Six months were to elapse, however, before Congress was moved to act on the Emergency Price Control Bill. Nor was this merely obstructionist foot-dragging. A proposal to place the normal allocative functions of a price system in abeyance raised legitimate questions that merited thoughtful consideration. Alternatives deserved to be examined as well. Bernard Baruch was at hand to challenge the feasibility of a selective control system and to champion the all-embracing approach instead. Irving Fisher, for quite different reasons, was also critical of the administration's plan. In a statement submitted to the House Committee on Banking and Currency, he expressed sympathetic support for proper measures to prevent both inflation and profiteering in strategic commodities. But the bill's preoccupation with controlling specific prices failed to get to the root of the matter. As Fisher put it, "individual price control, if it is restricted to keeping the individual prices in line with the general level of prices, is, I believe, an appropriate remedy for the profiteering problem, but I emphatically do not think it is

26. J. M. Clark to Henderson, August 18, 1941, as reproduced in ibid., pp. 697–8.
27. OPA also engaged a number of academic economists as part-time consultants. J. M. Clark, for example, had this status. So also did George J. Stigler, then an assistant professor of economics at the University of Minnesota. OPA's legal staff included a recent graduate of the Duke University Law School, Richard M. Nixon.

appropriate for the inflation problem." And he reiterated his view that "price inflation is almost uncontrollable as long as there is monetary inflation."[28]

The months of testimony on the Emergency Price Control Bill also brought to light the considerable degree of congressional uneasiness about its possible implications for farm prices. At last, markets seemed to be working in favor of farmers. Those lobbying for their interest argued with some passion that no steps should be taken that would set the prices of agricultural products below those that were attainable through the standard workings of supply and demand. Voices that had long called for price floors now opposed price ceilings. On January 30, 1942, some seven weeks after Pearl Harbor, the Emergency Price Control Act became the law of the land. One of its provisions stipulated that the Office of Price Administration was proscribed from fixing a price for farm outputs at a level below 110 percent of parity.

3   Post-Pearl Harbor designs for macroeconomic management

America's entry into the war reordered the agenda. No longer was the question of achieving full employment part of the discussion, as it had been in 1941. The central problem became one of directing the allocation of resources between civilian and military demands when the economy was stretched to its limits. In principle, a restrictive monetary policy might have formed part of the macroeconomic policy mix. In practice, this was not to be. The Federal Reserve had forfeited its autonomy by agreeing to support the government bond market to ensure that the Treasury's debt issues were placed.

No one questioned the importance of curbing civilian spending, but councils within government were divided on how that could best be done. The divisions reflected, in part, differences in the social and political convictions of senior policy makers. But there were also analytic divergences about the way the economic mechanism could work. These intramural controversies, in turn, sparked fresh thinking on points of economic theory and policy.

The issues dividing Keynesians at the Bureau of the Budget and the Office of Price Administration from Secretary of the Treasury Morgenthau and his economic advisers were joined in earnest in April 1942. All parties to the discussion agreed that stringent economic control measures were necessary in wartime, but they did not share a common reading of what the optimal mix should be. The Keynesians supported fiscal constraints through tax increases and were sympathetic toward tax measures that were specifically aimed at reducing consumption, such as a general sales tax. In addition, they called for a universal compulsory savings program: A scheme to absorb 5 percent of after-tax income, later to be increased to 10 percent, was then mooted. These forced savings would be placed in "non-negotiable bonds payable after the war when

28. Fisher, Testimony submitted for the record, October 20, 1941, ibid., pp. 1972–81.

hard times begin."[29] These recommendations were in keeping with the program Keynes had proposed for the United Kingdom.

In presenting the Treasury's position, Morgenthau informed the president that "there are radical points of difference between our conclusions and those of Harold Smith's group." He registered strong objection to the use of sales taxes on the grounds that they would bring hardship to the lower-income groups, adding that a presidential recommendation for such legislation would probably encourage Congress "to make drastic cuts in the Administration's proposals for increases in personal and corporate incomes and profits (taxes)." He also took strong exception to proposals for compulsory savings. In his judgment, they were mistaken for two reasons: They would kill the Treasury's voluntary saving program and would probably lead to liquidations of war bonds already sold to the public. The Treasury supported a program of "strict rationing" to frustrate potential consumption spending and to swell the volume of funds flowing into voluntary purchases of bonds.[30]

Economists at the Bureau of the Budget found all these arguments to be flawed. From a Keynesian perspective, a central task of wartime economic management was to reduce private demand, and reduction of private demand meant that tax policy should bite the incomes of those with the highest propensity to consume. In normal circumstances, progressive taxation might be desired. But, "in the present situation ... we must resort to the absorption of mass purchasing power because taxation of the upper-income brackets does not have the requisite anti-inflationary effect." Similarly, a compulsory universal saving plan had merit because it would "collect most of its receipts from the lower and middle bracket incomes while the voluntary savings originate largely in the higher income brackets." Nor was the Treasury's faith in general rationing well founded: Rationing and price controls could not be effective unless fiscal constraints drained off excess demand.[31]

Two divergent intellectual perspectives shaped these exchanges. The Keynesians focused attention on aggregate demand management through the

29. These proposals were presented to Roosevelt in "A Memorandum for the President Urging an Anti-Inflation Program" on April 18, 1942, signed by Claude R. Wickard (Secretary of Agriculture), Leon Henderson, Marriner Eccles, Harold D. Smith, and Henry Wallace (Vice-President), FDRPL. Morgenthau, who had been appointed to this interdepartmental group to devise an antiinflation program, refused to endorse these recommendations.
30. Morgenthau to Roosevelt, April 3, 1942, and April 10, 1942, FDRPL.
31. Bureau of the Budget, "Comments on the Letter and Memorandum of the Secretary of the Treasury to the President," April 1942, Records of the Bureau of the Budget, NA. Budget Director Smith lamented that: "The truth is [the Secretary of the Treasury] is avoiding facing the real issues in fiscal policy. I am beginning to think he doesn't even understand them." (Harold D. Smith, April 16, 1942, Harold D. Smith Papers, FDRPL.)

manipulation of the macroeconomic variables. In their analyses, it was self-evident that the task of suppressing consumption required targeting incomes of those with the highest propensities to spend, and they were prepared to suspend some of the freedoms consumers normally enjoyed in order to accomplish their purpose. The Treasury position, in contrast, was rooted in a different philosophical tradition. Despite the urgencies of war, Morgenthau fought for minimal compromise in his vision of the New Deal's commitment to a progressive tax structure. And, despite his enthusiasm for direct controls, he sought to preserve a measure of individual freedom of choice in consumption–savings decisions.[32]

One of the by-products of this clash in perspectives in 1942 was a Treasury initiative in packaging an innovative approach to wartime fiscal management: an expenditure tax. Strictly speaking, the analysis underlying it was not new; in one form or another, the idea had been around since at least the early 1920s. The context of World War II, however, gave renewed vitality to this concept. Fisher had revived it in mid-1941 when proposing a tax reform in which savings would be immune from taxation as income. Instead, the tax – scaled progressively – would be levied exclusively on consumption expenditures. This plan, Fisher informed Roosevelt, "would help mitigate the depletion of resources by defense and also facilitate savings for the private subscriber to government bonds which ... would help avoid inflation."[33] Fisher elaborated the analytic justification for this scheme in a book entitled *Constructive Income Taxation* (which appeared in 1942). Meanwhile he actively pressed his findings on Treasury officials with responsibility for tax policy. Fisher's thinking on a counterinflationary tax strategy in wartime, it should be noted, was not informed by a Keynesian perspective. On the contrary, it stemmed from a position he had worked out in *The Nature of Capital and Income* in 1906, a work in which he had insisted that savings should be excluded from the definition of income.

Fisher received a respectful hearing for his views from Treasury economists, who then faced the challenge of devising a tax program that would minimize burdens on lower-income groups, while raising more revenue and discouraging consumption. Initially, however, they had been attracted to a plan of "expenditure rationing," which, it was held, could be implemented without

---

32. For his part, Morgenthau did not disguise his disdain for Keynesian economists in Washington:

> They think that the Government can do the thing one day by pumping money in, and the next day they think the Government can do the thing by putting the brakes on the lower income groups, but I have yet to see a single one of them make a success of anything they have undertaken. [Morgenthau, as quoted in John Morton Blum, *From the Morgenthau Diaries: Years of War 1941–1945* (Boston: Houghton Mifflin, 1967), pp. 37–8.]

33. Fisher to Roosevelt, June 4, 1941, FDRPL.

further legislation. Under this projected scheme, total consumer spending power would be limited to an amount "roughly equal to the aggregate of available consumers' goods at present prices." Each person would receive a "ration allowance" and its magnitude would vary with income and family size. Thus, those at the lowest end of the income distribution might be permitted to spend without limit, whereas the fraction of income that could be spent would diminish as income rose.[34] The Treasury was soon to turn its back on the administrative complexity of this scheme and to support something closer to Fisher's conception of tax strategy.

The expenditure tax, which the Treasury recommended to the Senate Finance Committee in September 1942, proved to be a nonstarter. Conceptually, it nonetheless contained a number of attractive features. Not only did it promise to raise tax receipts; it provided a deterrent to consumption and an incentive to saving. Spending on necessities would be exempt, and households in the higher consuming brackets would be assessed at higher rates than those in lower ones. Because savings would be immune from this levy, adoption of this tax program would enhance the willingness of the public to purchase war bonds voluntarily. Congress, however, was unmoved. The expenditure tax idea nonetheless lived on in discussions among professional economists.[35]

Fisher remained ready to volunteer advice on other techniques for inflation fighting as well. In midsummer 1942, he suggested that consumers be required to buy 5 cents worth of savings stamps (with which war bonds could be purchased) for each dollar of retail purchases, describing this as a "mixture of voluntary and involuntary savings." In addition, he advanced an ingenious variation on his stamped scrip proposal of 1932–33, now adapted to a quite different economic environment. He proposed a 1 percent stamp tax on all checks. The point of this, he informed Roosevelt, was to lower the velocity of monetary circulation which "ought to reduce the inflation pressure enormously."[36]

4   Microeconomic interventions, post-Pearl Harbor

America's entry into the war obviously gave urgency to the formulation of a microeconomic strategy appropriate to all-out mobilization. Thurman Arnold seized the moment to press for a still more vigorous antitrust program. In his view, this was essential because "conspiracies" in the com-

---

34. "Expenditure rationing" was exhaustively discussed in the Treasury Staff Conference of July 30, 1942; see the Morgenthau Diaries of that date, Box 55, FDRPL. Among those providing sympathetic support to this scheme were Milton Friedman, Jacob Viner, and Roy Blough.

35. Fisher continued to champion it, as did Milton Friedman who argued its merits in "The Spendings Tax as a Wartime Fiscal Measure," *American Economic Review,* March 1943, pp. 50–62. On the recommendation of Nicholas Kaldor, it was given a not altogether satisfying practical run in India in the late 1950s.

36. Fisher to Roosevelt, July 30, 1942, FDRPL.

mercial structure "had suppressed the production of critical materials, deprived the Allies of weapons of war, and unwittingly divulged military secrets and vital production data to foreign governments."[37] This view did not prevail. Roosevelt, responding to arguments that antitrust prosecutions and investigations threatened to hamper production for war, ordered that these activities be suspended for the duration unless the Secretaries of War and of the Navy certified that the war effort would not thereby be placed in jeopardy. Under the terms of this arrangement, some 25 antitrust cases were postponed. Violators, however, would not be immune from prosecution after the cessation of hostilities.[38]

On the congressional front, Pearl Harbor finally led to action providing legislative foundations for a program of selective price controls. The ultimate enactment of the Emergency Price Control Bill on January 30, 1942 was, at best, only a partial victory for the administration. Congressional insistence that farm prices could not be capped at levels below 110 percent of parity was at odds with the bill's central purposes. Henderson alerted Roosevelt to the destabilizing consequences of this provision:

> ... [F]ood and fibre price increases, by making wage increases inescapable, will force OPA to increase industrial prices, which as you know will raise the parity price. We will then be in the vicious spiral – and forbidden by law to do anything about it! In other words, we are worse off with this bill than we are under your Executive Order![39]

The selective control strategy that had inspired the Emergency Price Control Act was to be short-lived. As Henderson had anticipated, the exemption of farm products from OPA jurisdiction spelled disaster. Cracks in the fabric were abundantly in evidence by April 1942: In the four months after Pearl Harbor, food prices rose by nearly 5 percent and clothing prices by 7.7 percent.[40] Guided primarily by advice from economists at OPA and the Bureau of the Budget, Roosevelt called for new legislation to seal the parity price for farm products as the maximum and to authorize substantial increases in taxes. At the same time, he ordered that ceilings be fixed on "prices which consumers, retailers, wholesalers, and manufacturers pay for the things they buy" and on "rents for

---

37. Thurman Arnold and J. Sterling Livingstone, "Antitrust War Policy and Full Production," *Harvard Business Review,* Spring 1942, p. 265.
38. Roosevelt, PPA, Vol. 11 (1942), pp. 181–4. Samuel I. Rosenman, who had acted as the White House intermediary on this issue, reported on Arnold's reluctance to accept this presidential order as follows: "I had several amusing conversations with the President in which I humorously suggested that it would be easier to make Thurman Arnold a Captain in the Navy than to convince him of the necessity of deferring his anti-trust prosecutions which interfered with the war, until victory was in sight." (Ibid., p. 185.)
39. Henderson to Roosevelt, January 12, 1942, FDRPL.
40. Roosevelt, PPA, Vol. 11 (1942), p. 224.

dwellings in all areas affected by war industries."[41] OPA responded on April 29, 1942 by issuing a General Maximum Price Regulation, under which the highest price charged for all nonagricultural goods in March 1942 was established as the ceiling. Narrowly focused interventions aimed at breaking specific bottlenecks had fallen by the wayside. OPA's new *modus operandi* came much closer to the Baruch model of comprehensive control that Henderson and Galbraith had opposed throughout 1941.

This turn of events was driven by circumstances, not by a preconceived design. OPA had been obliged to improvise and it lacked a model to guide its conduct. Moreover, the economists charged to administer the General Maximum Price Regulation were acutely conscious of the risk of failure. This was reflected in the choice of language in the Statement of Considerations issued when the Regulation had been promulgated: "Without [adequate taxation, savings and wage stabilization] the ceiling would in the long run become administratively unenforceable and socially harmful."[42] Galbraith subsequently observed that these *caveats* were inserted "partly in the hope of stimulating collateral action on taxes and wages, partly as a warning against what was deemed to be excessive reliance on price-fixing, and partly in the tenuous hope that they might, in the event of failure of the regulation, protect the professional reputations of those responsible."[43]

After the fact, experience with the General Maximum Price Regulation was to stimulate the formulation of a model of sorts. As Galbraith pieced it together, the challenge to the price fixer needed to be understood in the context of the structure of particular markets. Control of prices under conditions of imperfect competition could be regarded as a reasonably straightforward proposition. In such markets, prices tended to be fairly stable in any event. Moreover, the fact that the number of sellers was small obviously simplified the administrator's task. As Galbraith explained the issue to members of the American Economic Association in January 1943, imperfect competition meant that it was "relatively easy to come to grips with prices or more particularly with the production cost and profit information for which the price fixer must have regard." Markets in which conditions of perfect competition were approximated, by contrast, was another matter altogether. With large numbers of sellers to deal with, the control authorities could expect frustrations.[44] Galbraith's diagnosis of differential complexities in price control as a function of market structures proved to be prescient. OPA's subsequent successes and fail-

41. Ibid., p. 219.
42. As quoted in Galbraith, *A Theory of Price Control* (Cambridge, Mass.: Harvard University Press, 1952), p. 7.
43. Ibid., p. 7.
44. Galbraith, "Price Control: Some Lessons from the First Phase," *American Economic Review Supplement,* March 1943, p. 254. Galbraith expanded on these themes in 1952 in *A Theory of Price Control.*

ures can readily be understood in these terms. Galbraith's days as a Price Administrator, however, were numbered. Economists in official roles that obliged them to say "no" to politically influential interests made easy targets. Henderson was forced to resign under congressional pressure in December 1942. Galbraith followed him out the door in May 1943.

OPA's track record, nonetheless, was readily interpretable within the Galbraithian framework. The imperfectly competitive markets were indeed the more manageable. The price fixers could take justifiable pride in their treatment of a number of industries in which strategic commodities were supplied by only a few firms. For example, prices of copper, lead, zinc, mica, and tin were kept in check by underwriting high-cost domestic output with subsidies. This was a considerable advance over World War I practice: In the typical case then, the market price would be allowed to rise to a level sufficient to yield a normal profit to the high-cost producer. The situation in the markets closer to the perfectly competitive environment was indeed more problematic. As of October 1942, an amended version of the Emergency Price Control Act repealed the original stipulation prohibiting caps on farm prices below 110 percent of parity and set the parity price as the limit instead.[45] Thereafter, most farm prices were within OPA's legal reach. Even so, the escalation of food prices in early 1943 pushed up the cost of living, sparked labor unrest, and pressed the stabilization effort itself to the brink of collapse. On April 8, 1943, Roosevelt responded with an executive order, known as the "hold the line" order, in which all items affecting the cost of living were brought under control. OPA henceforth targeted to contain – and, if possible, to reduce – prices to which the consumer price index was sensitive. Shortly thereafter, prices of some 39 commodities were rolled back.[46] Perhaps the most widely publicized intervention in 1943 was the allocation of some $450 million as rollback subsidies to reduce the prices of meat and butter.[47]

On the first anniversary of the hold-the-line order, officials heading the economic stabilization effort could report to the president that "the cost of living as a whole [was] slightly lower than it was a year ago."[48] The behavior of

45. This rollback encountered formidable congressional resistance. Congress was persuaded to act by Roosevelt's threat to invoke presidential war powers if necessary to accomplish this result.

46. Roosevelt, PPA, Vol. 12 (1943), p. 155. In late July 1943, Gilbert estimated that "steps already taken in the case of meats, butter, cabbage, lettuce, and fresh fish, have already reduced the cost of living by 1.6 percent." (Gilbert to Prentiss M. Brown, July 27, 1943, Gilbert Papers, FDRPL.)

47. Richard V. Gilbert to Chester Bowles, September 13, 1943, Gilbert Papers, FDRPL.

48. Fred M. Vinson (Director, Office of Economic Stabilization), Chester Bowles (Administrator, Office of Price Administration), Marvin Jones (Administrator, War Food Administration), and William H. Davis (Chairman, National War Labor Board) to Roosevelt, April 7, 1944, FDRPL.

clothing prices, however, had been troubling, though price increases for these items had been more than offset by reductions elsewhere, particularly for foods. With its large numbers of producers, the textile sector did not lend itself to facile control. In 1943, economists at OPA were in the vanguard in pressing for the adoption of a novel technique to suppress upward price pressure on textiles. This scheme, referred to as the War Models Program, called for simplification in product specifications and for production "in the most economical way possible, stripped of practices, styling and varieties that are wasteful in wartime and taking the fullest advantage of mass production techniques."[49] Here were echoes of ideas from 1934, when Ezekiel and Lubin attacked product differentiation in the automobile industry and saw stripped-down specifications as a route toward high-volume and low-price production. Indeed one of the economists engaged in the War Model exercise, Dexter M. Keezer, was an NRA veteran.[50] The controls over production needed to make a war model textile program work failed to materialize. In their absence, OPA's price regulations tended to have a perverse effect on supply. As Gilbert lamented in mid-1944, "our price regulations at all stages of production have permitted and even encouraged a shift from low-price, low-profit to high-price, high-profit production. The consequence has been a really savage cut in the supply of low- and medium-priced items and a sharp increase in the actual cost of clothing the family."[51]

5   The upshot

Measured by the criterion that mattered most – military victory – America's economic mobilization in World War II was a huge success. Professional economists made a substantial contribution to that achievement. Strategies they helped to put in place enabled the nation to allocate roughly half of its GNP to the prosecution of war while still sustaining the standard of living of the civilian population. Meanwhile, despite a shaky start, some extraordinary measures to suppress increases in the consumer price index had proved to be effective. These were no mean accomplishments.

Results, it would appear, indicated that economists in government had earned their salt. Even so, there were some casualties along the way. The fates of Henderson and Galbraith, for example, were reminders of their vulnerability when cast in politically exposed operational roles. Conditions of war also

49. Howard Coonley (War Production Board), Edward D. Hollander (War Manpower Commission), Dexter M. Keezer (Office of Price Administration), and Samuel Lubell (Office of Economic Stabilization) to James F. Byrnes (Director, Board of Economic Stabilization), May 19, 1943, FDRPL.
50. The War Model idea had been borrowed from Britain where a program of standardized and low-cost "utility" consumer goods had been developed. Keezer had been assigned to survey British practice in late 1942.
51. Gilbert to James G. Rogers, Jr., Gilbert Papers, June 22, 1944, FDRPL.

saw the elimination of some institutional bases within the bureaucracy where economists had formerly enjoyed hospitality. The National Resources Planning Board, which had come to be regarded as a safe haven for Keynesians, was terminated by a Congress that turned its back on Roosevelt's pleas for its renewal. In addition, war-induced prosperity for farmers left a mark at the Department of Agriculture. From the perspective of the farm lobbies, the intellectuals associated with the Bureau of Agricultural Economics (and particularly those identified with land use planning) had worn out their welcome.

Though the war had focused the attention of economists on common objectives, it by no means followed that earlier doctrinal differences disappeared. To the contrary, conflicting perspectives on economic analysis and policy remained alive and well. Their vitality was to be abundantly in evidence in debates about the shaping of the postwar world.

10

Designs for the postwar world

By mid-1940, a domesticated version of Keynesian-style macroeconomics – though certainly not unchallenged – was in the ascendant among economists operating within the Washington establishment. The threat of war (and subsequently its reality) meant, however, that Currie's vision of an American econ-omy structured to achieve full employment through high consumption and low saving was put on hold for the duration. Successful economic mobilization instead required the deployment of policy tools to constrain private demand. Nevertheless, ingredients of the "official model of 1940" were expected to come into their own with the cessation of hostilities. Mass unemployment on the scale of the 1930s, it was feared, would again become a real and present danger. If the world was to enjoy a brighter future, the postwar economic order, on both the domestic and the international scenes, needed to be reorganized to keep that from happening.

1   Envisioning the postwar international order
Systematic thinking about the shaping of the postwar international economic system gathered momentum in early 1941. The "special relationship" between the United States and Britain was then in its infancy; in fact, it dated from the unexpected fall of France in May 1940. Before that, relations between the two countries had not been particularly close, and indeed there had been considerable intergovernmental testiness in the 1930s. Their collaboration was a by-product of the French defeat. The two countries then needed one another. Britain was dependent on American support if it was to sustain a war effort, and the United States had a big stake in keeping resistance to Hitler alive.

The guiding perspective – and a shared one – in this collaboration was that the experience of the interwar years should not be repeated. This point of view controlled the form in which the U.S. response to the British request for aid was packaged. Lend-lease was artfully crafted as something different from a loan: Rhetorical camouflage notwithstanding, no cash repayment was really expected. The U.S. government thus demonstrated that it had absorbed a lesson from earlier experience with intergovernmental finance in wartime. The world payments system would not again be burdened by the servicing of war debts, as it had been after 1918, and by the souring of intergovernmental relations that had accompanied it. But ingenuity on the American side was required for a further reason. U.S. law, dating from 1934, prohibited the American government from lending to any country in default on its World War I debts (as Britain was). Aid to Britain thus had to be packaged as a noncommercial transaction.

While the Roosevelt administration was prepared to waive financial compensation for lend-lease aid, it did not follow that this act of unconventional generosity should lack a quid pro quo. The Department of State, under the leadership of Secretary Cordell Hull, assigned high importance to one string: a commitment on Britain's part to forswear Imperial Preferences in its trading arrangements. This condition, which came to be known as the "consideration," reflected Hull's diagnosis of the Great Depression. In this reading of the economic history of the interwar years, artificial barriers to normal commerce had closed markets and cost jobs. The Hoover administration's Smoot-Hawley Tariff of 1930, which had provoked widespread retaliation, had been especially malevolent. A prescription for a happier future followed readily: Priority should be assigned to systematic reduction in trade barriers on a global basis. While this line of thinking insisted on freer trade, it did not require elimination of all restrictions. It was, however, uncompromising on one point: the principle of nondiscrimination within a multilateral system. Countries unable to open their doors completely to the world's commerce should not be selective in their choice of trading partners. Market access had to be open to all and on common terms, a condition at odds with the Imperial Preference system which Britain had constructed.

There was formidable British resistance to this condition. Foot-dragging was based in part on a recognition that Britain's competitive position by war's end would be severely weakened, even in the most favorable of circumstances. The British official posture was also informed by a different perception of the Great Depression's central message for a reordering of the world economy. This interpretation (heavily influenced by Keynes's views) emphasized that mass unemployment had bred trade restrictions, and this causal linkage was more important than a relationship the other way around. Whether or not a multilateral order would be within reach depended crucially on success in securing a world of high employment. From the British point of view, there seemed to be grounds for doubting the capacity of a postwar American government to assure that precondition for multilateralism. The historic propensity of Americans to lean more toward laissez-faire than to governmental management in the domestic economy was a matter of record. Quite apart from sentimental attachments to Imperial Preference, a comprehensible British case could be made for safeguarding that system as a buffer against destabilizing repercussions of an American postwar slump.

Anglo-American conversations on the consideration as a condition for lend-lease were close to stalemate in the summer and autumn of 1941, and those were among the darkest hours of the war. The log jam was broken in the month after Pearl Harbor with a compromise set out in Article Seven of the lend-lease agreements. The two governments then committed themselves to the following understandings:

(1) "agreed action by the United States of America and the United Kingdom, open to participation by all countries of like mind, directed to the expansion, by appropriate international and domestic measures, of production, employment, and the exchange and consumption of goods ...";

(2) "the elimination of all forms of discriminatory treatment in international commerce, and to the reduction of tariffs and other trade barriers ...";

(3) the initiation of "conversations ... between the two Governments with a view to determining, in light of governing economic conditions, the best means of attaining the above-stated objectives by their own agreed action and of seeking the agreed action of other like-minded Governments."[1]

This language amounted to a genuflection to both points of view. It also put in place a framework within which a rethinking about the future international economic order could proceed. Article Seven stopped short of a firm British commitment to abandon discriminatory commercial practice as a condition for lend-lease (as the original State Department drafts would have required), but it kept the issue on the table.

The conceptualization of a design for the future was shaped by a reading of the past. Keynes, who had served as a senior British Treasury official from 1915 to 1919 and did so again in World War II, articulated this state of mind as follows: "In 1918 most people's only idea was to get back to pre-1914. No-one today [in mid-1942] feels that about 1939. That will make an enormous difference when we get down to it."[2] The thought of most American officials was then cast in a similar mold. There was to be no going back to the rigidi-

1. Article Seven of the Anglo-American Mutual Aid Agreement, January 1942, as quoted by Richard N. Gardner, *Sterling-Dollar Diplomacy in Current Perspective: the Origins and Prospects of Our International Order,* new expanded edition (New York: Columbia University Press, 1980), pp. 58–9.
2. John Maynard Keynes to Pethick-Lawrence, 21 June 1942, as quoted by Donald Moggridge, *Maynard Keynes: An Economists' Biography* (London and New York: Routledge, 1992), p. 295.

ties of a gold standard that obliged countries to put clamps on their domestic economies to correct imbalances in their external accounts. Nor should there be a return to the destructive economic warfare of the 1930s, when countries manipulated the exchange value of their currencies for competitive advantage. Addressing these problems pointed toward the need for an international institution to perform two primary functions: (1) to enhance international liquidity and (2) to monitor exchange rates.

As thinking about postwar international monetary arrangements took on coherent form in 1943 and 1944, key strategists on both sides of the Atlantic – notably, Harry Dexter White of the U.S. Treasury and Keynes in Britain – were in broad agreement about the nature of the problem to be solved. When it came to details, they did not see eye to eye. Keynes's conception called for an International Clearing Union, empowered to offer generous credit lines to countries experiencing balance-of-payments deficits. In its underlying theoretical rationale, this scheme amounted to an extension to a global scale of arguments he had set out in *The General Theory* in 1936. The task, as now construed, was to create an environment in which the goal of full employment could be pursued on a worldwide basis. Countries would no longer need to abort domestic economic programs when facing external deficits, nor would they be forced to impose trade and exchange controls to protect their reserves. With foreign exchange available through the facilities of an international monetary authority, regular economic activity need not be seriously disrupted while adjustments in external accounts were being made. Countries with deficits would still have to correct them, but they would have some breathing room when doing so. Creditors, as well as debtors, would have an incentive to speed the necessary adjustments: Both would be assessed interest charges on imbalances.

The American approach, drafted by White, was far less grandiose in conception. In the first instance, the resources at the disposal of a new international lending facility were to be more modest: White envisaged a capital sum of some $5 billion (as opposed to the $26 billion in credit lines Keynes had projected). In addition, borrowing privileges available to debtors would be far more restricted. By contrast with Keynes's conception of open-ended overdraft facilities, the White scheme limited a borrower's drawing rights to the sums initially subscribed to the facility. And there was another important difference: The White Plan imposed no charges on surplus countries, a point to which Keynes had assigned importance as a spur to adjustment. The American draft was more explicit about changes in exchange rates: Devaluations were entertainable, but only when a deficit country demonstrated to the international body that its accounts were in "fundamental disequilibrium" and received the institution's approval for this course of action.

The architecture of the International Monetary Fund, as it emerged from Anglo-American draftsmanship in mid-1944, bore more resemblance to the White blueprint than to the one supplied by Keynes. Aided by the insertion of a "scarce currency clause," a basis for joint action by the two countries was found. This provision entitled deficit countries to discriminate against surplus ones when the Fund's supply of the latter's currency had been drawn down. Thus, when circumstances warranted, discrimination could still be legitimate. This escape hatch offered comfort to an omnipresent British anxiety. Keynes himself appears to have believed that the "scarce currency clause" would never be activated, on grounds that American dedication to nondiscrimination would prompt the United States to supply the world with enough dollars to prevent this situation from arising.

This compromise was crucial to the convergence of the two countries on the shape of two novel institutions: the International Monetary Fund and its companion, the International Bank for Reconstruction and Development (which was to underwrite long-term capital flows). The United States and Britain then invited the rest of the world to sign on. The gathering convened for this purpose was carefully stage-managed to achieve a timely result. The conference was held in August 1944 at Bretton Woods, New Hampshire. A resort hotel, closed down during the war, was reopened, but on the understanding that its facilities would be available for two weeks only. The delegates were thus on notice that they were expected to do their business with dispatch and to clear out.

The United States and Britain, in effect, rewrote the rules for the rest of the world. It is unlikely that a maneuver of this type could have been executed at any other moment in history. That it happened when it did was a by-product of the political reality of 1944. Other potentially significant players in world trade and finance were either enemy countries or had been emasculated by enemy occupation. Initiatives on an international scale, if they were to be undertaken at all, were in the hands of the partners in the wartime "special relationship."

In July 1945, in the afterglow of V-E day euphoria, the United States Congress acted with uncharacteristic speed when ratifying the Bretton Woods instruments. Opposition to this departure from tradition was not lacking. Champions of old-fashioned isolationism argued that membership in the new international institutions amounted to pouring money down a rat hole, and some conservative bankers feared that it would make the world safe for irresponsible debtors. Among the economists who had been prominent in the 1933 round of debates over international monetary matters, the handiwork at Bretton Woods received mixed reviews. Edwin W. Kemmerer regarded it as a step backward and was uncompromising in his conviction that "the only hope of international monetary stability on a wide scale is in a return to the international gold standard."[3] O. M. W. Sprague, on the other hand, supported both the Fund and the Bank, holding that "if an attempt were now made to return

3. Edwin W. Kemmerer, Testimony before the Committee on Banking and Currency, House of Representatives, 79:1, May 2, 1945, p. 837.

to the gold standard, no one would believe that it would hold."[4] Irving Fisher endorsed the Bretton Woods institutions as the foundation stones for fundamental improvements in the world monetary system, but faulted the drafters for failing to push monetary reforms still further. When congratulating Keynes on his accomplishments, Fisher urged him to press for the adoption of 100 percent money. He had a "hunch," Fisher informed Keynes, "that, if you could express to Eccles the idea that he in America and you in England might buttress the international plan by national 100% reserve plans, you might follow success internationally by success nationally. In this way one of the greatest, if not the greatest, economic problem might be solved 'in our time' with you in the leading role again."[5]

2   American Keynesians and designs for a postwar order on the domestic front

Even before Pearl Harbor, some preliminary thinking on the problems of a "post-defense" economy was set in motion. Within the bureaucracy, the National Resources Planning Board, which had engaged Alvin H. Hansen as a consultant, played a leading role in this exercise. As might have been expected, Hansen's analyses had a strong flavor of "secular stagnationism." Because private spending in normal circumstances was believed to be insufficient to generate a full-employment level of aggregate demand, it would again fall to government to close the spending gap. It was thus prudent to have useful public works projects "on the shelf" and to lay the groundwork for other spending programs as well, i.e., for federal funding for health and education, improved support for the aged, slum clearance and the provision of low-cost housing, construction of express highways, and flood control projects. Hansen directed his focus primarily to innovative ways in which to finance such employment-sustaining outlays. He anticipated that some $3 to $5 billions in the "post-defense budget" could be covered by selling government bonds to thrift institutions – insurance companies, savings banks, trust funds, educational institutions – "without resort to borrowing from the banks." Indeed, he held that their accumulations provided a "natural basis" for deficits of that magnitude. Hansen further drew attention to a possible financing scheme with a Fisherine quality (though Fisher's name was not mentioned). Part or all of the deficit could be financed, he observed, by issuing greenbacks against the gold certificates held by the Federal Reserve banks and spending them. This would lead to the accumu-

4. O. M. W. Sprague, Testimony before the Committee on Banking and Currency, House of Representatives, 79:1, May 10, 1945, p. 1209.
5. Fisher to Keynes, July 4, 1944, YUA. Keynes replied, noting that he had "some considerable reservations" about 100 percent money. In Keynes's judgment, "deflation is in the near future a much more dangerous risk than inflation. I am afraid of your formula because I think it would, certainly in England, have a highly deflationary suggestion to a great many people." (Keynes to Fisher, July 7, 1944, YUA.)

lation of excess bank reserves, but "these could be 'written off' by raising reserve requirements until a 100 percent reserve were reached."[6]

After the United States had become a belligerent, the staff of the National Resources Planning Board embarked on a project to mobilize support for postwar full employment policies. This undertaking proceeded from the premise that "government should provide work for adults who are willing and able to work, if private industry is unable to do so." From the tone of *After the War – Toward Security* (a National Resources Planning Board document published in September 1942), it was apparent that its authors believed that the public mind needed to be reconditioned. A successful full employment program, it was noted, "may well involve government in certain fields traditionally regarded as the preserve of private enterprise." Moreover, the nation's long-standing "reluctance to countenance large expenditures" to provide jobs needed to be overcome. On this point, the war-time experience itself was seen as having educational value: "Hereafter it will be difficult to argue either that a relatively small deficit of $3 to $4 billion will weaken the financial standing of the country, or that public spending does not influence the tempo of economic life."[7] This language did not enhance the National Resources Planning Board's survival prospects. Congress turned a deaf ear to Roosevelt's entreaties and terminated appropriations for the NRPB in mid-1943.

With NRPB's demise, leadership in the discussion of post-war economic policies shifted to the Bureau of the Budget. By early 1944, the issues in managing the post-war domestic employment problems began to be articulated rather differently. The Keynesians in Washington anticipated that the prospective end of hostilities would necessarily lead to sharp reductions in government spending for military purposes and that demobilization would swell the civilian labor force. They recognized that the combination of pent-up consumer demand for durables and the extraordinary volume of household liquidity associated with wartime savings would provide a short-term stimulant to consumption spending. But what would happen when the force of this stimulus wore off? In light of the accumulated learning on income determination, the Keynesians were convinced that large-scale unemployment was a distinct threat, but also that it could be avoided.

At the Bureau of the Budget, the first phases of the discussion of the post-war employment problem involved preliminary studies of the possible size of a "deflationary gap." Arthur Smithies of the Bureau's Fiscal Division made one such calculation in February 1944. Although he cautioned that his estimates of consumer spending out of disposable income were based on prewar

6. Alvin H. Hansen, "Financing Post-Defense Public Improvements," January 30, 1941, transmitted to Roosevelt by Frederic A. Delano, Chairman, National Resources Planning Board, February 1, 1941, FDRPL.
7. National Resources Planning Board, *After the War – Toward Security* (Washington, D.C.: U.S. Government Printing Office, 1942), pp. 20, 21, 22.

relationships (and thus might need to be revised), he was persuaded that they were solid enough to support a judgment that "there would be a large deflationary gap in the post-demobilization period."[8] Attention should thus be turned to measures to spur spending. Many familiar possibilities were resurveyed: accelerated spending on useful public works, federal subsidies to the construction of residential housing, and federal guarantees to minimum income standards and social welfare programs. But a fresh note was also struck: Generous provision of benefits to veterans was now seen as a device for easing the postwar employment problem. The G.I. Bill of Rights, which was to fund education and training, grew out of this analysis. This also precluded a repetition of the headaches created by the Veterans' Bonus that followed the First World War.

In August 1944, thinking on these issues entered a new phase. The Keynesians, encouraged by Eccles at the Federal Reserve Board and Smith at the Budget Bureau, set to work on an American white paper on full employment, with Harvard's Alvin Hansen (then a consultant at the Federal Reserve Board) serving as the coordinator of its drafting committee.[9] As this document evolved, some novel emphases were introduced. Government was called on to make a formal commitment to responsibility for economic stabilization, which included attacking both deflationary and inflationary gaps. And when it needed to spur aggregate demand, it should not do so only as a spender. Attention should also be given to variations in tax rates to spur private spending. But to do the job properly a major overhaul in administrative machinery was needed. The draft report of August 17, 1944, proposed the following:

> It will be necessary to set up ... a national investment board or a fiscal authority to cooperate closely with a joint congressional fiscal committee. Under a broad legislative grant a program of public construction should be laid out for a period of 5 to 10 years. The national investment board or fiscal authority should be allowed to adjust and fluctuate the total expenditure so appropriated according to the requirements of economic stability. ... The public investment board or fiscal authority should, moreover, operate within a broad grant of power by Congress and, within specified limits imposed by Congress, should be empowered to make variations in income tax rates and in social security pay roll taxes as a means to regularize the flow of total expenditures and to promote economic stability.[10]

8. Arthur Smithies, "The Economic Problem in 1950," February 21, 1944, Records of the Bureau of the Budget, NA.
9. Others participating in this exercise included Richard Gilbert, Gerhard Colm, Emile Despres, Arthur Smithies, and Walter Salant.
10. Alvin H. Hansen to Weldon Jones, August 18, 1944, with attached draft of "Postwar Employment Program" (dated August 17, 1944). Records of the Bureau of the Budget, NA.

This daring scheme amounted to a grand design for a "Fisc" with discretionary powers to execute fiscal policy analogous to the powers the "Fed" enjoyed over monetary policy. That it could be proposed at all reflected the confidence of the Keynesians that they now possessed the knowledge needed to manage the economy.

3   Responses to a proposed "full employment" bill, version 1945

The high aspirations of American Keynesians to become discretionary managers of fiscal policy faded quickly. The powers to tax and spend, after all, are the meat and potatoes of the political process. Congress had no taste for delegating its authority over these matters to self-proclaimed experts who had never carried a precinct. The Full Employment Bill, introduced as S. 380 in January 1945 by Senator James E. Murray (Democrat of Montana), was thus a disappointment to some. Yet it also contained attractive features. The bill would commit the government of the United States to assuring that "all Americans able to work and seeking work would have the right to useful, remunerative, regular, and full-time employment." It would charge the president to submit a National Production and Employment Budget to the Congress each year. In the event that the Budget estimates indicated that aggregate demand would be insufficient to sustain a "full employment volume of production," the president would be required to submit a program to offset the prospective deficiency. Similarly, should projected expenditure exceed the amounts needed to generate full employment, the president was instructed to present a program to "forestall inflationary economic dislocations."[11] Notably absent was any reference to the conception of a Fisc in which appointed officials enjoyed flexibility to manipulate the fiscal dials.

S. 380, if enacted, would still represent a major departure from historic practice in the American polity. Were the federal government to assume responsibility for assuring jobs to all who sought them, the usual jurisdictional domains of the private and the public sectors would have to be redrawn. In the context of 1945, the political salability of the type of planning implied by the draft of the Full Employment Bill was very much an open question. Only two years earlier Congress had killed the National Resources Planning Board for venturing into this terrain. With the end of hostilities apparently near at hand, public opinion on the future direction of economic policy was sharply divided. At one extreme, the visible hand of government was held to be essential to a satisfactory reconversion from war- to peacetime. But strong

11. The Full Employment Bill, as originally introduced, is reproduced in Stephen K. Bailey, *Congress Makes a Law: The Story behind the Employment Act of 1946* (New York: Columbia University Press, 1950), pp. 243–8. Bailey's study remains the definitive work on the legislative history of the Employment Act.

views were expressed as well about an imperative to be attached to a speedy return to a world in which the economy's fate should be entrusted to the private sector's initiatives.

By the time serious deliberations on the Full Employment Bill began in earnest, Roosevelt had died and Harry S Truman had succeeded to the presidency. Transition at the White House, however, did not affect the bill's treatment in the legislative branch. The Senate Committee on Banking and Currency, under the Chairmanship of Senator Robert Wagner (Democrat of New York), opened public hearings on S. 380 in late July. As a preliminary to that process, Wagner solicited the views of some 1500 citizens identified as "opinion makers." Questions on which he invited comment included the following:

1. What should be the basic responsibilities of the federal government in the maintenance of continuing full employment after the war?
2. What specific improvements in S. 380 might be considered by the Banking and Currency Committee?
3. If you believe S. 380 should not be enacted, what alternative can you suggest?[12]

A fair number of academic economists were among the approximately 300 respondents to this invitation. They certainly did not constitute a representative sample of the profession. Nevertheless, dimensions of the spectrum of contemporary professional opinion came through loudly and clearly in the reactions of the notables within their ranks.

Columbia's John Maurice Clark offered a qualified endorsement of S. 380, subject to the proviso that its language be modified. In his view, an appropriate bill should "not purport 'to assure full employment' unconditionally." Emphasis should instead be placed on "full employment opportunity." Government's proper role was to maintain "a high level of employment and provision for whatever residue of unemployment may persist." When circumstances were such that government was "forced to fall back on increased public spending," it should still "renew its efforts to get results in other ways." In particular, it should be mindful of burdens it imposed on the job-creating ability of private enterprise. Clark further criticized S. 380's apparent confidence in statistical projections and suggested "laying less stress on forecasts, which are likely to be little more reliable than such forecasts have been in the past, and more stress on prompt flexibility in meeting current fluctuations of the actual figures." He further faulted S. 380 for its inattention to aspects of market structure that could influence the volume of employment.

12. Wagner's letter of invitation appears in the Hearings before a Subcommittee of the Committee on Banking and Currency, U.S. Senate, 79:1, 1945, pp. 973–4. Wagner had taken a similar step in 1932 when asking academic economists to comment on an Emergency Public Works Bill that he had introduced.

In his judgment, "flexibility versus stickiness of prices and wages [was] one of the central problems."[13]

Harvard's Gottfried Haberler also advanced suggestions to improve S. 380. He took issue with "the general tenor of the bill," which suggested that "unemployment [could] be effectively prevented or eliminated ... by regulating aggregate expenditure." Increasing total effective demand, he argued, could not deal with pockets of unemployment specific to particular industries or regions without endangering price stability. He further objected to the bill's preoccupation with government spending. "[I]t should be made clear," he wrote, "that the Government can supplement the flow of total private expenditure either by varying its expenditures or by varying its revenues from taxes and other sources with expenditure remaining unchanged."[14]

Joseph A. Schumpeter of Harvard provided only a cursory one-paragraph response. He endorsed the general principles of the bill, but drew attention to the importance of "creating employment opportunity as distinguished from actual full employment as promised in the Beveridge plan" in Britain. "[A]ctual full employment can be guaranteed, indeed, but not without a good deal of compulsion all around."[15]

Chicago's Henry C. Simons struck a sharply negative note, describing the bill as "misguided and ill-conceived." In his view, full employment was "not a proper or desirable rule of fiscal policy." Priority should instead be assigned to a rule for monetary stabilization "to prevent deflation as a cause of unemployment." In light of Simons's views on 100 percent money, it was in character for him to find the bill deficient because it "ignore[d] crucial problems [of] financial reform, especially in banking, which reform is indispensable to a sound program of monetary-fiscal stabilization (and to a sound debt policy)." Simons challenged the presuppositions underlying S. 380 on yet another ground: "The bill contemplates excessive reliance on a kind of statistical forecasting of national income and outlay which [forecasting] is as unreliable as it is currently fashionable among Washington economists of extremist (hyper-Keynesian) persuasions."[16]

Enactment of the bill was vigorously opposed as well by others who shared an anti-Keynesian monetarist perspective. Harry Gunnison Brown of the University of Missouri, for example, maintained that much in the bill "was beside the point or positively harmful." Monetary stabilization was instead the route to full employment.[17] New York University's Willford I. King was no less out-

13. John Maurice Clark to Senator Robert F. Wagner, June 13, 1945, Hearings before a Subcommittee of the Committee on Banking and Currency, U.S. Senate, 79:1, pp. 1029–32.
14. Gottfried Haberler to Senator Robert F. Wagner, May 18, 1945 in ibid., pp. 1092–3.
15. Joseph A. Schumpeter to Senator Robert F. Wagner, May 9, 1945 in ibid., p. 1208.
16. Henry C. Simons to Senator Robert F. Wagner, May 9, 1945 in ibid., pp. 1210–12.
17. Henry Gunnison Brown to Senator Robert F. Wagner, April 26, 1945 in ibid., pp. 1014–18.

spoken. The right monetary program would mean that public works spending to bolster employment would be unnecessary. He held that "the action that is recommended by Mr. Keynes and other people of that type who want the Government to go into debt deeper and deeper and deeper, is the type of action that I contend will wreck any government, because, as the Government goes deeper and deeper into debt it tends to inflate the currency."[18] Irving Fisher was not in Senator Wagner's network of correspondents, but he protested elsewhere against the bill's fiscal orientation. He found it "strange" that the bill nominally drafted to solve the unemployment problem virtually omitted the money issue, treating it "as if it were something entirely on the side that might be considered, but not very important. It seems to me it is like Hamlet with Hamlet left out."[19]

Strong supporters of S. 380 among academic economists were also identified in Wagner's correspondence. For the most part, the advocates were members of a younger professional generation who had grown up with *The General Theory*. One of the coauthors of the Harvard-Tufts Keynesian manifesto of 1938, Alan Sweezy, writing in 1945 from Williams College, welcomed the bill with enthusiasm.[20] Harvard's Seymour E. Harris offered congratulations, as did Oscar Lange (University of Chicago) and Richard A. Lester (Duke University).[21] Lloyd G. Reynolds (Johns Hopkins University) held that the bill did "a very good job of erecting a framework within which private and Government investment might be coordinated at a level sufficient to maintain full employment." He took note of the difficulties in estimating prospective surpluses or deficiencies in a "national budget" but was "sure that we already know enough to make a start on it and that the techniques of estimate could be greatly improved after a few years of experience."[22]

18. Willford I. King, Testimony before the Subcommittee of the Committee on Banking and Currency, August 28, 1945 in ibid., pp. 544–52. King had been invited to appear before the Subcommittee in his capacity as Chairman of the Committee for Constitutional Government, Inc., an anti-New Deal lobbying group. A pamphlet issued by this organization attacked S. 380 with the following language: "If not amended, with its most dangerous features removed, this mislabeled 'Full Employment' bill (really bigger government – more debts – more taxes) may turn America permanently from constitutional private enterprise toward a system of collectivist statism" (as quoted by Bailey, *Congress Makes a Law,* p. 145).
19. Irving Fisher, Transcript of a Talk on the "Velocity of Circulation of Money" to the Econometric Society, Cleveland, Ohio, January 27, 1946, YUA.
20. Alan Sweezy to Senator Robert F. Wagner, May 2, 1945, Hearings before the Subcommittee of the Committee on Banking and Currency, U.S. Senate, p. 1221.
21. Seymour E. Harris to Senator Robert F. Wagner, May 3, 1945 in ibid., pp. 1095–1100; Oscar Lange to Senator Robert F. Wagner, April 27, 1945 in ibid., pp. 1111–12; Richard A. Lester, July 20, 1945 in ibid., pp. 1120–5.
22. Lloyd G. Reynolds to Senator Robert F. Wagner, May 15, 1945 in ibid., 1188–9.

Wagner's decision to solicit written comment only from economists in the academy, it should be noted, meant that the champions of a Full Employment Bill within the profession were considerably underrepresented. The large numbers in government service (or in the armed forces) in 1945 were voiceless in his sample. Even an academic economist serving as a part-time government consultant, such as Alvin Hansen, was not a participant. Hansen, of course, required no assistance from Congress to make his views on the proposed legislation a matter of record. His writings when wearing his professorial hat had enabled him to give public expression to his position. An American counterpart to Britain's Beveridge Report, with its declaration of governmental responsibility for full employment, engaged his sympathies. But the maintenance of postwar full employment in the United States, he had written, made it "necessary to improve our governmental machinery" in a manner that "permits quick action when necessary." A lingering attachment to the Fisc idea was in evidence when he wrote:

> A flexible compensatory policy requires that close attention be paid
> to the timing of expenditures and to changes in the basic income tax
> rate. Having authorized a long-range investment program, Congress
> could set the limits within which the expenditures could be timed
> according to the requirements of stability and also the limits within
> which the standard tax rate could be varied.[23]

As the Full Employment Bill proceeded through the Congressional pipeline, it was expected that the views of economists associated with the bureaucracy would be reflected in the presentations made by the heads of departments and agencies to Congressional committees. The high concentration of pro–S. 380 economists at the Bureau of the Budget were certainly well served by their director. Harold D. Smith put the case for the fiscal orientation as follows:

> Fiscal policy will be one of our major weapons both in avoiding de-
> pressions and in combating inflation. I believe that fiscal policy,
> both on the revenue and the expenditure sides, is the most potent
> weapon we have for influencing markets and employment, especial-
> ly when we need quick results. It is also a means of action most
> consistent with free enterprise. Public finance must be our servant
> and not our master.[24]

4   From the Full Employment Bill of 1945 to the Employment Act of 1946

The American Keynesians suffered a rebuff when the design for a Fisc did not find its way into the Senate version of the 1945 bill. They were to

---

23. Hansen, "Stability and Expansion," in Paul T. Homan and Fritz Machlup, eds., *Financing American Prosperity: A Symposium of Economists* (New York: The Twentieth Century Fund, 1945), p. 209.
24. Harold D. Smith, Testimony before the Committee on Expenditures in the Executive Departments, House of Representatives, 79:1, September 25, 1945, p. 61.

encounter much heavier weather, however, when the House of Representatives attended to this legislation. Leadership of the House committee to which it was referred was in the hands of conservative Southern Democrats who had little enthusiasm for extending governmental responsibilities in peacetime and none for reincarnating a National Resources Planning Board.

In the hearings at the committee stage in the House of Representatives, the testimony of one of the most hostile critics of Hansen-style stagnationism was taken seriously. George Terborgh – then the research director of the Machinery and Allied Products Institute and formerly an economist with the Research Division of the Federal Reserve Board – had acquired considerable prominence as the author of a book entitled *The Bogey of Economic Maturity* (which appeared in mid-1945). This was structured as a root-and-branch attack on Hansen's teaching. In Terborgh's reading, "the four horsemen of the stagnationist apocalypse ... – the decline of population growth, the passing of frontier, the dearth of great new industries, and the increasing self-sufficiency of corporations" – were all fraudulent. He took it to be his duty to expose them because "a defeatist philosophy, if widely believed, can so debilitate the economy that it helps to produce the very condition it assumes." How had such erroneous doctrine been able to exert such influence and, in particular, to inspire strategies to discourage private saving and to promote government spending? The public, he maintained, had been skillfully brainwashed by propaganda unleashed through the hearings of the Temporary National Economic Committee. As Terborgh put it: "Ostensibly an unbiased search for truth, these hearings, so far as they dealt with saving, investment, and government spending, were carefully staged by a small group of Administration operatives to exclude all testimony in conflict with the philosophy it was their purpose to promote."[25]

This line of thinking informed part of Terborgh's recommendations on the disposition the Congress should give to the bill before it. It "should be purged," he insisted, "of the remaining vestiges of the right-to-a-job idea, its qualified but still persistent reliance on Government spending as a panacea, and the surviving remnants of its mandate for long-range (fiscal-year) forecasting."[26] But Terborgh's testimony gave a novel twist to the proceedings. Despite his disdain for stagnationist doctrine and his confidence in an abundance of investment opportunities in the American economy, he was no champion of unbridled laissez-faire. There was still a place for government in smoothing bumps in the economy, and its policies should be informed by expert analysis. But how those tasks were performed was a matter of concern. Terborgh expressed his discomfort with the status quo as follows:

25. George Terborgh, *The Bogey of Economic Maturity* (Chicago: Machinery and Allied Products Institute, 1945), pp. 4, 6, 173.
26. Terborgh, Testimony before the Committee on Expenditures in Executive Departments, House of Representatives, 79:1, October 23, 1945, p. 613.

... [B]oth the economic analysis and the economic policy may be prepared and promoted by men unknown to the public, whose appointment has not been confirmed by Congress, and who have no formal public responsibility. This set-up invites behind-the-scenes manipulation by Presidential advisers of the moment, possessed, it may be, both by a passion for anonymity and a passion for controlling economic policy. However able and high-minded these advisers may be, the arrangement is bad. If the Federal government is really serious about developing and implementing a full-employment policy – as it should be – it ought to make better organizational provision than is made in this bill.[27]

The "organizational provision" Terborgh had in mind took the form of the creation of a small and independent commission, charged "to make continuous study of the art of business stabilization through Federal action" and to issue periodic reports on its findings and recommendations to the president, Congress, and public. Members of the commission were to be appointed by the president and confirmed by the Senate. He anticipated that this reform would have a "most salutary influence on public policy, now too often dominated ... by the self-seeking demands of minority pressure groups, and by the opinions and philosophies of a changing coterie of Presidential advisers, operating in the obscurity of the Executive Offices."[28]

In the subsequent negotiations between conferees from the House of Representatives and the Senate on the ultimate shape of legislation concerning the employment issue, Terborgh's modest proposal took on some unanticipated dimensions. The more conservative participants – and especially those from the House delegation – stood firm in their insistence that a bill stop short of a commitment to "full employment" and that S. 380's mandate for policies controlling the "national budget" be eliminated. In exchange, they offered a concession: the creation of a Council of Economic Advisers, which would submit reports to a Joint Economic Committee of Congress but which would be denied any operational powers.

With the adjective "full" stripped from its title, the Employment Act of 1946 cleared both houses of Congress in February. This outcome was bitterly disappointing to the Keynesians who had set the original ball rolling. So great was the distance between their aspirations and the Congressional product that the Bureau of the Budget staff seriously considered advising President Truman to exercise the veto. In the end, they did not: A statute that affirmed governmental responsibility for "maximum employment, production, and purchasing power" could be regarded as an achievement, even if a dismayingly limited one. But when Truman offered Budget Director Harold D. Smith the post of

27. Terborgh in ibid., pp. 612–13.
28. Terborgh in ibid., p. 813.

Chairman of the Council of Economic Advisers, Smith declined. He perceived the job as "a very hazardous one." The public would expect much from the incumbent, yet he would lack the authority needed to meet those expectations. "I am willing to be expendable in a good enterprise," he told Truman, "but I want to be sure that the enterprise is a good one."[29]

There was something ironic about the upshot to all this. The initial Keynesian initiatives had been frustrated. But a new institution had emerged that elevated the status of economists in Washington's officialdom. The existence of the Council of Economic Advisers owed much to some side comments from an opponent of Keynesian designs for an Employment Act.

29. Harold D. Smith, "Conference with President Truman," February 8, 1946, Smith Papers, FDRPL.

Epilogue

> Government isn't infallible by any means. Government is only beginning to learn a lot of these new tricks. We are all going to school.
> – Franklin D. Roosevelt, remarks on his economic program during his 66th Press Conference, November 3, 1933

For a dozen years, Roosevelt did indeed provide the nation with a "school" for economic learning. One of its by-products was the emergence of a home-grown variant on Keynesian doctrine that was to become an agenda-setter in policy debate. This perspective on the management of the economy was a far cry from the chaos of the "policy mix" with which his administration began in 1933. The new "model" appeared to be serviceable in providing intellectual leverage on problems of actual or potential underemployment, on the one hand, and problems of inflation containment, on the other. Moreover, economists in government contributed much more to its analytic refinement in these years than did their colleagues who operated exclusively from ivory towers.

While a Keynesian-style way of thinking set the pace in the framing of economic policy issues – post-1940 – it by no means followed that its champions prevailed in all the battles in which they chose to engage. Even though they were at the cutting edge of analytic innovation, they still faced formidable opposition. The legislative achievement represented by the Employment Act of 1946 has sometimes been treated as a triumph for a Keynesian point of view. It needs to be underscored that such a reading of that event is mistaken. What emerged bore little resemblance to the design the enthusiasts for the "new economics" had proposed. Even the architecture of a new institution, the Council of Economic Advisers, owed less to their thinking than to the views presented by an economist hostile to Americanized Keynesianism.

169

While Roosevelt's "school" helped to further this "new economics," it also provided a seed bed for Keynesian critiques which gained momentum through time. Intragovernmental debates about "gap analysis" in 1941 and 1942, for example, exposed a methodological cleavage that was subsequently to be a focal point of professional debate. The central issue turned on the confidence level appropriate for economic projections. Was the economic universe ordered around a stable consumption function with predictable properties that would permit "fine-tuning" through policy (as the more doctrinaire of the American Keynesians claimed)? Or should economists be more humble, acknowledging the limitations of their knowledge and resisting temptations to intervene (as critics of Keynesianism recommended)? In the immediate postwar controversies, such matters were at the core of the vigorous attack on Alvin Hansen launched by Arthur F. Burns of Columbia and the National Bureau of Economic Research. Burns indicted Hansen-style Keynesianism for being "excessively mechanical," for "gloss[ing] over the turbulent life that goes on within aggregates," for "subjecting *ceteris paribus* to excessive strain," and for "slight[ing] in particular the instability of the consumption function."[1] To participants in the earlier exchanges about the magnitude of an "inflationary gap," such as Milton Friedman and Walter Salant, this was familiar ground.

Researches conducted in the government laboratory also provided ammunition for another line of Keynesian critique. From the earliest stages of debates over Roosevelt's recovery policies, the conceptual distance between monetarists, such as Fisher, and Keynes had been apparent and was to be sustained. Studies undertaken in one of the more obscure offices in Roosevelt's Washington were to reinforce the challenges from monetarism. Clark Warburton, as chief economist for the Federal Deposit Insurance Corporation, undertook the collection of empirical data that supported the claim that the behavior of the economy was driven by the behavior of the money supply. He initially drew on this material to attack the income approach of the Keynesians to the wartime "gap."[2] This version of anti-Keynesian monetarism had virtually no impact at that time. Warburton's location within the bureaucracy was remote from the nerve centers of power. Moreover, what he had to offer seemed irrelevant to policy making during wartime when the Federal Reserve had sacrificed its autonomy in order to support the government bond market. Indeed Warburton's findings passed largely unnoticed, even by some of the professionals who later embraced this position. Friedman, though early in establishing himself as a critic of Keynesianism, came only later to monetarism. When he did so, the debt to Warburton was recognized. As Friedman and his collab-

1. Arthur F. Burns, "Keynesian Economics Once Again," *Review of Economic Statistics,* November 1947, pp. 252–68.
2. See, for example, Clark Warburton, "Who Makes the Inflationary Gap?" *American Economic Review,* September 1943, pp. 607–12 and Warburton, "Monetary Expansion and the Inflationary Gap," *American Economic Review,* June 1944, pp. 303–27.

orator on *A Monetary History of the United States* observed: "Time and again, as we came to some conclusion that seemed to us novel and original, we found that he had been there before."[3] Thus, governmental "insiders" did more than just press forward the frontiers of domesticated Keynesianism. Some of them helped to spawn subsequent counterrevolutions.

In the immediate postwar years, a revolution of quite a different type was to be in the making. During the Roosevelt years, the bulk of the professionals based in the academy were hostile to his flirtations with heterodoxy. Most of them, and especially those who reached professional maturity before 1936, found little in *The General Theory* to commend it. The gap between economic learning (as understood in mainstream academia) and economic learning (as viewed from within the bureaucracy) thus tended to widen. There were, of course, some exceptions; Hansen's Fiscal Policy Seminar at Harvard was an obvious one, but it was atypical. After 1945, on the other hand, the "new economics" began to infiltrate the universities on a considerable scale, though still failing to make much headway at a number of institutions (such as the University of Chicago). This phenomenon was being fed by the migration of insiders from Washington, where they had assimilated the "new" learning, back to the universities, which were then undergoing major postwar expansion. This reversed the flow of the 1930s. In the depression decade, the collapse of the academic labor market had made Washington an attractive haven for aspiring young professionals.

Yet another variety of learning left its mark on the course of events in the administrations of Franklin D. Roosevelt. American society at large had absorbed some major lessons from the experiences that followed World War I. Thus, the crafting of lend-lease precluded a repetition of the headaches generated by intergovernmental war debts; the Bretton Woods instruments were designed to displace the rigidities of the classical gold standard; and the G.I. Bill of Rights meant that a veterans' bonus and the passions aroused by it would not again be on the public agenda. But the "societal learning" associated with the Roosevelt era may not always have been so fortunate. Viewed from the "Twin Towers" of the 1990s – i.e., the federal budget deficit and the balance-of-payments deficit – some legitimate questions can be raised. It is least arguable that American society has become too captivated by one of the teachings of domesticated Keynesianism, namely, that the United States should aim to become a high-consumption and low-saving economy.

3. Milton Friedman and Anna Jacobson Schwartz, *A Monetary History of the United States, 1867–1960* (Princeton, N.J.: Princeton University Press, 1963), p. xxii.

Bibliographical note

Much of the primary material drawn upon in this study is housed in the Franklin D. Roosevelt Presidential Library in Hyde Park, New York. Its holdings of the papers of the following contributors to New Deal "designs" have been particularly valuable. Adolf A. Berle; Mordecai Ezekiel; Richard V. Gilbert; Leon Henderson; Harry L. Hopkins; Isador Lubin; Gardiner C. Means; Henry Morgenthau, Jr.; Harold D. Smith; and Rexford Guy Tugwell. I have also benefited from opportunities to work with the papers of Irving Fisher (in the Manuscripts and Archives Collection of Sterling Library at Yale University), of Alvin H. Hansen (in the Pusey Library at Harvard University), and of Edwin W. Kemmerer (in the Mudd Library at Princeton University). Documents in the possession of the National Archives in Washington, D.C. have been helpful in illuminating a number of important topics.

All students of twentieth-century American history are grateful to Franklin D. Roosevelt for inspiring the publication of the *Public Papers and Addresses* series of American Presidents. In his own case, nine such volumes – covering the campaign of 1932 through 1940 – were published during his lifetime. The "explanatory notes" that he added to the materials compiled by Samuel I. Rosenman are the closest approximation to Roosevelt memoirs that we shall ever have. Four additional volumes of the *Public Papers and Addresses of Franklin D. Roosevelt* were published in 1950.

For insights into the thinking of economists during these disorderly times, study of the documents in archival collections should be supplemented by analyses of their writings in professional journals and, most particularly, of their presentations before Congressional Committees.

Works pertaining to the turbulence surrounding economic policy making in the Roosevelt years are vast in number. The following are especially rewarding:

172

Blum, John Morton. 1959–67. *From the Morgenthau Diaries: Vol. I: Years of Crisis, 1928–1938; Vol. II: Years of Urgency, 1938–1941; Vol. III: Years of War, 1941–1945.* Boston: Houghton Mifflin Company.

Brinkley, Alan. 1995. *The End of Reform: New Deal Liberalism in Recession and War.* New York: Alfred A. Knopf.

Chandler, Lester V. 1970. *America's Greatest Depression, 1929–1941.* New York: Harper & Row.

Eccles, Marriner S. 1951. *Beckoning Frontiers: Public and Personal Recollections.* New York: Alfred A. Knopf.

Feis, Herbert. 1966. *1933: Characters in Crisis.* Boston: Little, Brown.

Fite, Gilbert C. 1954. *George N. Peek and the Fight for Farm Parity.* Norman: University of Oklahoma Press.

Gardner, Richard N. 1980. *Sterling-Dollar Diplomacy in Current Perspective: The Origins and Prospects of our International Order* (new expanded edition). New York: Columbia University Press.

Hawley, Ellis W. 1966. *The New Deal and the Problem of Monopoly: A Study in Economic Ambivalence.* Princeton, N.J.: Princeton University Press.

Hyman, Sidney. 1976. *Marriner S. Eccles: Private Entrepreneur and Public Servant.* Stanford, Calif.: Stanford University Graduate School of Business.

Ickes, Harold L. 1953–4. *The Secret Diary of Harold L. Ickes* (3 vols.) New York: Simon & Schuster.

Johnson, Hugh S. 1935. *The Blue Eagle from Egg to Earth.* Garden City, N.Y.: Doubleday, Doran.

Kirkendall, Richard S. 1966. *Social Scientists and Farm Politics in the Age of Roosevelt.* Columbia: University of Missouri Press.

Lash, Joseph P. 1988. *Dealers and Dreamers: A New Look at the New Deal.* New York: Doubleday.

McKimsey, George. 1987. *Harry Hopkins: Ally of the Poor and Defender of Democracy.* Cambridge, Mass.: Harvard University Press.

Moley, Raymond. 1939. *After Seven Years.* New York: Harper & Brothers.

Ohl, John Kennedy. 1985. *Hugh S. Johnson and the New Deal.* DeKalb: Northern Illinois University Press.

Peek, George N. 1936. *Why Quit Our Own.* New York: Von Nostrand.

Richberg, Donald R. 1936. *The Rainbow.* Garden City, N.Y.: Doubleday, Doran.

Sandilands, Roger J. 1990. *The Life and Political Economy of Lauchlin Currie.* Durham, N.C.: Duke University Press.

Schwarz, Jordan. 1987. *Liberal: Adolf A. Berle and the Vision of an American Era.* New York: Free Press.

Schapsmeier, Edward L. and Frederick H. 1968. *Henry A. Wallace of Iowa: The Agrarian Years, 1910-1940.* Ames: Iowa State University Press.

Stein, Herbert. 1969. *The Fiscal Revolution in America.* Chicago, Ill.: University of Chicago Press.

Sternsher, Bernard. 1964. *Rexford Tugwell and the New Deal.* New Brunswick, N.J.: Rutgers University Press.

Tugwell, Rexford Guy. 1968. *The Brains Trust.* New York: Viking Press.

———. 1977. *Roosevelt's Revolution: The First Year – A Personal Perspective.* New York: Macmillan.

White, Graham and Maze, John. 1985. *Harold Ickes of the New Deal: His Private Life and Public Career.* Cambridge, Mass.: Harvard University Press.

Index